AMC'S BEST DAY HIKES NEAR BOSTON

WELCOME TO THE AMC

Welcome to the Appalachian Mountain Club! Founded in 1876, we are America's oldest conservation and recreation organization. We promote the protection, enjoyment, and wise use of the mountains, rivers, and trails of the Appalachian region. The AMC has twelve chapters from Maine to Washington, D.C., comprised of tens of thousands of outdoor enthusiasts like you.

By purchasing this book you have contributed to our efforts to protect the Appalachian region. Proceeds from the sales of AMC Books and Maps support our regional land conservation efforts; trail building and maintenance; air- and water-quality research; search and rescue; and environmental education programs for school-age children, at-risk youth, and outdoor enthusiasts.
The AMC encourages everyone to enjoy and appreciate the natural world because we believe that successful conservation depends on such experiences. So join us in the outdoors! We offer hiking, paddling, biking, skiing, and mountaineering activities throughout the Appalachian region for outdoor adventurers of every age and ability. Our lodging destinations, such as our state-of-the-art Highland Center, are Model Environmental Education Facilities, demonstrating our stewardship ethic and providing a place for you to relax off-trail and learn more about local ecosystems and habitats, regional environmental issues, and mountain history and culture.

For more information about AMC membership, destinations, and conservation and education programs, turn to the back of this book or visit the AMC website at www.outdoors.org.

AMC'S BEST **DAY HIKES** NEAR
BOSTON

Four-Season Guide to 50 of the Best Hikes
in Eastern Massachusetts

MICHAEL TOUGIAS

Appalachian Mountain Club Books
Boston, Massachusetts

AMC's Best Day Hikes near Boston

Editorial Direction: Sarah Jane Shangraw
Production: Belinda Thresher
Cover and Interior Design: Eric Edstam
Cartography: Ken Dumas
Front Cover Photographs: *Young hikers navigating bog bridges*, © David Brownell; *Step by step on showshoes*, by Gillian Gregory.
Back Cover Photographs: *Short hike in fall*, © Jerry and Marcy Monkman, www.ecophotography.com; *Curious fox*, by D. J. Santoro; *Halibut Point State Park*, by Michael Tougias.

Published by the Appalachian Mountain Club. Distributed by the Globe Pequot Press, Inc., Guilford, CT.

LIBRARY OF CONGRESS CATALOGING-IN-PUBLICATION DATA

Tougias, Mike, 1955–
AMC's best day hikes near Boston: four-season guide to the 50 best trails in Eastern Massachusetts, Middlesex Fells, Blue Hills, Cape Cod and more / Michael Tougias.—1st ed.
p. cm.
Includes index.
ISBN-13: 978-1-929173-66-2 (alk. paper)
1. Hiking—Massachusetts—Guidebooks. 2. Massachusetts—Guidebooks. I. Title: Four-season guide to the 50 best trails in Eastern Massachusetts, Middlesex Fells, Blue Hills, Cape Cod and more. II. Title: Guide to the 50 best trails in Eastern Massachusetts, Middlesex Fells, Blue Hills, Cape Cod and more. III. Title: Guide to the fifty best trails in Eastern Massachusetts, Middlesex Fells, Blue Hills, Cape Cod and more. IV. Title.

GV199.42.M4T68 2006
917.4404'4—dc22

2005036048

The paper used in this publication meets the minimum requirements of the American National Standard for Information Sciences—Permanence of Paper for Printed Library Materials, ANSI Z39.48–1984.∞

Due to changes in conditions, use of the information in this book is at the sole risk of the user.

Printed on recycled paper using soy-based inks.
Printed in the United States of America.

10 9 8 7 6 5 4 3 2 07 08 09 10

ACKNOWLEDGMENTS

I'VE BEEN WRITING ABOUT special outdoor places in Massachusetts for a number of years now, and I often take them for granted. But every now and then, when I'm out in the woods, I stop and look around and say to myself, "Thank God somebody had the foresight to protect this beautiful place." Usually, I have no idea who that "somebody" was, but I'd like to acknowledge the men and women who, long ago, made the effort to save some open space for future generations. Today, more and more people are realizing the benefits of protecting wild places, and the work goes on.

A great number of individuals and organizations lent me a helping hand in the research for this book. The Appalachian Mountain Club, The Trustees of Reservations, Massachusetts Audubon Society, Essex County Greenbelt Association, The Nature Conservancy, Sherborn Forest & Trail Association, Massachusetts Department of Conservation and Recreation, U.S. Fish & Wildlife Service, and a number of town conservation commissions all provided me with maps and helpful suggestions. I am especially grateful to Tom Foster and Wayne Mitton, regional supervisors for the Trustees of Reservations, who answered my many questions and shared their knowledge of the land and its wildlife.

This book grew out of two books in AMC Books' Nature Walk series, namely *Nature Walks in Eastern Massachusetts* and *More Nature Walks in Eastern Massachusetts*. A special thanks to Carol Tyler, who drew the original maps, and to my then editor, Gordon Hardy, whose knowledge and enthusiasm made this a better book. Current AMC Books staff includes Belinda Thresher, production manager, and Laurie O'Reilly, senior marketing manager. While this book was in development, Sarah Jane Shangraw was editor-in-chief. Brandon Crose, Katherine McKracken, Katrina Schroeder, and Molly Shangraw assisted in editorial development.

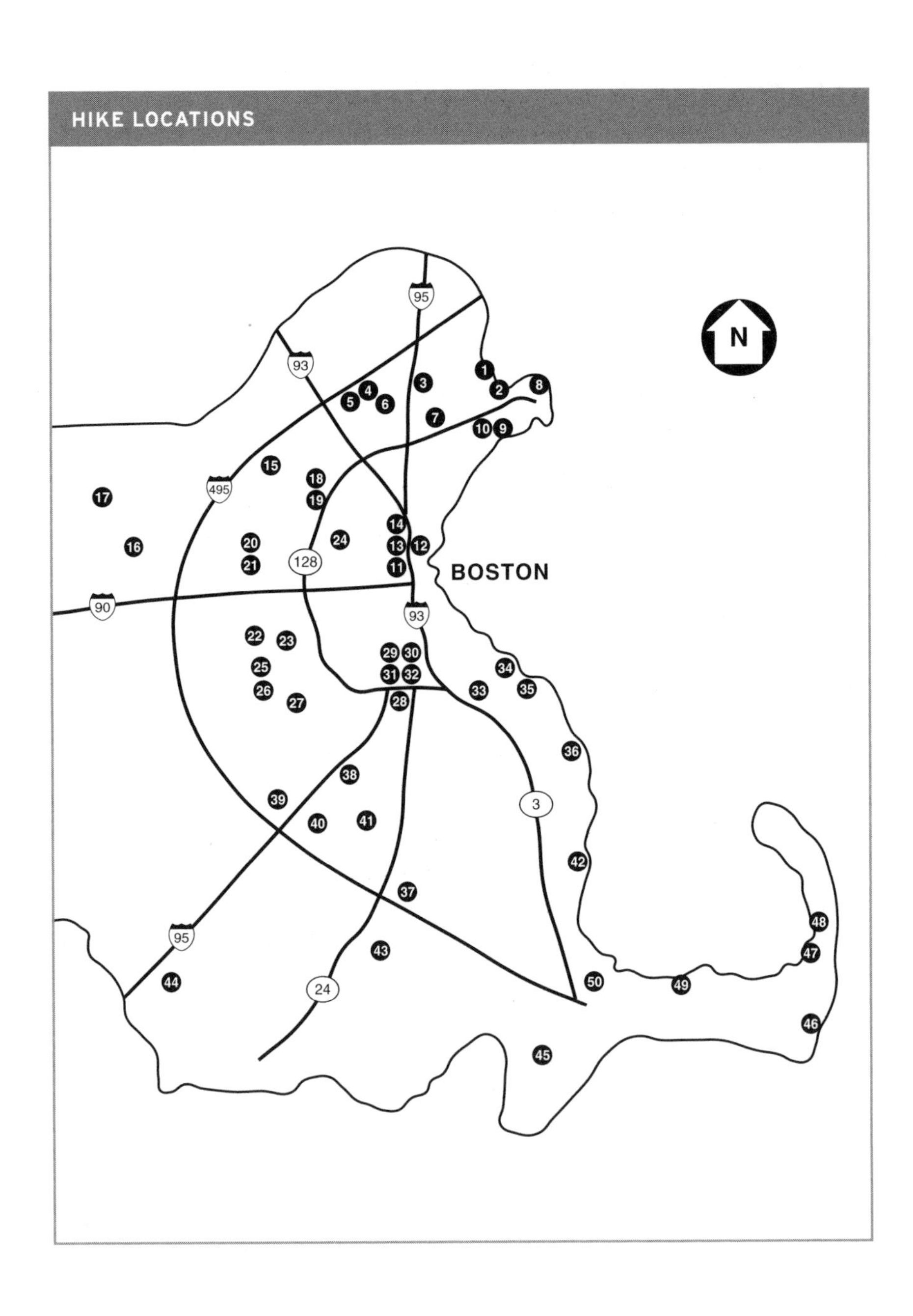
HIKE LOCATIONS
N
BOSTON
95
93
495
128
90
93
3
95
24
1
2
3
4
5
6
7
8
9
10
11
12
13
14
15
16
17
18
19
20
21
22
23
24
25
26
27
28
29
30
31
32
33
34
35
36
37
38
39
40
41
42
43
44
45
46
47
48
49
50

CONTENTS

APPENDICES

AT-A-GLANCE TRIP PLANNER

#	Trip	Page	Location (Town)	Difficulty	Distance	Estimated Time	Fee
1	Parker River National Wildlife Refuge	3	Newburyport	Easy to Moderate	2–3 mi	1–1.5 hr	•
2	Crane Beach Loop	7	Ipswich	Moderate	5 mi	2.5 hr	•
3	Ipswich River Wildlife Sanctuary	10	Topsfield	Easy to Moderate	4 mi	2 hr	•
4	Weir Hill Reservation	15	North Andover	Moderate	2.5–3 mi	1.5 hr	
5	Ward Reservation	18	Andover	Easy to Moderate	0.5–4 mi	30 min–2 hr	
6	Bald Hill Reservation	23	Boxford	Moderate	3.5 mi	1.5 hr	
7	Appleton Farms Grass Rides	26	Hamilton	Moderate	4 mi	2–2.5 hr	•
8	Halibut Point State Park	30	Rockport	Easy	1.5 mi	1 hr	•

Good for Kids	Scenic Vista	Ocean, Lake, or River	Trip Highlights	Property Owner/ Manager
•		•	Plum Island is a premier destination for birding in the Northeast. These two short hikes feature the island's natural barrier beach—one hike takes you to Sandy Point and the other takes you over an interpretive nature trail.	National Wildlife Refuge System
		•	Crane Beach consists of 1,233 acres of white sand beach and dunes along both sides of Castle Neck, a finger of land extending into the sea. More than 5 miles of marked trails explore the area, some on elevated walkways to protect the environment.	The Trustees of Reservations
•		•	Hike a wide path through this forest circling a pond on your way to the Rockery. Children will have fun exploring the maze of paths, bridges, and tunnels.	MassAudubon
•	•	•	A peaceful walk along the banks of Lake Cochichewick and up Weir Hill for scenic hilltop views of open meadows.	The Trustees of Reservations
•	•	•	View a quaking bog, a fascinating natural place to see rare and unusual plant life. Later on explore the Solstice Stones and observe the abundant wildlife on Holt Hill.	The Trustees of Reservations
•		•	Sprawled over three towns in central Essex County, Bald Hill covers 1,700 acres of forested hills and low-lying swamp protected as conservation land.	Massachusetts
•			Meander through meadows, wetlands, and woodlands by foot or, in winter, by cross-country skis.	The Trustees of Reservations
•	•	•	Enjoy magnificent views of the ocean and a walk along the rocky coastline.	The Trustees of Reservations and State

#	Trip	Page	Location (Town)	Difficulty	Distance	Estimated Time	Fee
9	Coolidge Reservation	35	Manchester-By-The-Sea	Easy	3 mi	2 hr	
10	Ravenswood Park	39	Gloucester	Easy to Moderate	2.5 mi	2.25 hr	
11	Middlesex Fells Reservation: Cross Fells Trail	43	Stoneham/ Medford/ Winchester/ Melrose/Malden	Strenuous	8.6 mi	5 hr	
12	Middlesex Fells Reservation: Rock Circuit Trail	46	Stoneham/ Medford/ Winchester/ Melrose/Malden	Strenuous	4 mi	3.5 hr	
13	Middlesex Fells Reservation: Skyline Trail	49	Stoneham/ Medford/ Winchester/ Melrose/Malden	Strenuous	6.8 mi	5 hr	
14	Middlesex Fells Reservation: Reservoir Trail	52	Stoneham/ Medford/ Winchester/ Melrose/Malden	Moderate	5.5 mi	3 hr	
15	Great Brook Farm State Park	56	Carlisle	Easy	3 mi	1.5 hr	•
16	Wachusett Reservoir and Reservation	59	Boylston/West Boylston	Easy	Limitless	1-4 hr	
17	Mount Pisgah Conservation Area	63	Northborough	Easy	2 mi	1.5 hr	
18	Minute Man National Historical Park–Battle Road Trail	66	Concord/ Lincoln/ Lexington	Moderate	5 mi	3 hr	
19	Walden Pond	70	Concord	Easy	3 mi	1.5 hr	
20	Lincoln Conservation Land (Mount Misery)	73	Lincoln	Moderate	3 mi	1.5 hr	
21	Lincoln Conservation Land (Sandy Pond)	77	Lincoln	Moderate	3.5 mi	2.25 hr	

Good for Kids	Scenic Vista	Ocean, Lake, or River	Trip Highlights	Property Owner/ Manager
•		•	Come on a Saturday when the Great Lawn is open and relax for a while, taking in the magnificent view.	The Trustees of Reservations
•			Historic and ecologically diverse pocket of wilderness with a rare magnolia swamp.	The Trustees of Reservations
		•	The blue-blazed Cross Fells Trail is a good connecting trail between the eastern and western sections of the Middlesex Fells Reservation, because it touches every major trail in the reservation.	Massachusetts
	•	•	This rugged and rocky trail offers the best views in the reservation, including those from White Rock and Melrose Rock.	Massachusetts
	•	•	This hike, which loops the western side of the Fells, has some steep ascents to afford great views of Boston.	Massachusetts
	•	•	A very pleasant circuit around the three Winchester reservoirs.	Massachusetts
•		•	More than 10 miles of trail through historic and ecologically rich farmland.	Massachusetts
•		•	Approximately 8,000 acres of water and woods, maintained by the Department of Conservation and Recreation, offer tremendous hiking, cross-country skiing, snowshoeing, and wildlife watching.	Massachusetts
•	•		Hike along old stone walls to the summit of Mount Pisgah and enjoy views of Hudson and Marlborough.	Local
			An historic woodland and meadow trek that doesn't stray far from settled areas but is quaint and pleasant nonetheless, particularly in the fall.	National Park Service
•		•	Although the pond is not remote and you won't be alone, you somehow feel miles away from civilization. Indeed, you are at the heart of the beginnings of the American conservation movement.	Massachusetts
•		•	The Mount Misery conservation land provides excellent views of the Sudbury River and Fairhaven Bay while passing through a deeply shaded hemlock forest and a patch of open marsh.	Local
•		•	A scenic loop around Sandy Pond in the footsteps of Thoreau.	Local

#	Trip	Page	Location (Town)	Difficulty	Distance	Estimated Time	Fee
22	Broadmoor Wildlife Sanctuary	81	Natick	Moderate	3 mi	1.5–2 hr	•
23	Noanet Woodlands	84	Dover	Moderate	3.5 mi	1.75 hr	
24	Wilson Mountain Reservation	88	Dedham	Easy	2 mi	1.5 hr	
25	King Philip and Rocky Narrows	92	Sherborn	Moderate	3 mi	1.5 hr	
26	Rocky Woods Reservation	97	Medfield	Easy to Moderate	1–3.5 mi	30 min–1.5 hr	•
27	Noon Hill Reservation	100	Medfield	Moderate	2 mi	1 hr	
28	Blue Hills Reservation: Ponkapoag Pond	104	Canton	Easy	4 mi	2 hr	
29	Blue Hills Reservation: Observation Tower Loop	109	Canton	Moderate	2 mi	1.5 hr	
30	Blue Hills Reservation: Great Blue Hill Green Loop	113	Milton/Canton/ Randolph/ Braintree/ Dedham/Quincy	Moderate	2.8 mi	2.5 hr	
31	Blue Hills Reservation: Houghtons Pond Yellow Loop	116	Milton/Canton/ Randolph/ Braintree/ Dedham/Quincy	Easy	1 mi	1 hr	
32	Blue Hills Reservation: Skyline Trail	118	Milton/Canton/ Randolph/ Braintree/ Dedham/Quincy	Strenuous	9 mi	6 hr	
33	Great Esker Park	121	Weymouth	Easy	1.5 mi	1 hr	
34	World's End Reservation	126	Hingham	Moderate	4.5 mi	3 hr	•
35	Whitney and Thayer Woods	130	Hingham	Easy	3 mi	1.75 hr	
36	North Hill Marsh Wildlife Sanctuary	134	Duxbury	Moderate	3.5 mi	1.5 hr	•

Good for Kids	Scenic Vista	Ocean, Lake, or River	Trip Highlights	Property Owner/ Manager
•		•	Broadmoor is a sanctuary rich in both wildlife and history. Walk by the remains of a grist mill that the Native Americans allowed to be owned and operated in the area.	MassAudubon
•	•	•	An extensive network of trails leads to a millpond and waterfall and up to modest Noanet Peak.	The Trustees of Reservations
•	•		Enjoy a stroll to a hilltop overlook and explore trails adjacent to wetlands.	Massachusetts
•	•	•	Walk or paddle to the rugged hillside slopes of the remote Rocky Narrows on the Charles River.	The Trustees of Reservations and Local
•	•	•	Three walks with opportunities to fish, picnic and, in the winter, cross-country ski.	The Trustees of Reservations
•	•	•	Heavily wooded Noon Hill is secluded with a diversity of wildlife. Few people even know of its existence, and as an added bonus it abuts the Henry L. Shattuck Reservation with an additional 225 acres along the Charles River.	The Trustees of Reservations
•		•	A short hike to a quaking bog through the Avenue of Maples offers hikers a chance to see diverse and rare plant species.	Massachusetts
•	•	•	A hike to the observation tower takes you through a variety of woodland terrain and affords a tremendous view at the top.	Massachusetts
•	•	•	This 2.8-mile loop meanders through the Great Blue Hill section of the reservation. It generally follows the cols between the hills, never ascending to any of the summits.	Massachusetts
•	•	•	This easy, 1-mile trail is a popular walk for families with small children.	Massachusetts
	•	•	This trail, marked by blue rectangular blazes, is the longest in the Blue Hills Reservation, extending from Fowl Meadow in Canton east to Shea Rink on Willard Street in Quincy.	Massachusetts
•		•	The esker runs parallel to a salt marsh, making it interesting for exploring, and offers an excellent opportunity to see a wide variety of birds.	Local
•	•	•	Tremendous views, rolling fields along the ocean's edge, and an impressive assortment of flora and fauna make for a beautiful walk.	The Trustees of Reservations
•			Hike and cross-country ski these well-maintained yet removed woodland trails.	The Trustees of Reservations
•		•	Take a hefty walk around a large freshwater pond that is teeming with birds and waterfowl.	MassAudubon

#	Trip	Page	Location (Town)	Difficulty	Distance	Estimated Time	Fee
37	Camp Titicut Reservation	138	Bridgewater	Easy	1.5 mi	1 hr	
38	Moose Hill Wildlife Sanctuary	142	Sharon	Moderate	1.75–2.5 mi	1–2 hr	•
39	F. Gilbert Hills State Forest: Blue Triangle Loop	146	Wrenthan/ Foxboro	Easy	1.5 mi	45 min	
40	Wheaton Farm Conservation Area	149	Easton	Easy	2.5 mi	1.5 hr	
41	Borderland State Park	153	North Easton	Moderate	3.5 mi	1.75 hr	•
42	Ellisville Harbor State Park	156	Plymouth	Easy	3 mi	1.75 hr	
43	Freetown/Fall River State Forest	160	Assonet	Easy to Moderate	0.5–3.5 mi	20 min–2 hr	
44	Caratunk Wildlife Refuge	165	Seekonk	Easy to Moderate	2–2.5 mi	1–1.5 hr	•
45	Lowell Holly Reservation	169	Mashpee/ Sandwich	Moderate	2 mi	1 hr	
46	Fort Hill	172	Eastham	Easy	2 mi	1 hr	
47	Wellfleet Bay Wildlife Sanctuary	175	South Wellfleet	Easy	3 mi	1.5 hr	•
48	Great Island	180	Wellfleet	Moderate	4 mi	2.5 hr	
49	Sandy Neck Circuit	184	Barnstable	Moderate	1.6–13 mi	4 hr 40 for 4 mi option	
50	Myles Standish State Forest: Easthead and Bentley Loop	187	Plymouth/ Carver	Moderate to Strenuous	3–7.5 mi	2–4 hr	•

Good for Kids	Scenic Vista	Ocean, Lake, or River	Trip Highlights	Property Owner/ Manager
•		•	A small, but scenic conservation area situated along the banks of the Taunton River.	Massachusetts
•	•		Moose Hill Wildlife Sanctuary covers 1,435 acres of quiet trails and secluded hilltops.	MassAudubon
•		•	A number of rocky ridges, swamps, and secluded ponds provide the hiker with diverse scenery.	Massachusetts
•		•	A relatively easy ramble through level terrain that features a white pine forest, shallow ponds, and open fields.	Local
•		•	Six ponds and hilly, rocky terrain make this park worth a visit.	Massachusetts
•		•	Walk by an abandoned Christmas tree farm on your way to the rocky coastline.	Massachusetts
•	•	•	Good vistas, trout fishing in Rattlesnake Brook, and cross-country skiing in the winter are just a few possibilities here.	Massachusetts
•		•	Set on 195 acres with ponds, fields, streams, a small bog area, and boulder-strewn woodlands, Caratunk is a hidden gem just waiting to be discovered.	Audubon of Rhode Island
•		•	Enjoy a walk through primarily wild woods and along scattered beaches.	The Trustees of Reservations
•	•	•	An ocean-side hike through the Cape Cod National Seashore, with panoramic views.	National Park Service
•		•	Excellent birding and diverse plant life abound along Silver Springs Brook.	MassAudubon
•		•	The combination of pine woodlands and coastal dunes makes Great Island a special place to walk.	National Park Service
		•	Sandy Neck is a 6-mile-long barrier beach bordering Cape Cod Bay.	National Park Service
•		•	At more than 14,000 acres, Myles Standish State Forest is one of the largest reservations in the state park and offers many recreational activies.	Massachusetts

INTRODUCTION

WHILE EASTERN MASSACHUSETTS IS HOME to a large urban area—Boston and its suburbs—there are a number of "pockets" of wilderness near the city where you can walk in solitude. Many of the locations described here are not well known and can give the feeling of a remote area. Others are more popular, but they have "hidden" trails where few visitors bother to go. The reservations range in size from just 30 acres to well over a thousand. All of them are surprisingly rich in wildlife.

For me, hiking combines the physical joy of walking with the thrill of seeing wildlife. A special day in the woods can make your spirits soar. Maybe it's during a walk on a crisp, colorful autumn day, or a winter's trek just after a heavy snow, or perhaps the first warm day of spring when all the earth seems to be awakening.

Of course, seeing a fox, coyote, or deer at close range can make any walk a special one. I've included some of my more memorable wildlife encounters in the book, such as the goshawk I saw at Bald Hill Reservation or the ruffed grouse that tried to draw me away from its chicks at Rocky Narrows. Just about every wild species that is found in the state can also be found at the reservations detailed here.

Each description includes directions, suggested trails, a map, potential wildlife to be seen, estimated hiking time, trail conditions, scenic views, and nearby points of interest where appropriate. We also note if trails are suitable for snowshoeing or cross-country skiing, and if the reservation abuts a river, pond, or lake, we discuss canoeing and fishing possibilities.

I'm fond of quoting Thoreau because he spent much of his life exploring eastern Massachusetts, and he liked nothing better than a long tramp through the woods or a paddle up a river. He viewed walking as a way to lose oneself: "What business have I in the woods, if I am thinking of something out of the woods?" He walked often and far afield: "I think that I cannot preserve my health and spirits, unless I spend four hours a day at least—and it is commonly more than that—sauntering through the woods and over the hills and fields, absolutely free from all worldly engagements." And if Thoreau saw wildlife, all the better. It was not unusual for him to sit and wait patiently for some creature to appear, or stop his walk to watch wildlife for the rest of the day. I've found my own hikes to be infinitely more enjoyable if I follow Thoreau's examples.

My lifelong passion has been to explore Massachusetts, looking for off-the-beaten-path places. At first glance it would appear that this book and my prior books are giving away my secrets and bringing more people to these secluded spots. But I've learned that people protect the things they love. I am pleased to share some of my special places with you and hope that by raising appreciation for nature we can protect more wild places before they are forever lost to development.

HOW TO USE THIS BOOK

THIS BOOK INCLUDES 50 SCENIC HIKES in special natural settings within a couple hours drive of Boston, with many much closer to the city and accessible by public transportation. Use the Trip Locator Map (page vi) and the At-a-Glance Trip Planner (pages x–xvii) to help you choose a trip based on location, distance of hike, difficulty, or natural features you will encounter along the way.

Each trip is described in detail, with:

- A summary containing the degree of difficulty, the length of the trail (including return trip, if the trail is not a loop), elevation gain, and how long it should take;
- Symbols indicating whether the trail is appropriate for snowshoeing, cross-country skiing, and/or hiking;
- A brief summary of highlights of the trail or property, such as outstanding natural features;
- Directions—how to get to the trailhead from major roads and towns;
- Detailed hiking directions for the trail;
- A general trail map showing the locations of various features;
- Nature Notes—natural history, scenery, human history, and special activities, such as swimming or exploring a quarry.

The approximate time it takes to make the recommended walk is given at the beginning of each entry. The time-to-mileage ratio used in this book is about 30 minutes for each mile, but you might want to allow more time to enjoy the environment. This ratio was used in some cases to figure approximate trail mileage.

Take this book with you to use the map for your hike. A bold letter **P** designates the parking area found at the entrance to each site. Each map shows north to orient you, and we have included an approximate scale in either feet or miles. A heavy dashed line indicates the route described in the text, and the lighter dashed line indicates other trails in the area.

Conditions of trails do change from time to time and we would appreciate hearing about any changes you find. See the note "AMC Book Updates" at the back of this book for more information, and check out our updates page on the web at: www.outdoors.org/publications/books/updates.

The AMC's *Massachusetts Trail Guide* is a wonderfully comprehensive guide to each and every Massachusetts trail network and would be a great companion to this book, especially if you are interested in traveling or hiking farther, or even camping and backpacking overnight.

We hope you enjoy this book and that it is a useful companion on many great outings.

SAFETY TIPS

THE FOLLOWING ARE RECOMMENDATIONS for the hikes in this book, which are on properties with limited extents.

- To make your hikes more enjoyable, bring binoculars, a camera, and a snack (food always tastes better in the outdoors).
- Unfortunately, it's not advisable for women to hike alone. Ask a friend who shares your love of the environment, or better yet, find a friend who spends more time in the malls than the woods, and introduce her or him to the joys of walking in the great outdoors.
- Getting lost in the woods is no fun. If you are unfamiliar with an area, allow plenty of time before dark when you set out. Even at the smaller reservations it's possible to get lost—I have. Always tell someone what reservations you plan to explore and what time you expect to be home. It's a good idea to carry water with you, even in cold-weather months.
- The tiny deer ticks that can carry Lyme disease are found throughout New England. Always wear long pants, preferably with the pants tucked beneath your socks. Avoid fields of tall grass during the warm-weather months. And to be on the safe side, give yourself a "tick check" after every hike by examining yourself all over, especially the scalp, neck, armpits, groin, and ankles.
- Be on the lookout for poison ivy—identified by its three shiny leaves. Again, long pants are recommended.

- During warm-weather months I carry a small backpack or fanny pack with water and bug spray.
- During cold-weather months I layer my clothes, taking my outer coat off as I heat up, but leaving on my hat.
- During the fall deer-hunting season, I wear a blaze-orange hat to be on the safe side—even when I'm in a no-hunting area.

WHAT TO BRING

Ten essential items you should carry on every trip:

- Map
- Compass
- Warm clothing including hat and mittens
- Extra food and water
- Flashlight or headlamp
- Matches/firestarter
- First-aid kit
- Whistle
- Rain/wind gear
- Pocket knife or multitool

TRAIL COURTESY, TRAIL MAINTENANCE

RESPECT FOR NATURE involves a few basic rules.

- Follow the "carry-in, carry-out" principle when it comes to trash.
- Do not remove any plants from the woods.
- Keep to the established trails.
- Give wildlife a wide berth. Binoculars and a telephoto lens on your camera will allow you to view the wildlife without forcing it to flee.

By becoming involved in local conservation efforts, we can all help to keep our woods and waters in a clean, natural state where wildlife has a chance to flourish. Besides local conservation commissions and watershed associations, there are also statewide organizations such as the Appalachian Mountain Club, the Trustees of Reservations, and Massachusetts Audubon Society that have active conservation programs. Many organizations, including the AMC, provide opportunities to become part of a volunteer trail crew. For information on finding trail work or "adopt a trail" programs through the AMC, visit www.outdoors.org/trails.

HIKING WITH CHILDREN

A HIKE OR WALK IN THE WOODS WITH A CHILD can be a wonderful experience or a potential nightmare. The most important step you can take is simply to be flexible. High expectations can ruin any trip. Be ready to turn back anytime, and don't force your goals on a child. When a child shows signs of fatigue, take a rest—then turn back, or you might find yourself carrying the child back to the car. And remember that walking in the snow, sand, or mud can use up twice as much energy as a walk of the same length on hard ground.

A little preparation goes a long way in ensuring that both adult and child have a good time. Bring a snack; oftentimes the child will be more interested in the snack than in the natural world. (There's nothing wrong with that; the idea here is to have fun and make the trip a pleasant one.) Bring a field guide to birds, animals, reptiles, and plants. A guide enables the child to work with you in identifying the natural world around him. Binoculars are always a big hit (there are some sturdy and inexpensive models for children), and if you do spot wildlife, binoculars might allow the child to see much more than a fleeting glimpse. Let the child hold the map, and have her help decide which way to go while you teach her how to interpret it. You might also want to bring a small backpack with some extra clothing for him to carry on your adventure.

Spending a day outdoors with a child is a great way to simultaneously become closer and teach him a respect for nature. You can show him responsibility through your own actions, such as picking up trash—even if it's not yours. Try to see the world through her eyes and enjoy the simple things that feed her enthusiasm. (If the location has water, it's a good bet the child will want to spend some time throwing twigs or stones.) When you take a rest, that's a good time to tell stories about nature or browse through the field guide together. Remember to praise and encourage the child each time he learns something new or completes a walk.

AMC'S BEST DAY HIKES NEAR BOSTON

TRIP 1
PARKER RIVER NATIONAL WILDLIFE REFUGE

LOCATION: Newburyport
RATING: Sandy Point, Moderate; Hellcat Swamp Nature Trail, Easy
DISTANCE: Sandy Point, 3 miles; Hellcat Swamp Nature Trail, 2 miles
ESTIMATED TIME: Sandy Point, 1.5 hours; Hellcat Swamp Nature Trail, 1 hour
OTHER ACTIVITIES: Birding, fishing, swimming

Plum Island is a premier destination for birding in the Northeast. These two short hikes feature the island's natural barrier beach—one hike takes you to Sandy Point and the other takes you over an interpretive nature trail.

The Parker River National Wildlife Refuge on Plum Island, a natural barrier beach, is a place nature lovers should try to visit in all seasons. It is one of the premier birding spots in the Northeast. More than 270 species of migratory and local birds have been spotted at the refuge. Spring and fall are the preferred birding months because of the many migrants that fly low over the dunes, but a winter walk is recommended when white snow, golden-brown salt grass, and beach sand mix together in subtle beauty. A winter walk here is a sure cure for cabin fever and may just give you the inspiration to venture out every weekend.

DIRECTIONS

From I-95, take Exit 57 and follow Route 113 east. Head into Newburyport for 2.5 miles, and then Route 113 feeds into High Street, which becomes Route 1A. Proceed south for 1.2 miles. Turn left onto Water Street (there will be a sign for Plum Island), and follow this road to its end. Then turn right on Plum Island Turnpike and proceed for about 2 miles (crossing the Parker River), turning right on Sunset Road to the entrance gate.

If you miss the left turn from Route 1A onto Water Street, you can take a left on Rolfe's Lane to Plum Island Turnpike and proceed to the refuge.

TRAIL DESCRIPTION

The trail begins at Lot 4, which is 3.8 miles down the entrance road from the main gate. There is also an observation blind near the parking area, and it's a

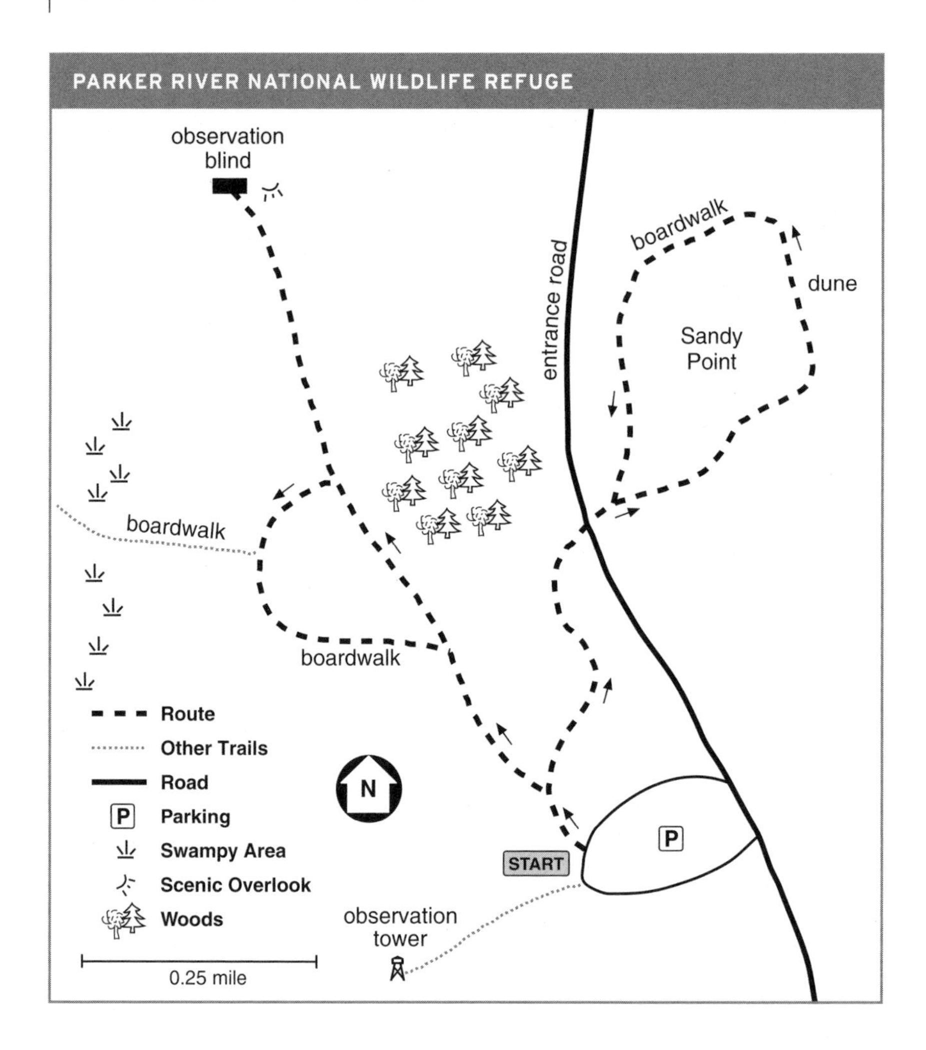

good idea to stop here first to see the lay of the land and birds in the freshwater marsh. The short path to the observation tower is at the rear of the parking lot. From the top of the tower you can see the dunes, marshes, ocean, and the mainland. Look for black ducks, green-winged teal, pintails, great blue herons, and green-backed herons in the warmer-weather months.

The Hellcat Swamp Nature Trail, most of which is a boardwalk, begins at the north side of the parking lot and forks only a couple minutes down the trail. To first visit Sandy Point, take the right fork through scrub oaks and freshwater marsh, and follow this for 0.25 mile until you reach the entrance road. Cross the road and continue on the trail, where it soon climbs stairs to a panoramic view of the dunes. If you are here in September, you may be rewarded with the sight of dozens of monarch butterflies migrating through the refuge. The open

No one knows for sure how woodchucks got here. They cannot tolerate salt water, so swimming across from the mainland seems unlikely. Could they have traveled at night along the roadway that leads to the island?

Atlantic is just 0.25 mile to the east from the top of the dune.

As the steps and boardwalk carry you through the dunes, woodlands, and along the small pockets of freshwater swamp, the trail forms a loop. A 1-mile walk from the beginning of the boardwalk completes the loop on the east side of the entrance road. Turn right here to cross back over the road and retrace your steps back to the intersection by the parking lot.

Turn right at this intersection, heading north, northwestward. Proceed on this trail, and stay to the right past two forks in the trail, and you will soon reach the observation blind. Here you can observe birdlife at a freshwater marsh without being seen by the birds.

From the observation blind, retrace your steps to the south, then at the first intersection, turn right onto the marsh trail. A boardwalk will lead you through wetlands where tall reedgrass and cattails line the path. A side boardwalk leads farther out into the marsh for more exploration. The purple-flowering plant that blooms in August is the purple loosestrife, a nonindigenous plant that is taking over the wetlands.

Once you have circled the marsh, the boardwalk intersects with the main trail where you should turn right to return to the parking lot.

For those who want to continue walking, many more trails and possibilities await. A walk along the beach is always a good bet. You can examine the various flotsam that has washed ashore, and listen to the surf—pounding and angry one day, gently lapping in rhythmic wavelets the next.

NATURE NOTES

Plum Island was formed by glaciers, and additional sculpturing occurred as the Merrimack River brought silt to the Atlantic, which was swept onto Plum Island. When the first Europeans arrived in the region, the island was covered with mature forest. Colonists quickly cleared the land—they used white pine for ship masts and other lumber for wood fires (heat), and set their sheep to graze on the rest of the vegetation. Today, Plum Island has trees again but only a few that approach 50 feet tall. The trees have gained a foothold in the hollows, where they are sheltered from the wind and closer to the ground water. Plants closest to the beach are those that can tolerate the salt spray: beach grass, seaside goldenrod, dusty miller, beach pea, and seabeach sandwort.

Autumn is a good time to see rough-legged hawks and harriers hunting for small mammals, and falcons wheeling in the sky as they migrate south. Lucky birders in the winter are sometimes rewarded with the sight of a snowy owl, a visitor from the Arctic. Although the snowy owl breeds in the tundra, they move south at irregular intervals to winter in New England. Plum Island and the Boston Harbor Islands are the two best locations to see a snowy owl, particularly from December to the end of February. Some years they are fairly common at Plum Island where they hunt in the open salt marshes. They will feed on meadow voles and smaller birds.

Be on the lookout as well for the piping plover, an endangered bird that is successfully reproducing on Plum Island. Piping plovers are small sand-colored birds that nest right on the beach and are therefore susceptible to being crushed by beach vehicles and disturbed by beachgoers. At nesting times in the early part of the spring and summer, sections of the beach may be closed for their protection. Harbor seals can also be seen bobbing in the surf beyond the breakers. Shorebirds, such as greater yellowlegs and willets, work the shoreline looking for invertebrates to feed on.

SAFETY NOTES

If you go in the summer be sure to wear a hat; bring sunscreen and plenty of water. There are no lifeguards on the beach, and caution should be taken when swimming due to undertow. Ticks are common year-round, so avoid walking through tall grass, and tuck pant legs inside socks when walking in woods. Greenhead flies are present from mid-July to mid-August.

MORE INFORMATION

Open year-round; fee or annual pass; rest rooms at lot 4; pets prohibited. The refuge parking lots can fill up on summer weekends, so arrive early. Hunting is allowed, so always wear blaze orange in the fall and winter. Beach is often closed from April 1 into August due to nesting piping plovers. For more information, contact refuge headquarters, 978-465-5753; FW5RW_PRNWR@FWS.gov.

TRIP 2
CRANE BEACH LOOP

LOCATION: Ipswich
RATING: Moderate
DISTANCE: 5 miles
ESTIMATED TIME: 2.5 hours
OTHER ACTIVITIES: Birding, swimming
PUBLIC TRANSPORTATION: Crane Beach is connected to the Ipswich Train Station (Commuter Rail linked to Boston) by the Ipswich Essex Explorer bus. For schedule and rates, visit www.ipswich-essexexplorer.com.

Crane Beach consists of 1,233 acres of white sand beach and dunes along both sides of Castle Neck, a finger of land extending into the sea. More than 5 miles of marked trails explore the area, some on elevated walkways to protect the environment.

DIRECTIONS

From MA 128 take Exit 20A and follow MA 1A north for 8 miles to Ipswich. Turn right onto MA 133 east and continue 1.5 miles, then turn left onto Northgate Road. Travel 0.5 mile, turn right onto Argilla Road, and drive 2.5 miles to the entrance at the end of the road (1,300 cars maximum).

TRAIL DESCRIPTION

Two trails start from the right side of the beach parking lot: a short, well-marked nature trail, and a longer, less well-defined "low-impact" trail marked by posts in the dunes. Take a pleasant round trip of about 5 miles by following the posts up and down the dunes. Exact location of the posts may change

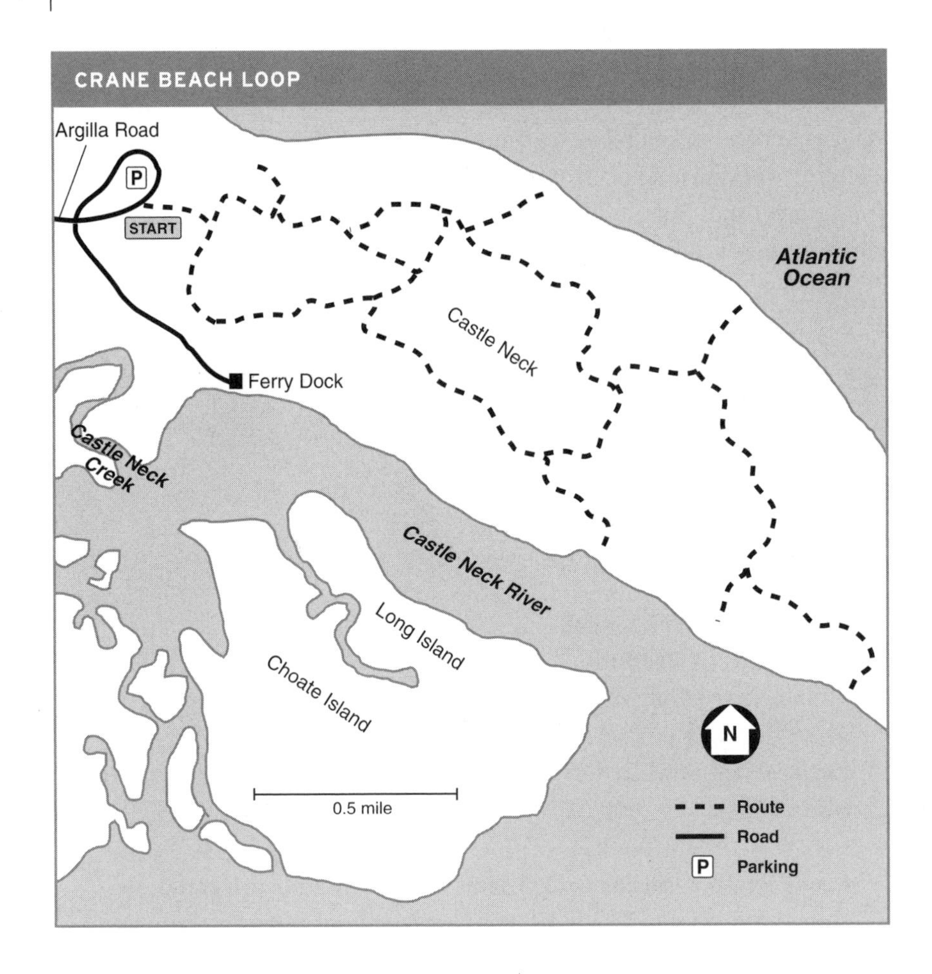

occasionally to minimize the impact of foot traffic. (When the path emerges on the bank of the Castle Neck River, you may turn left and follow the riverbank around the point to the barrier beach, and then follow the beach back to the parking lot.) During peak season (Memorial Day through Labor Day) Crane Beach is a popular albeit expensive swimming beach. (Admission fees are lower for cyclists.) Summer weekends can be particularly crowded.

NATURE NOTES

The area is one of the most important nesting sites for the endangered piping plover. (Dogs are not allowed between April 1 and September 30.) An extensive pitch pine forest, carnivorous plants, and cranberries can all be found here. The area is also known for its bird watching and fall foliage. Note: This area is ecologically fragile. The dunes, which prevent the land from being engulfed by the sea, are held together by the long, connected roots of plants. Stay

Choate Island viewed from Crane Beach. Photo by Alex Wilson

on the marked trail and do not walk along the crests of the dunes, slide down the dunes, or step on the vegetation.

MORE INFORMATION

Near Crane Beach is the Crane Wildlife Refuge The Trustees of Reservations (TTOR), which consists of 697 acres of islands, salt marsh, and intertidal environments. More than 3 miles of trails explore this area, where over 200 species of birds have been observed. For more information about Crane Beach, visit www.thetrustees.org.

TRIP 3
IPSWICH RIVER WILDLIFE SANCTUARY

LOCATION: Topsfield
RATING: Easy to Moderate
DISTANCE: 4 miles
ESTIMATED TIME: 2 hours
OTHER ACTIVITIES: Birding, paddling, swimming
WINTER ACTIVITIES: The trail is flat and well-maintained, excellent for cross-country skiing

Hike a wide path through this forest circling a pond on your way to the Rockery. Children will have fun exploring the maze of paths, bridges, and tunnels.

The Ipswich River Wildlife Sanctuary has both water and rock formations. The area called the Rockery is a man-made maze of rocks and boulders formed into paths, bridges, and tunnels adjacent to a picture-perfect pond, surrounded by azaleas, rhododendrons, and mountain laurel. Ten miles of trails wind through meadows, ponds, marsh, forest, and alongside the Ipswich River. (Maps with labeled trails are available at the office.)

The outing described here is a solid 2-hour walk. If you are exploring with young children, you may want to shorten the walk, yet still visit the features most appreciated by children, by walking to Waterfowl Pond and then going on to the Rockery, bypassing the loop of Averill's Island (see map).

DIRECTIONS

From I-95, take Exit 50 (Route 1–Topsfield) and go north about 3 miles on Route 1 to its intersection with Route 97. Turn right (south) on Route 97 and proceed 0.6 mile, then turn left on Perkins Row. Go 1 mile to the entrance on the right.

TRAIL DESCRIPTION

From the parking lot, follow the path toward the office and turn left on the driveway by the red buildings. Look for the sign for the Innermost House Trail. Follow this wide grassy trail to the northeast, passing through goldenrod, Queen Anne's lace, and milkweed, but be careful of poison ivy (shiny green leaves in groups of three).

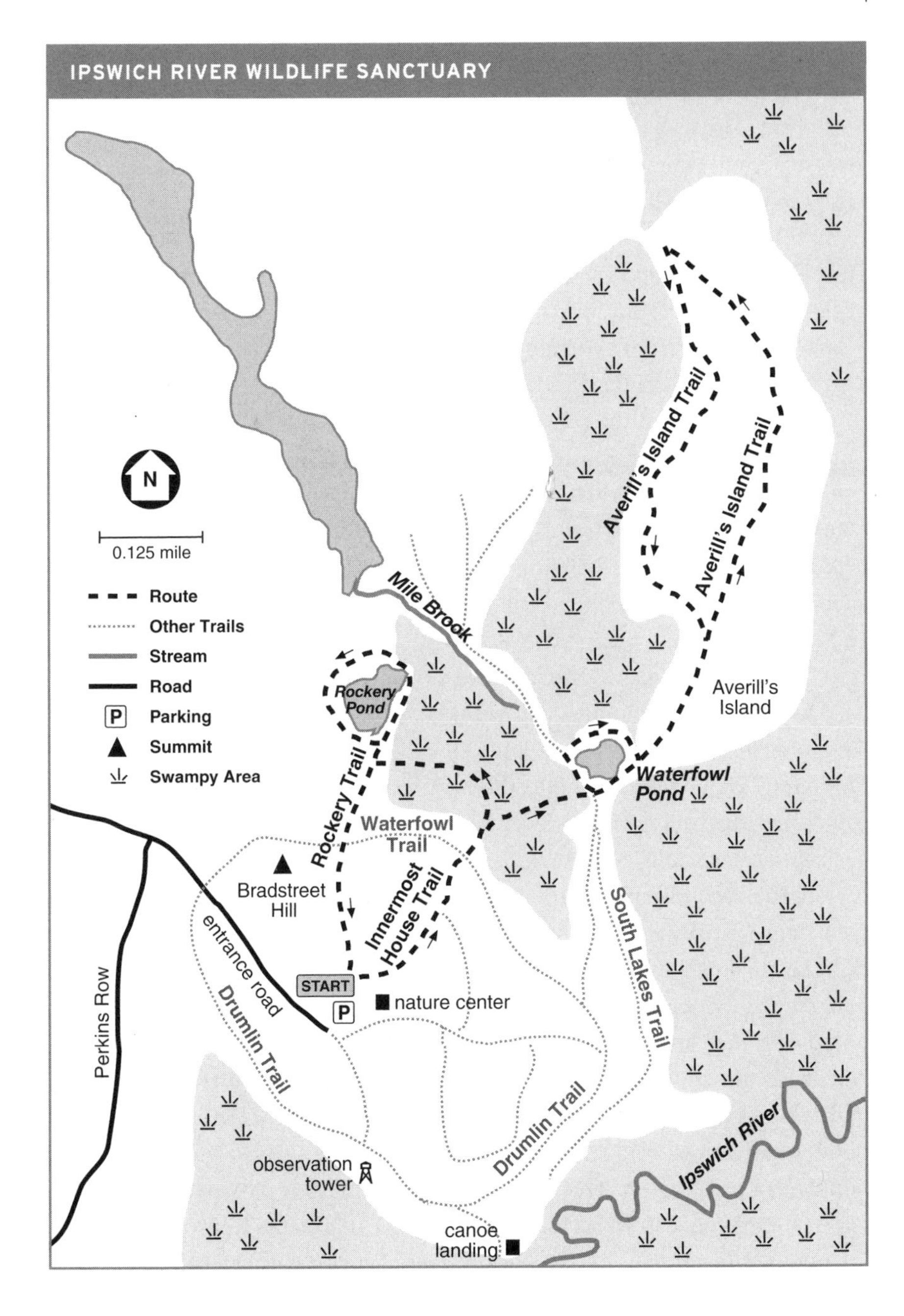

After walking roughly 50 feet, you will pass a side trail on the right, but you should bear left here, following the Innermost Trail that leads downhill through foliage that has formed a tunnel. In three minutes, you will pass a side trail on the right, but you should continue straight on this trail, passing beneath white pines and maples. Within a couple minutes, you will reach an intersection with the Drumlin Trail, but you should continue walking straight ahead on the Innermost Trail. The trail crosses a boardwalk through a swamp of cattails, purple loosestrife, and swamp maples, soon reaching an intersection. Turn right, passing by more wetlands where dead timber rises from the lowlands.

In 0.125 mile, you will arrive at an intersection at the Stone Bridge Trail. Turn left to get a good view of Waterfowl Pond from a small, handsome stone bridge. Look for wading birds, such as great blue herons and night herons. Scan the water for frogs and painted turtles. Just a few feet past the bridge, take a right on a small trail that circles the pond.

At the back end of the pond, the trail intersects with Averill's Island Loop Trail. Go left, heading toward Averill's Island. Passing beneath white pine, hemlock, and an occasional beech tree, the trail swings to the north. About a quarter mile down the trail is a fork in the trail, where the loop of Averill's Island begins. Bear right, passing towering white pines that give the forest an enchanting quality. In about half a mile you can see an open marsh on the right and just beyond that, the Ipswich River.

The trail now angles to the northwest through mixed woodland.

After about five minutes, you will reach the northern end of Averill's Island; turn left to complete your loop. (If you were to go straight on the White Pine Loop Trail, you'd head into the northernmost end of the sanctuary, but sometimes the trails are flooded from beaver activity.) Head south to arrive back at the Waterfowl Pond in 0.75 mile, completing your loop of the island.

For the second part of the walk to the Rockery, bear right and retrace your steps past Waterfowl Pond, all the way to the Waterfowl Pond Trail. Bear right again, and the Waterfowl Pond Trail will take you through the heart of a marsh. In five minutes you'll arrive at the Rockery Trail. Turn right onto a boardwalk that brings you to Rockery Pond. Circle the pond in a counterclockwise direction by bearing right. Mountain laurel and rhododendrons make this an especially appealing walk in the late spring. At the back end of the pond, cross a small bridge, walk through cedars and spruce, and arrive at the boulders of the Rockery. This spot offers a peaceful view of the pond's tranquil waters, but if you visit with children, they will run into the Rockery, exploring the nooks and crannies. In one section slabs of rock have been placed over the path, making you walk through a dark tunnel. It's a magical place, made more so by the many evergreens.

To return to the parking lot, walk from the rock tunnel and retrace your steps over the boardwalk to the intersection of the Waterfowl Pond Trail and the Rockery Trail. Stay straight on the Rockery Trail, as it mostly goes uphill through woods and then brings you to the field by the parking lot. It's about a 0.5-mile walk from the Rockery to the parking area.

There are many more miles of trails to explore on future trips, including a walk to the southern end of the property, where there is an observation tower overlooking Bunker Meadows, and a trail that brings you to the banks of the Ipswich River.

NATURE NOTES

The parking lot and nature center rest atop Bradstreet Hill, a glacial drumlin formed during the last ice age when the glacier deposited its debris and shaped it into a smooth, elongated mound. Also on the property are eskers, long ridges of sand and gravel. Eskers form when meltwater streams within the glaciers deposit their load of debris within the ice, leaving raised streambeds after all the ice melts.

Children love the boardwalks through the wetlands.

If you are walking in May, inspect the edges of the path near the pond for recent signs of digging. Snapping turtles lay their eggs in the dry ground adjacent to the pond where the digging is easy. Snappers can be found in just about every body of water, from dark mudholes to clear lakes. Once her eggs are laid into the shallow depression, the female covers them with dirt, but skunks and raccoons still manage to find many nests. Snappers play an important role in the health of ponds by eating dead fish, so teach children not to harm them. Much of the reptile population in Massachusetts is at risk, and they need all the help we can give them.

The portion of the Ipswich River that runs through the sanctuary is great for flatwater canoeing and particularly scenic, with 8 miles protected from development. But like other rivers in eastern Massachusetts,

Pond lilies cover Waterfowl Pond near a stone arch bridge.

the Ipswich is being threatened by water withdrawals; fourteen communities draw water from the Ipswich River Basin. The need for water conservation programs is immediate if we are to protect the river and its aquatic life from the stresses of reduced flow.

The Rockery was cleverly designed in 1902 by Shintare Anamete, a Japanese landscape architect. It was commissioned by Thomas E. Proctor, the former owner of the area, as a setting for his collection of exotic shrubs, trees, and flowers. Constructed by immigrant Italian laborers, it took seven years to build. Proctor bought rocks from surrounding farms because there were no boulders or glacial erratics on this property. Some of the boulders were transported by horse and cart from more than 10 miles away. The Rockery's beauty appears to have been created by nature, but if you look closely, you will see stone steps and sitting stones angled perfectly to offer unencumbered views of the pond, which is also man-made. Massachusetts Audubon bought the sanctuary from the Proctor family in 1951.

MORE INFORMATION

Open dawn to dusk, Tuesday through Sunday. Closed Mondays (open Monday holidays); admission fee for nonmembers; rest rooms; nature center programs. Canoe and cabin rental for members. For more information, contact the Ipswich River Wildlife Sanctuary, 978-887-9264; ipswichriver@massaudubon.org.

TRIP 4
WEIR HILL RESERVATION

LOCATION: North Andover
RATING: Moderate
DISTANCE: 2.5–3 miles
ESTIMATED TIME: 1.5 hours
OTHER ACTIVITIES: Birding, horseback riding
WINTER ACTIVITIES: Trails are flat and well-maintained, excellent for cross-country skiing and snowshoeing

A peaceful walk along the banks of Lake Cochichewick and up Weir Hill for scenic hilltop views of open meadows.

Weir Hill Reservation combines the best of woodlands, fields, and water. A hiker gets treated to views not only from the hilltop but also from the shores of beautiful Lake Cochichewick, a water-supply reservoir. The reservation got its name from the fish weirs the Indians once constructed in nearby Cochichewick Brook. The weir (usually a woven fence) would trap migrating fish on their way to the lake.

DIRECTIONS

From I-495 take Route 114 east. Follow Route 114 into North Andover for about a mile, then take a left on Route 133 east and stay on this for roughly a mile. Turn right on Massachusetts Avenue. Pass the Common on the right, then turn left at the white church on Great Pond Road. After one block, turn left on Stevens Street. Continue 0.8 mile to the Weir Hill entrance on the right.

From I-93, get off at Exit 41 and take Route 125 north 7.5 miles. Turn right at the lights on Andover Street. Follow Andover Street 0.6 mile. Bear right at the fork and drive 0.2 mile to Old North Andover Center. Go straight for 0.1 mile, then left on Stevens Street for 0.8 mile to the entrance on the right.

TRAIL DESCRIPTION

Weir Hill is one of the few reservations where you can reach a scenic vista in just a ten-minute walk. From the parking area take the wide path, heading in a northeasterly direction, that leads to Stevens Trail and turn right. A slow and steady climb takes you beneath huge oaks. After walking 1,500 feet you will enter an upland meadow with magnificent views to the west. This hill is a drumlin, rising 300 feet above the surrounding countryside. Weir Hill, located a few hundred yards to the south, is roughly the same size. Walk the perimeter of the reservation by continuing on Stevens Trail southward toward Lake Cochichewick, a 2.5-to-3-mile walk.

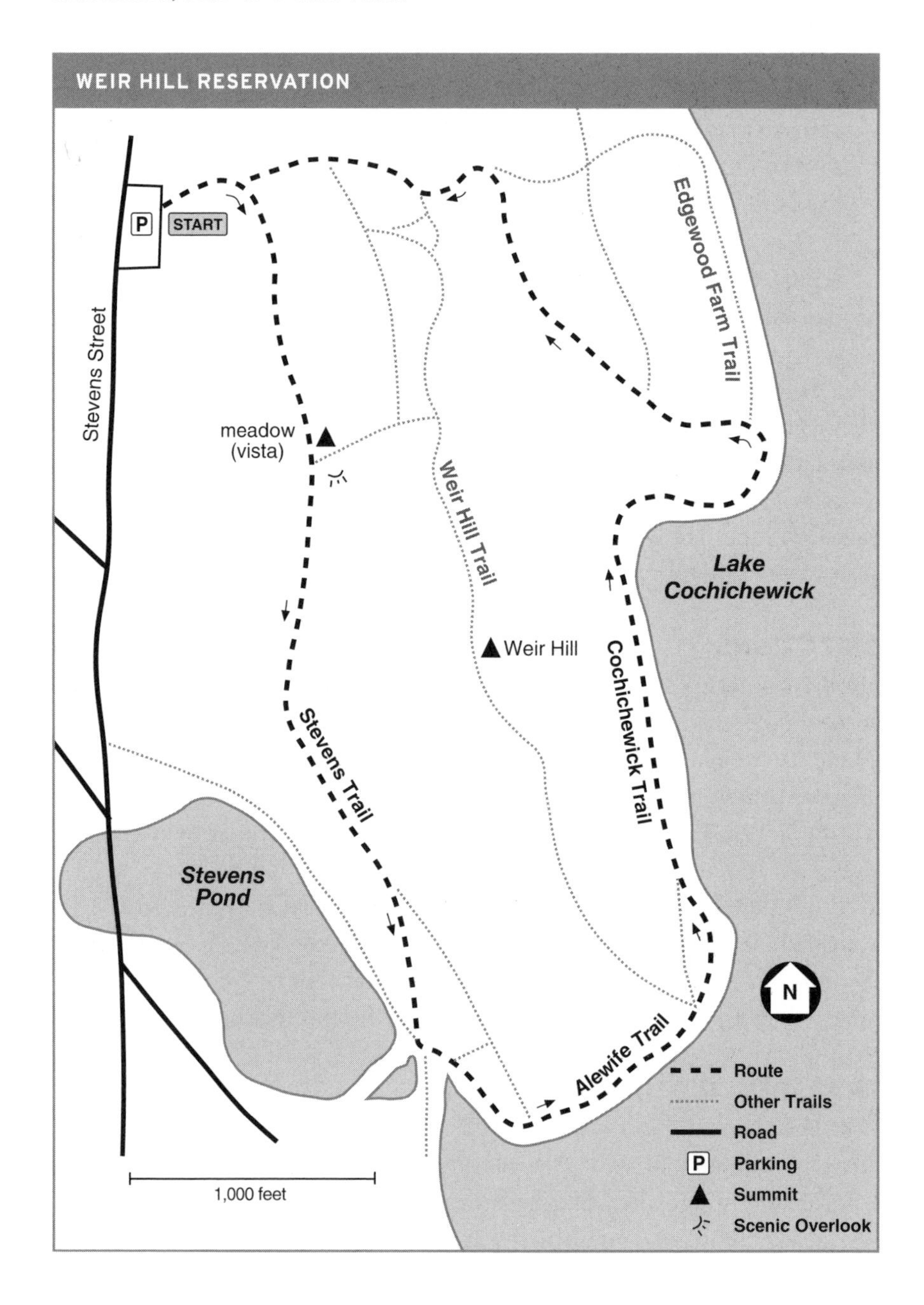

After leaving the meadow, continue on Stevens Trail as it heads down the south side of the drumlin. From the meadow vista it is about a half mile along the Stevens Trail until it brings you to a strip of land that separates Stevens Pond from Lake Cochichewick. There is an interesting stone arch bridge at this spot. (To stay on the Stevens Trail, bear left, and do not cross the strip of land separating the bodies of water.)

As Stevens Trail passes Lake Cochichewick, the name of the trail changes to the Alewife Trail. It's a quiet, peaceful walk by the banks of the lake, made especially appealing in the spring when the shadbush blooms with white flowers.

The perimeter loop trail we are following along the edge of the lake changes names again after an eighth of a mile and is called Cochichewick Trail. The Cochichewick Trail then intersects with a wider trail/dirt road where an old foundation can be seen on the shoreline. Go left, following this road as it angles back, gradually climbing up a hill away from the water. You will pass an impressive stand of large white birch on your right.

Stay left where the dirt road forks about 600 feet up. You will soon come to a scenic open meadow. Just before the trail enters the meadow, there is a small path on the left (Edgewood Farm Trail) that will lead to a parking lot, passing over a wooden footbridge and then beneath tall pines.

NATURE NOTES

At one time all the land around Weir Hill was open meadow to allow grazing for sheep and cattle. The early settlers of North Andover began clearing the virgin forests in the seventeenth century. (The settlers' axes and saws were busy throughout the state, and today there are only small, scattered stands of old-growth timber remaining.)

One of the more interesting features of the reservation is the difference in tree species between the east and west sides. The west side tends to be a bit warmer and drier from the sun while the east side stays cooler, with more moisture from the lake. You will notice that along the western Stevens Trail are a combination of oak and pitch pine, while on the east side are maple, beech, aspen, white pine, white birch, and shagbark hickory. The fruit of these trees, especially the hickory and beech, provides food for a variety of animals that live on the reservation, such as ruffed grouse, opossum, and raccoon.

MORE INFORMATION

Open 8 A.M. to sunset; no fee; dogs allowed on leash. For more information, contact the Trustees of Reservations, 978-682-3580; neregion@ttor.org; www.thetrustees.org.

TRIP 5
WARD RESERVATION

LOCATION: Andover
RATING: Bog Nature Trail, Easy; Holt Hill and Northern Section, Moderate
DISTANCE: Bog Nature Trail, 0.5 mile; Holt Hill and Northern Section: 4 miles
ESTIMATED TIME: Bog Nature Trail, 30 minutes; Holt Hill and Northern Section, 2 hours
OTHER ACTIVITIES: Biking, birding, horseback riding
WINTER ACTIVITIES: Trails are flat and well-maintained, excellent for cross-country skiing and snowshoeing

View a quaking bog, a fascinating natural place to see rare and unusual plant life. Later on explore the Solstice Stones and observe the abundant wildlife on Holt Hill.

Featuring a quaking bog, fantastic vista, and miles of woodland trails, the Ward Reservation requires a full day to explore all its trails. The two walks in this chapter will include the bog, Holt Hill, and the northern section of woodlands.

DIRECTIONS

From I-93 take route 125 north 5 miles and then go right on Prospect Road. Follow Prospect Road 0.3 mile to the parking area on the right.

From I-495 take Route 114 east about 2 miles and then go right on Route 125 south 1.6 miles. Go left on Prospect Road and travel 0.3 mile to the parking lot on the right.

TRAIL DESCRIPTION

Before starting the Holt Hill and Northern Section walk, take a short walk to the bog. From the parking area, cross the grassy area to the south past a private residence on your left. After walking 150 feet through the field with the woods on your right, you will come to the beginning of the trail that leads into the woods. Follow this woodland trail and be on the lookout for low-growing club mosses, poison ivy (three shiny green leaves), and Indian pipe. The woodland

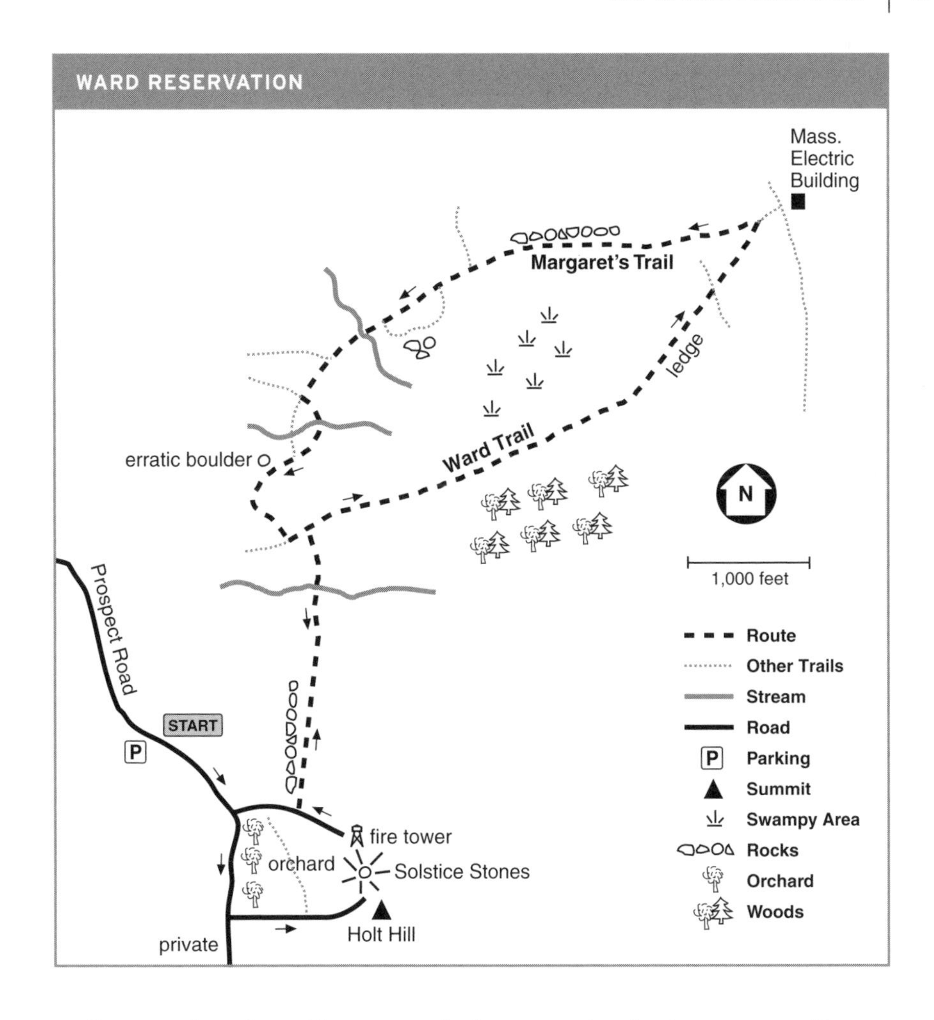

trail goes only a short distance, and after a couple of minutes you will soon pass a wet area on the right. Shortly afterward you will reach a T-intersection where you should turn right onto a boardwalk.

As soon as you begin walking on the boardwalk you will smell the dank earth, spruce, and hemlock. The boardwalk rests on a mat of vegetation and below that is at least 19 feet of muck (as measured during the creation of the boardwalk). Look for cattail, cotton grass (a member of the sedge family that has a cottony tuft in late summer), and highbush blueberries, which prefer the acidic soil of the bog.

It is only a bit over a quarter mile to the bog pond, where the boardwalk ends. Ringed by dark cedars, the bog is particularly appealing in the fall when the golden grasses along its edge frame the black water.

A great horned owl watches us closely. Photo by John Hayes

The bog Nature Trail has interpretive numbers at various intervals. For those who seek an in-depth review of the bog, call the Trustees of Reservations, 508-921-1944, to purchase an interpretive booklet.

To return to the parking area or begin the Holt Hill and Northern Section walk, simply retrace your steps.

From the parking lot go up the paved road 200 feet, where a road enters on the left. Continue straight, climbing uphill, passing an apple orchard on the left. If you are here in the early morning, scan the orchard for deer, particularly when there is fruit on the trees. Approach a large birch tree on the right where there are partial views looking back down toward the bog. Turn left at the chained-off path. Climb the hill through the orchard, then through an open field, and finally into woods. Stay straight, passing a trail on the left, and within a couple minutes you will enter a field again. Look for bluebirds, bobolinks, kestrels (a small hawk that primarily hunts insects), and other birds that prefer open meadows.

To your left you will see a radio tower. Take the path through the meadow that leads that way and you will quickly arrive at the Solstice Stones and the summit of Holt Hill. The Solstice Stones were assembled at the direction of the property's former owner, Mrs. Charles Ward. They are laid out like a compass, with the largest stones indicating the four primary points. (The north stone is marked.) The narrow stone in the NE quadrant points in the direction of the sunrise on the summer solstice, the longest day of the year, which is usually on June 21. The view is breathtaking from Holt Hill. At 420 feet, it is the highest hill in Essex County. Looking southward you can see the Boston skyline and the great Blue Hill in Milton. During the Revolutionary War the townspeople from Andover watched the burning of Charlestown from Holt Hill.

After enjoying the view, walk toward the radio tower and follow the paved road downhill about a quarter mile to a trail on the right with white blazes. Take this trail, which runs northward along a stone wall, indicating that this was once pasture. Large white pines have now grown here, and farther along the trail more oaks and maples appear. The trail gradually goes downhill, and after walking a little more than a quarter mile you will cross a tiny stream on wooden boards.

On the other side of the stream approach a three-way intersection. Turn right onto Ward Trail. After about a quarter mile, you will pass wetlands on the left. Look for tree swallows (dark on the top, white on the bottom) flying here.

After another quarter mile, approach a ledge of granite rock on the right. Next pass through an area of small white pines that crowd the trail, making for a tunnel effect. Deer use the same trail as they make their nocturnal rounds—see if you can spot their heart-shaped hoofprints in the ground. You will soon pass an intersection with a narrow trail. Continue straight until you see a Massachusetts Electric building. Turn left at an intersection just before the building (and before a trail map) to loop back toward the parking area. The trail, called Margaret's Trail, heads in a westerly direction alongside lowlands and a stone wall.

A side trail enters on the right about a half mile down, but you should continue straight, stepping up on exposed bedrock. In another couple hundred feet the trail forks. Stay straight (bearing right), following the trail to a tiny stream that drains the marsh on your left. Before crossing, you might want to go upstream to listen to the stream making four-inch drops over rocks. You can also explore the little side trail that loops back to a partial view of the wetlands by a semicircle of stones around a fire pit.

Back on the main trail, just beyond the stream, approach a fork and follow the trail to the left, where it is crowded by pines. In about 300 feet you'll arrive at a four-way intersection. Turn left and cross another small stream and then walk a couple minutes toward a trail on the right. Bear left here and pass the exposed ledge. A small glacial erratic boulder will be resting on the ledge. After a quarter mile you'll reach an intersection where you should turn left, then go right after 10 feet. You are now back on one of the original trails from the paved road. About 15 or 20 minutes of walking will bring you back to the parking lot.

NATURE NOTES

Indian pipe is a flowering plant that lacks the green pigment chlorophyll and is unable to manufacture its own food by photosynthesis. With the aid of a fungus that connects it to the roots of nearby trees, the Indian pipe collects its food from the host tree. The Indian pipe is 4 to 10 inches tall and its nodding flowers are white or pink, similar in shape to a pipe.

Tree swallows have a greenish-black sheen on their backs and are about 5 inches long. In spring they prefer to nest in cavities in standing timber and

A BOG'S LIFE

The bog formed 12,000–14,000 years ago when the last glacier retreated. It rests on a glacial kettle hole, a depression made when a huge block of ice from the glacier was left buried in the ground. Unlike other bodies of water, decay in a bog is extremely slow, and as the plants die they accumulate at the bottom of the bog, forming thick organic matter known as peat. In time, the open water in the bog will disappear as plants such as leather leaf and sphagnum moss take over.

Both black spruce and tamarack, which are usually only found in northern New England, grow in the bog. And although the trees are small, they are actually quite old. Sphagnum moss rings the bog, and it is this decayed moss that becomes peat. It is very spongy and absorbent. First used by the Native Americans to line their babies' diapers, it was later used as dressing for wounds.

Some of the rare plants here include rose begonia, bog orchids, and two insect-eating plants—the sundew and the pitcher plant. The pitcher plant attracts insects with the fluids that collect in its hollow leaves. The tiny hairs on the leaves allow the insect to enter but the same hairs block their escape. Then the plant's enzymes digest the insect, absorbing its nutrients. You can spot the pitcher plant by looking for a plant roughly 8 to 24 inches tall with a red flower hanging from the center of green or purplish pitcher-shaped leaves.

The sundew is a much smaller plant, with round leaves and white or pink flowers. It too traps insects in the sticky fluid, only this plant's leaves actually close around the insect, trapping it in the fluid. The insects provide the plants with some of the nutrients, like nitrogen, that are lacking in the bog.

are easily attracted to backyard birdhouses if you live anywhere near water. Tree swallows are very social birds and can provide hours of viewing pleasure as they dip and wheel in the sky, chasing each other or catching insects.

Look along the edge of the stream for animal tracks such as those made by the raccoons or minks that forage along wet areas. Mink can grow as long as 35 inches, including tail, yet the weight of a mink that size would be only about 2.5 pounds. They are crafty hunters that prey primarily on small rodents, but will also eat birds, snakes, frogs, crayfish, and even muskrat.

MORE INFORMATION

Open year-round, dawn to dusk; no fee; no rest rooms; dogs allowed. For more information, contact the Trustees of Reservations, 978-682-3580; neregion@ttor.org; www.thetrustees.org.

TRIP 6
BALD HILL RESERVATION

LOCATION: Boxford
RATING: Moderate
DISTANCE: 3.5 miles
ESTIMATED TIME: 1.5 hours
OTHER ACTIVITIES: Birding, swimming

Sprawled over three towns in central Essex County, Bald Hill covers 1,700 acres of forested hills and low-lying swamp protected as conservation land.

The different tracts of woods include John C. Phillips Wildlife Sanctuary, Boxford State Forest, and Boxford Woodlots. The area encompassing Bald Hill and Crooked Pond is generally known as Bald Hill Reservation. It lies within the town of Boxford near the Middleton and North Andover borders.

DIRECTIONS

Take I-95 to Exit 51. Head toward Middleton (south) and take the first right on Middleton Road. Follow this approximately 1.5 miles to a parking lot on the left, where there is a sign and a map welcoming you to Bald Hill.

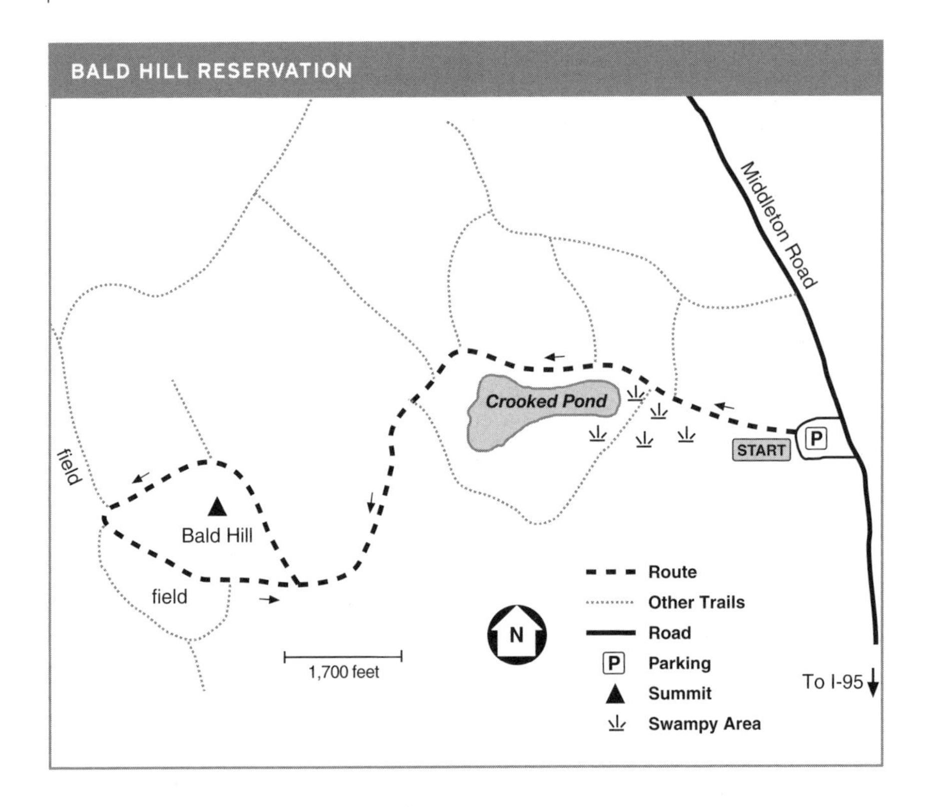

TRAIL DESCRIPTION

To begin your hike, follow the main trail leading away from the parking area. (The trail has numbered markers at various trail intersections.) Overhead, hemlock trees shade this wide, well-maintained trail as it heads in a westerly direction. About 0.25 mile into the walk, you will pass a small swamp on the left, followed by Crooked Pond, also on the left. There are a couple of openings to peer through the vegetation and scan this shallow pond's shoreline for great blue herons or visiting ducks.

Oaks, maples, and pines begin to join the hemlocks as you walk parallel to the pond. After you pass a trail that comes in from the right (at marker 13), the main trail begins a gradual climb toward Bald Hill. At marker 12, turn right to reach the summit in a short walk. The woods thin out farther up the hill and old apple trees can be seen among the small maples and oaks. There are no spectacular views, but an open field stretches along the ridge, providing a nice sunny spot to picnic (which is especially inviting in the autumn). From the summit, bear left as the trail goes downhill through the field. This leads to another open field, where the remains of an old fireplace and chimney sit.

To begin heading back to the parking lot, bear left after passing the old chimney and walk in a southeasterly direction around the base of the hill. This brings you to the main trail, at marker 12. After marker 12, more adventurous walkers might want to take a small path that makes a wide loop of Crooked Pond. The path is marked by a maroon dot on a tree and is between markers 12 and 13 or 13A. The trail is rugged and hilly and adds about 20 minutes to your walk.

NATURE NOTES

Because there are more than 1,700 protected acres, wildlife abounds: Ruffed grouse, goshawks, barred owls, woodcock, deer, fisher, and coyote all live here. The uncommon pileated woodpecker has also been seen. It is one of the largest woodpeckers in North America and can be identified by its red head and loud, rasping call. Also keep an eye out for the elusive native American turkey, a large bird that inhabits these woods.

The largest member of the accipiter family of hawks, the goshawk is a rapid-flying hawk that feeds on birds and small mammals, including gray squirrels. It can negotiate its way through thick forest understory or fly just above the treetops. It is a magnificent and rather uncommon bird. If you are ever fortunate enough to see one, you won't forget the way it stares at you with its red eyes—they can make anybody into an avid bird-watcher.

MORE INFORMATION

Open dawn to dusk; no fee; no rest rooms. For more information, call the Boxford State Park information line at the Division of Conservation and Recreation regional headquarters, 978-369-3350.

TRIP 7
APPLETON FARMS GRASS RIDES

LOCATION: Hamilton
RATING: Moderate
DISTANCE: 4 miles
ESTIMATED TIME: 2–2.5 hours
OTHER ACTIVITIES: Biking, birding
WINTER ACTIVITIES: Trails are flat and well-maintained, excellent for cross-country skiing and snowshoeing
PUBLIC TRANSPORTATION: Commuter Rail to Ipswich, then a shuttle to Appleton Farms; call Appleton Farms Grass Rides at 978-356-5728 for more information

Meander through meadows, wetlands, and woodlands by foot or, in winter, by cross-country skis.

The reservation offers a nice combination of fields, wetlands, and wooded areas comprised of pine, oak, maple, cedar, and my personal favorite, the dark-green majestic hemlock. This area is covered by a confusing network of trails, but don't let that stop you from paying a visit to this reservation. It has an extensive wildlife habitat, and the trails are so wide and the slopes so gentle that it is a perfect place for cross-country skiing.

DIRECTIONS

From Route 128, take Exit 20N. Go north on Route 1A for 4.5 miles. Take a left onto Cutler Road and drive 2.2 miles to the intersection with Highland Street, where there is a parking area on the left. To enter the reservation, park and walk across Cutler Road and follow the sign and trail that are at the edge of the field opposite the parking area.

Public Transportation. From North Station, take the Newburyport Commuter Rail line to Ipswich Station. The Ipswich-Essex Explorer operates from the station to Appleton Farms roughly every two hours during normal weather conditions. Visit www.ipswich-essexexplorer.com for schedules and hours of operation.

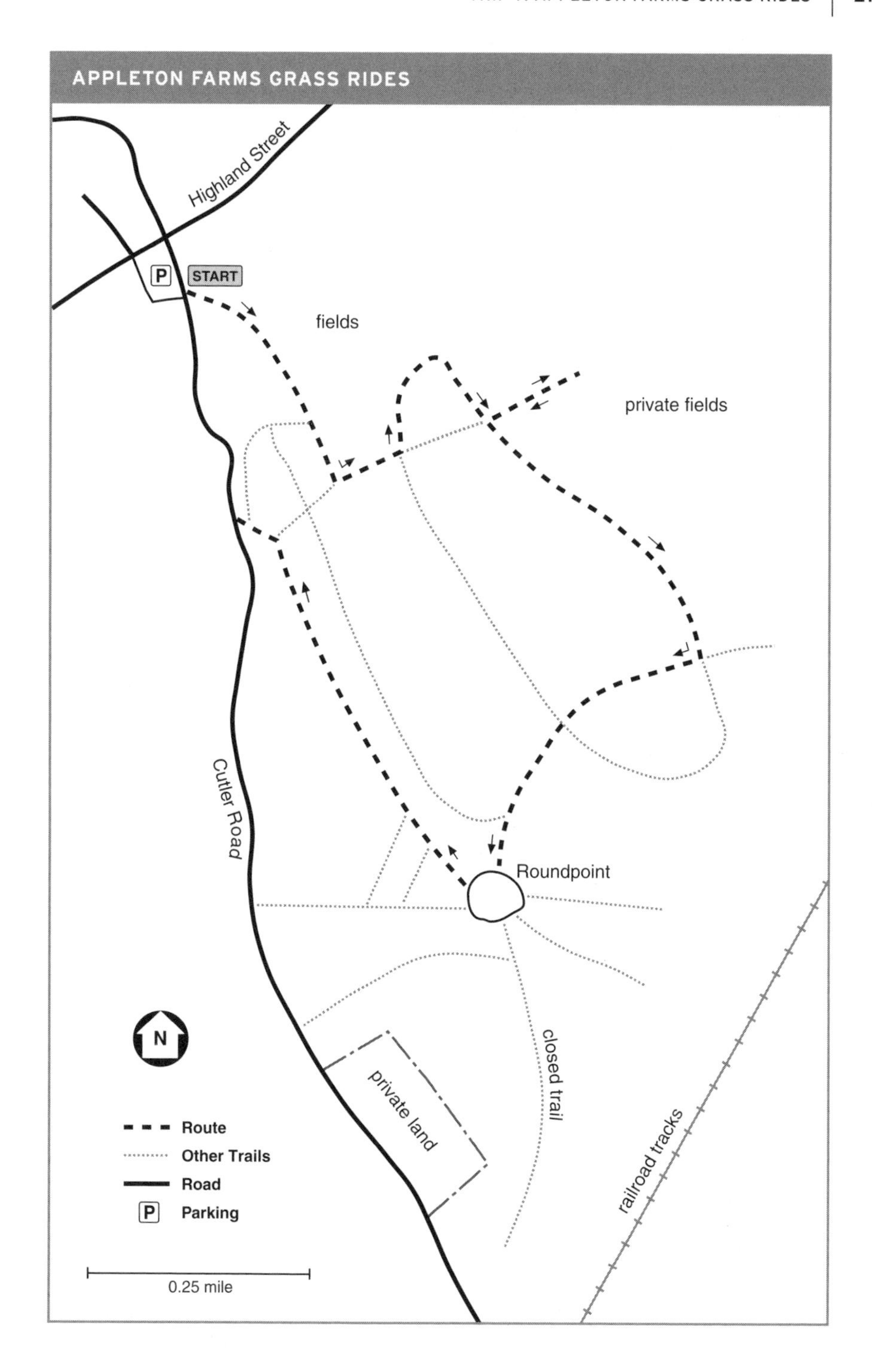
APPLETON FARMS GRASS RIDES
Highland Street
P
START
fields
private fields
Cutler Road
Roundpoint
closed trail
private land
railroad tracks
N
Route
Other Trails
Road
P Parking
0.25 mile

A chipmunk rests on a stone wall.

TRAIL DESCRIPTION

This walk is a circuit of the northern portion of the property. Start by following the signs from the parking lot that direct you onto a path that begins on the other side of Cutler Road and heads southeastward through a meadow. The trail soon enters the woods; by taking the first left, you reach the higher ground. At the next two intersections, bear left again. The trail soon follows the edge of the woods where it meets private fields.

Retrace your steps a short distance to the last intersection, located just before the trail curves toward the field. Follow this trail to the southeast, past one intersection that appears quickly, and go about 0.4 mile to the second intersection, where you turn right. About fifteen minutes down this trail, you arrive at Roundpoint. This circular area is like the center of a wheel with spokes (trails) heading out in various directions.

To return to the parking area, stand at the end of the trail you just walked down and face Roundpoint. Take the trail immediately to your right. This will lead to Cutler Road after about 0.5 mile of walking. When you reach Cutler Road go right (north); from there it is a short walk back to the parking area. Allow yourself plenty of time before dark when you embark on this hike, which takes only about 2 to 2.5 hours, but the maze of trails could get you temporarily lost.

NATURE NOTES

Appleton Farms is believed to be the oldest farm in continuous operation in the United States. Its plantings date back to 1638, when the town of Ipswich granted the land to Thomas Appleton. The descendants of the original owner gave some of the land to the Trustees of Reservations in 1970; today, it is open for all to enjoy. In 1998, adjacent Appleton Farms was opened to the public with an additional 4 miles of trails and community-supported agriculture.

The name "Grass Rides" came from the original use of the land as carriage roads. (The word "ride" comes from Europe to designate a path made for horseback riding.) Horse-drawn carriages raced here in the late 1800s and early 1900s, which is why the main trails loop.

The areas near private fields are good places to catch a glimpse of wildlife, such as fox or coyote, which visit in search of mice. While these predators are primarily nocturnal, they are often seen in the middle of the afternoon.

Keep an eye out for ruffed grouse, deer, and woodchucks, which are fun to watch. After hibernating all winter, woodchucks have a voracious appetite and will eat almost every kind of flower and vegetable, preferring to dine on cold-weather crops like peas first. When threatened they seek the safety of their burrows, which can extend underground for many yards and usually have two entrances.

Notice the wide assortment of wildflowers, which include lady's slipper, Canada mayflower, starflower, violet, and wild indigo. Saint John's wort, meadowsweet, bluets, and other wildflowers that thrive in clearings can be seen in the field near the parking area.

MORE INFORMATION

Both Appleton Farms Grass Rides and Appleton Farms are open year-round daily from 8 A.M. to sunset; fee. Dogs are permitted on the Appleton Farms Grass Rides trails, but not at Appleton Farms. Tours and programs are available periodically throughout the year. For more information, contact Appleton Farms Grass Rides, Highland Street, Hamilton, MA, 978-356-5728; www.thetrustees.org.

TRIP 8
HALIBUT POINT STATE PARK

LOCATION: Rockport
RATING: Easy
DISTANCE: 1.5 miles
ESTIMATED TIME: 1 hour
OTHER ACTIVITIES: Birding, fishing
PUBLIC TRANSPORTATION: Cape Ann Transit Authority (CATA) offers service; the stop needs to be requested (between Pigeon Cove post office and the Rockport train station) as there is not a scheduled stop at Halibut Point; for more information contact the CATA at 978-283-7916 or www.canntran.com.

Enjoy magnificent views of the ocean and a walk along the rocky coastline.

On the Cape Ann coastline, more reminiscent of Maine than Massachusetts, Halibut Point offers walkers, beachcombers, birders, and history buffs a wonderful network of trails to explore. The State Park and the adjacent shoreline owned by the Trustees of Reservations combine for a unique area of open space on this rocky headland known as Halibut Point. Originally called "haul about" by sailors (because they had to tack around this mass of rock), Halibut Point was the site of numerous quarry operations that began in 1840 when the 450-million-year-old granite was cut for the next 100 years.

DIRECTIONS

From the intersections of Routes 128 and 127, take Route 127 north (Eastern Avenue) toward Rockport. Follow route 127 for 6.1 miles and then go left on Gott Avenue a couple hundred feet, where you will see a large parking lot for the State Park. If you are coming from Rockport Center take Route 127 north for 0.5 mile to Gott Avenue on the right.

TRAIL DESCRIPTION

The trail begins just across the street from the parking lot and rest rooms. Dense foliage crowds the path, forming a tunnel of green, as you walk in a

Hiking the rugged granite shoreline of Halibut Point.

northerly direction heading toward the open Atlantic. The trail is wide and flat, with a covering of woodchips. Red cedars, wild apples, dogwoods, oaks, mountain ash, wild cherry, and the draping vines of grapes line the path. At the end of the trail, after a quarter-mile walk, you will reach a T-intersection overlooking the Babson Farm Quarry, now filled with water.

Turn right at the quarry and follow the path around the edge of the quarry, stopping to read the interpretive signs along the way. On your left is marker 3 at a piece of granite with groves along the edge that were the side of holes drilled to split the rock.

Follow the path halfway around the quarry just past marker 5 to a fork in the trail where you should turn right and follow a sign to an overlook. The jumble of rocks you are standing on is called the Grout Pile, which are discarded pieces of granite dumped over the years, now forming the perfect vantage point to view the coastline and ocean. On clear days you can see the New Hampshire coast and even Mount Agamenticus in Maine. With binoculars you can scan the shoreline for seals or watch the lobstermen in small boats check their traps. Should you see a seal on the rocks below do not walk down

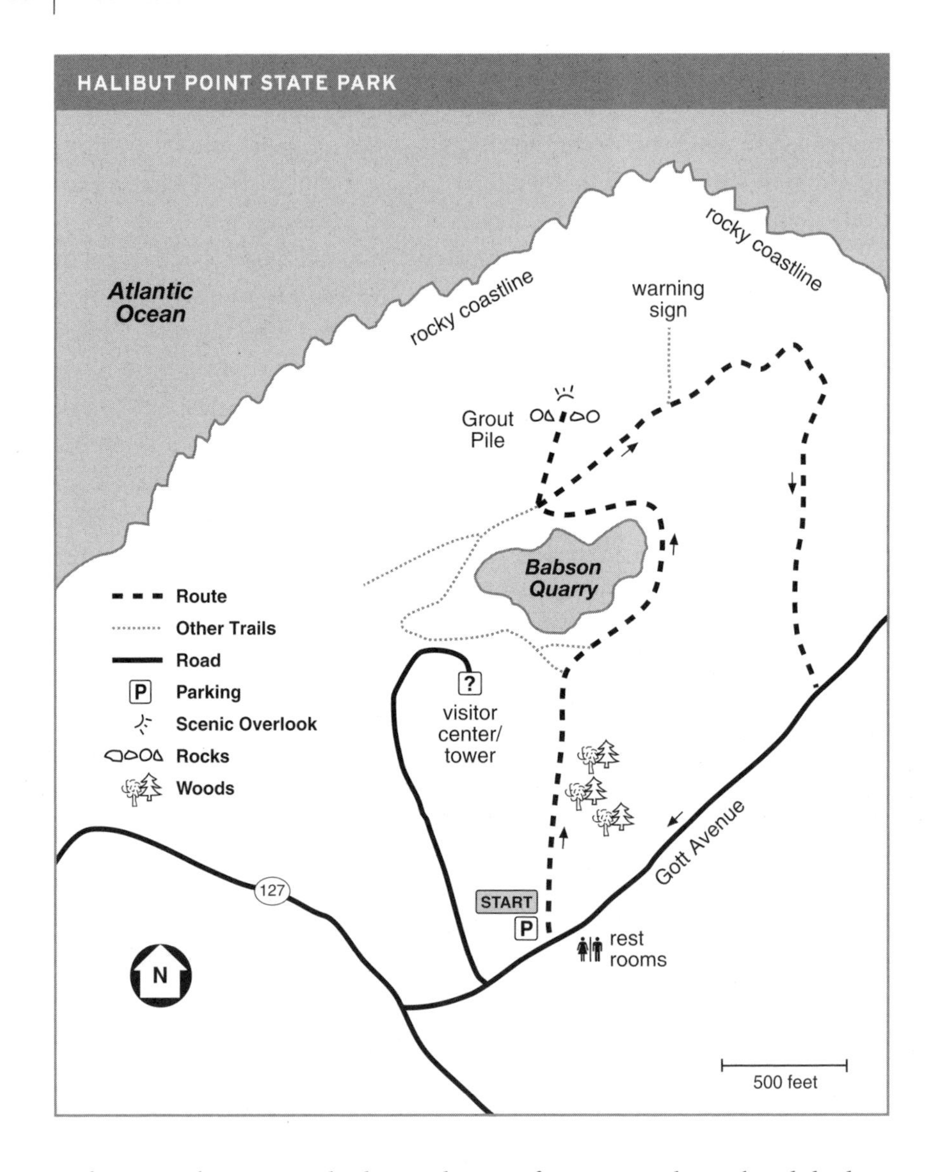

and get too close. Young harbor seal pups often rest on the rocks while their mothers continue to feed offshore. The pups will nap then later return to the sea and join their mothers. Disturbing the seals may cause them to return to the ocean when they are still fatigued and they can drown.

Once you have enjoyed the overlook, retrace your steps a couple hundred feet to the intersection near the quarry and this time follow the path and sign that reads "To Ocean." The path slopes downward, first through an area of small scrub oaks and shadbush then to a more open area of large rocks. There

The common loon winters off Halibut Point, although it does not make its haunting cry in winter and its distinctive black and white patterned plumage is replaced by a dull brown color on the back with the throat and chest white. Loons migrate in small flocks and continue to dive beneath the water surface hunting for fish. Other wintering ducks seen here include the buffleheads, red-breasted mergansers, white-winged scoters, and common eiders.

is a warning sign that reads "This ocean shoreline is hazardous," due to the pounding surf that can sweep over the rocks. Look for wildflowers such as trout lily, violet, asters, and goldenrod growing in the rocky soil.

Once you have enjoyed picking your way through the rocks near the ocean, return to the warning sign and follow the path back up to the intersection and head east (to your left). The trail is difficult to follow because it often crosses exposed rock, but if you continue heading eastward, paralleling the ocean toward a lone house that you can see farther down the coast, you will reach another sign in about a quarter of a mile. The sign marks the border of the reservation's boundary and points to the "Sea Rocks," a right-of-way path owned by the town of Rockport along the water. Our walk goes to the right to make a loop back to the parking lot. Follow the path through the vegetation of small trees for about five minutes until it intersects with a dirt road. The first right turn leads to a private home. You should walk straight ahead for about 20 feet and then bear right on the roadway. Follow this road for 0.25 mile and you will arrive back at the parking lot.

NATURE NOTES

During low tide you will be able to observe the marine organisms that survive in this harsh, open space by clinging to rocks. Starfish, barnacles, and algae can sometimes be seen in the tidal pools.

Prominent bird species include northern gannet, loons, scoters, red-breasted mergansers, and red-necked and horned grebes.

MORE INFORMATION

Open year-round, dawn to dusk; parking fee; portable rest rooms; no bicycling; pets allowed on leash. Park headquarters: 978-546-2997. For more information, contact the Trustees of Reservations: neregion@ttor.org; www.thetrustees.org.

ROCK OF AGES

Between Cape Cod and Cape Elizabeth in Maine, Cape Ann is the largest outcrop of rocky headland, resistant to wave erosion unlike the sand spits and dunes comprising the rest of the Bay State's coastline. The boulders along the shore are of various sizes. The slablike granite rocks and toppled ledges at Halibut Point are a statement to the ice sheet that moved through the land 15,000 years ago. The bedrock tended to break along parallel cracks, which is why the granite slabs look layered in appearance. Just a few hundred feet farther inland evidence of the glaciers is seen in the huge round boulders that litter the landscape. The boulders, called glacial erratics, were deposited haphazardly by the retreating glaciers, and Cape Ann has an abundance of these boulders.

TRIP 9
COOLIDGE RESERVATION

LOCATION: Manchester-By-The-Sea
RATING: Easy
DISTANCE: 3 miles
ESTIMATED TIME: 2 hours
OTHER ACTIVITIES: Birding, fishing, swimming
WINTER ACTIVITIES: Trails are flat and well-maintained, excellent for cross-country skiing and snowshoeing
PUBLIC TRANSPORTATION: Rockport Commuter Rail line to West Gloucester

Come on a Saturday when the Great Lawn is open and relax for a while, taking in the magnificent view.

Established in 1992, Coolidge Reservation is one of the Trustees of Reservations' newer ones. It has two very different parcels of land connected by a right-of-way for walkers. The northern portion closest to the parking lot features hilly woodlands and a pond, while the southern section (open only on Saturdays) includes the Great Lawn, an awe-inspiring open space above the ocean. The walking is easy on the well-maintained trails and, except for the path to the summit of Bungalow Hill, it is flat.

DIRECTIONS

From Route 128, take Exit 15 and follow signs to Manchester. In 0.5 mile, at the small white sign for Magnolia and Gloucester, take a left onto Lincoln Street. Go about a half mile to its end. At the stop sign, take a left onto Route 127 North. Proceed 2 miles to parking area on the right.

TRAIL DESCRIPTION

Start your walk by entering the woods at the trail adjacent to the signboard at the back of the parking lot. Following the trail to the right, you can quickly climb Bungalow Hill. The trail is shaded by the forest and passes an exposed granite ledge and small boulders. Pass a faint trail on the left that is a shortcut to the hilltop and continue on the wider trail, which soon curls around the crest of the hill and leads to a small overlook. The view is to the southeast, where you can see a portion of Clark Pond in the foreground and Magnolia Harbor beyond.

To descend the hill and connect with the reservation's main trail, simply follow the path off the hill to the east (in the direction of Clark Pond). The trail snakes downhill, passing a closed trail on the right and arriving at a fork where you should bear right. This will bring you to the main trail. Follow it to the right to walk along the edge of Clark Pond, passing through a tunnel-like canopy of small trees and bushes.

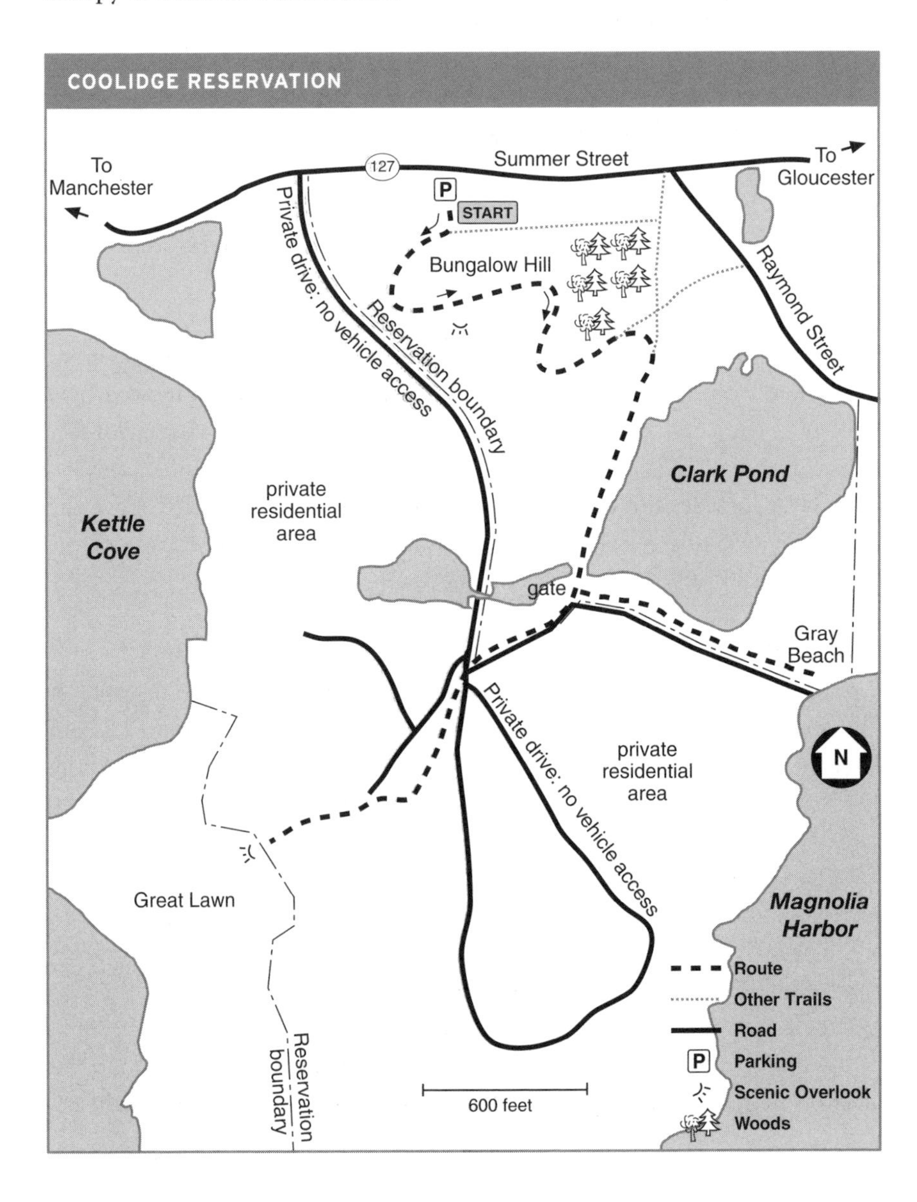

It's only 0.25 mile along the pond's edge and over a small stone bridge to the end of the pond, where there is an intersection in the trail at a metal gate. Turning left, walk east for another 0.25 mile to arrive at Grey Beach on Magnolia Harbor. This is a fine place to rest, soak up the sun, and listen to the surf before pushing on toward the Great Lawn, if you are fortunate enough to be visiting on a Saturday.

Retrace your steps to the metal gate and go left. After about 300 feet, the path crosses a road onto private property, so please stay on the designated trail. Follow the trail for roughly 0.25 mile to a breathtaking view above the ocean. Before you are acres of rolling lawn and magnificent trees. This is the Great Lawn, with Kettle Cove to the northwest and the Atlantic Ocean to the south. Simply retrace your steps to return to the parking area.

NATURE NOTES

Thomas Jefferson Coolidge, the great-grandson of President Thomas Jefferson, purchased the Great Lawn in 1871 for $12,000. He built a large white

A seawall runs along the edge of the Great Lawn.

clapboard country home in 1873 and also sold several lots to relatives, friends, and business associates. In 1902, Coolidge had a grand cottage, known as the "Marble Palace," built on the Great Lawn. It featured Roman columns favored by Thomas Jefferson; the entire brick and white-marble house measured 230 feet in length. (It was razed in the 1950s.) Numerous dignitaries stayed at the Marble Palace, including President and Mrs. Woodrow Wilson, who were given the house for a week in 1918.

The Coolidge family donated 41.6 acres to the Trustees of Reservations in 1990 and 1991. In 1992, the Essex County Greenbelt Association donated an additional 16.2 acres that had been given to it earlier. With these gifts, most of the original land purchased by Thomas Jefferson Coolidge is now protected by the Trustees of Reservations for conservation and historic preservation.

The lawn slopes gently down to the ocean, and at the water's edge is a flat-topped cement breakwater that makes an excellent walkway. The Great Lawn is open for picnicking, and there are a few large trees, one of which is an enormous beech tree with spreading branches that provide a shady spot to spread a blanket. If you walk to the tree's trunk and look up, you will see that the main branches of the tree are wired together to prevent splitting.

Another especially scenic spot is the very southern tip of the Great Lawn, where there is a granite bluff offering sweeping views of the offshore islands. Scan the water for harbor seals and birds such as eiders, scoters, and cormorants. There are few places as peaceful and scenic as this!

MORE INFORMATION

Open year-round, dawn to dusk; no fee (but donation recommended); no rest rooms; dogs allowed. For more information, contact the Trustees of Reservations, 978-682-3580; neregion@ttor.org; www.thetrustees.org.

TRIP 10
RAVENSWOOD PARK

LOCATION: Gloucester
RATING: Easy to Moderate
DISTANCE: 2.5 miles
ESTIMATED TIME: 2.25 hours
OTHER ACTIVITIES: Biking, birding
WINTER ACTIVITIES: Trails are flat and well-maintained, excellent for cross-country skiing and snowshoeing

Historic and ecologically diverse pocket of wilderness with a rare magnolia swamp.

Ravenswood is a pocket of wilderness within the suburbs of the North Shore. The large hemlock trees, the miles of winding trails, and the magnolias in the swamp are all reasons to visit this 500-acre property owned by the Trustees of Reservations. History lovers will enjoy the story of Mason A. Walton, the "Hermit of Gloucester" who lived in Ravenswood Park for 33 years.

DIRECTIONS

From Route 128, take Exit 14/Route 133. Follow Route 133 east for 3 miles to Route 127. Turn right on Route 127 and proceed south for 2 miles. Look for sign and parking area on the right.

TRAIL DESCRIPTION

When you arrive at the parking lot, pause for a moment to read the signboard. It has a series of maps of the property, each one showing the mileage for a different walk. Our walk is a 2.5-mile one that first goes through Magnolia Swamp, then leads to the hermit marker before looping back to the parking area through an area of old trees and rocky terrain. From the parking lot, follow the wide gravel road called Old Salem Road that leads into the woods.

Within 0.25 mile, you pass the Ledge Hill Trail on the right; a couple minutes farther, you'll see a sign for the Magnolia Swamp on the left. Take this left and follow the narrow Magnolia Swamp Trail beneath large hemlocks as it winds its way up and down small hills heading in a southwesterly direction. Just 300 feet down the trail, a narrow trail enters on the left, but you should

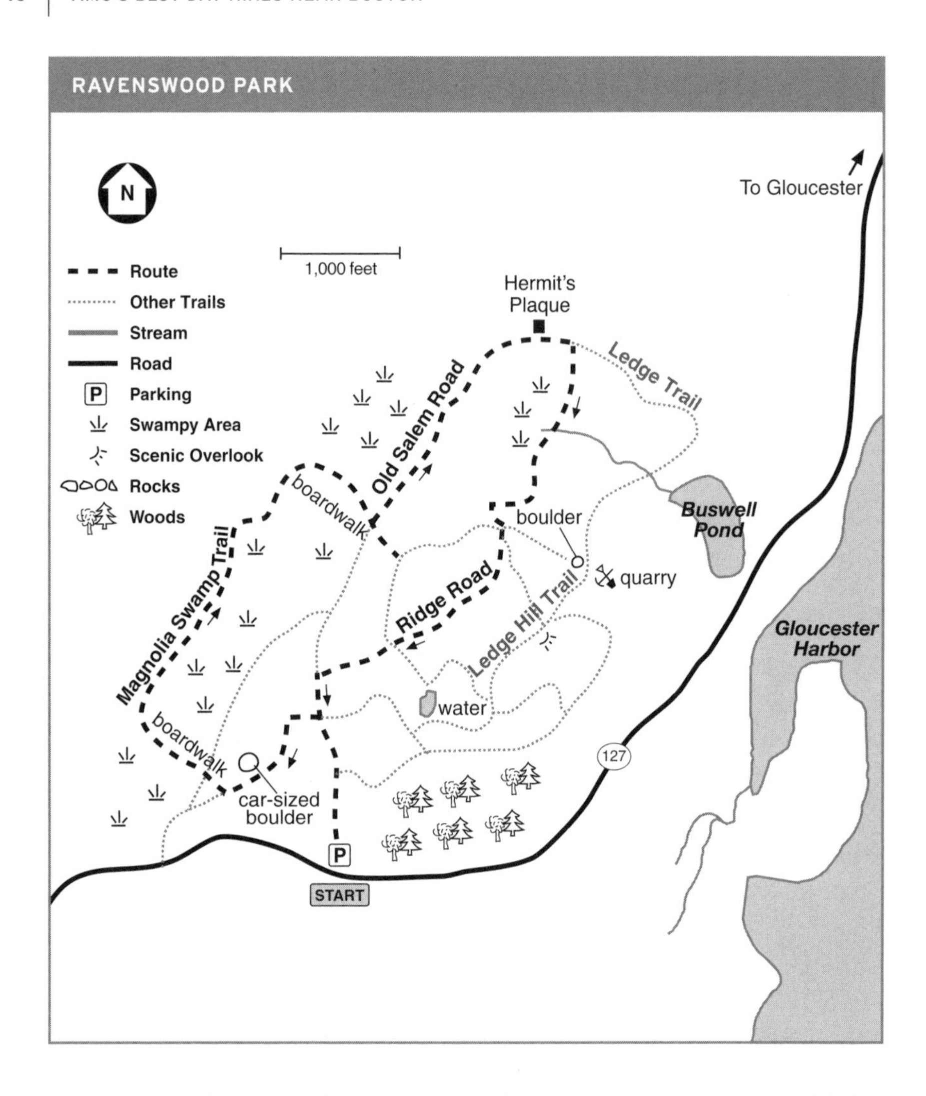

continue straight. In another 300 or 400 feet, you arrive at an exposed ledge of rock where a car-sized glacial boulder is perched on the bedrock. Such boulders are known as glacial erratics because of the haphazard way they were deposited by the glaciers roughly 15,000 years ago.

Follow the trail to the right of the boulder as the path curls to the right, heading toward the swamp and passing through an understory of mountain laurel and blueberries. You soon reach an intersection. Going straight will bring you to a new boardwalk that traverses the ferns and thick foliage in the wet area of the swamp. The boardwalk is a short one and you reach dry ground in 0.25 mile. The trail forks; bear right, following the edge of the swamp in a northerly direction. More large hemlocks and exposed rock are along the trail and it takes about 0.5 mile to reach the next boardwalk that recrosses the swamp.

After you cross the second boardwalk and wind your way uphill past more hemlocks with winterberry growing beneath, you reach the carriage road, Old Salem Road, where you should turn left. In about 0.25 mile, the road forks; stay to the left. Look for a few yellow birch off to your left, followed by another wet area where red maple and a few white pines grow. Stone walls lace the woods, indicating this was pasture or farm land at one time. By the looks of the number of stones and boulders scattered on the ground, chances are the soil was too bony for growing crops and was used instead for sheep or cattle pasture.

A boardwalk leads into the Magnolia Swamp.

After 0.5 mile of leaving the Magnolia Trail, you arrive at a boulder with a plaque dedicated to the Hermit of Gloucester, Mason. A. Walton. This scholarly man initially came to Gloucester to cure himself of tuberculosis; as his health improved, he built a cabin on the north side of Ravenswood and spent his days writing and studying wildlife. People came to his cabin to listen to him discuss the flora and fauna of the area.

From here, continue on the wide road, passing by a narrow trail that leads straight ahead where the wide road curls to the right. This wide trail is called Ridge Road. About five minutes farther down the road, the trail passes over a tiny stream where a nice stand of mountain laurel grows beneath the canopy of tall hemlocks. After 0.25 mile of walking, you will reach a road on the left. Turn left. About 75 feet farther, the road splits and you should bear right, continuing on Ridge Road. (On future trips, you may want to take an even longer walk by turning left here to visit a small former quarry, returning to the parking area via the Ledge Hill Trail—a narrow, snaking path through very rocky terrain.) Our walk stays on the well-maintained Ridge Road for about

0.5 mile, passing beneath more impressive-sized pines and hemlocks, until it intersects Old Salem Road. To reach the parking lot, turn left and follow the road for 0.25 mile.

NATURE NOTES

There are fisher cat here, and chances are, if there are fisher cat (or just "fisher") in the reservation, there are also porcupine. The fisher is a large member of the weasel family. Its muzzle is pointed, its ears broad and rounded, and its legs and feet are stout. Its glossy coat is brownish-black, with small white patches on the neck. Males can measure as much as 40 inches long, with a foot-long tail, although their maximum weight is only about 20 pounds. Fishers are one of the few animals that kill and eat porcupine. They do so by circling the porcupine, biting its exposed face, and tiring it before moving in for the kill. The hemlocks along the trail are a chief food source for the porcupine and the exposed ledges offer good denning areas. Look for porcupine tracks in the snow, when you can see the pigeon-toed paw prints, the tail drag, and even the marks left by their quills.

Red maples and sweet pepper grow along the boardwalk, and the low-lying swamp has a decidedly different feel than the upland trail. Magnolia trees also grow here (the nearby village of Magnolia gets its name from these trees). This is the northernmost stand of magnolias, and even Thoreau visited the swamp to see the trees. During the 1800s and early 1900s, magnolia plants were taken from the swamp and the population was on the verge of extinction before protective measures and replanting ensured the survival of a limited number of magnolias (they are on the state's endangered species list). In this northern climate, the magnolias are not very tall, and they are difficult to distinguish among the other trees. Perhaps the best time to spot one is in June, when they have creamy white flowers and give off a delicate scent. The species growing here is the sweet bay magnolia (*Magnolia virginiana*), which is native to lowlands and prefers rich, moist soil. Please be sure not to bend the trees to see the flowers up close, as this can damage growth.

MORE INFORMATION

Open year-round, dawn to dusk; no fee (donation recommended); no rest rooms; dogs allowed. For more information, contact the Trustees of Reservations, 978-526-8687; neregion@ttor.org; www.thetrustees.org.

TRIP 11 MIDDLESEX FELLS RESERVATION: CROSS FELLS TRAIL

LOCATION: Stoneham/Medford/Winchester/Melrose/Malden
RATING: Strenuous
DISTANCE: 8.6 miles (out and back)
ESTIMATED TIME: 5 hours
OTHER ACTIVITIES: Biking allowed on fire roads and designated mountain bike loop, marked by green blazes in the western area of the Fells
WINTER ACTIVITIES: Cross-country skiing
PUBLIC TRANSPORTATION: The eastern end of this trail is 0.6 mile north of the Oak Grove terminal of the MBTA Orange Line. To reach the trailhead in the eastern section of the Fells, follow Washington Street north to Goodyear Avenue

The blue-blazed Cross Fells Trail is a good connecting trail between the eastern and western sections of the Middlesex Fells Reservation, because it touches every major trail in the reservation.

DIRECTIONS

From I-93 take Exit 33 to MA 28, and travel south to Fellsway East. Turn right onto Glenwood Street, left onto Pleasant Street and then left onto Goodyear Avenue.

TRAIL DESCRIPTION

Follow Goodyear Avenue west (left) to the trailhead in Melrose, near the Melrose–Malden line. The trail climbs west along easy wooded grades to a high rocky ridge. Here it turns left (south) and follows the Rock Circuit Trail (white-blazed) and the Mini Rock Circuit Trail (orange-blazed) to Black Rock. The Cross Fells Trail continues some distance with the Rock Circuit Trail (but not with the Mini Rock Circuit Trail) before exiting right (west) to cross Black Rock Path (a bridle trail) and Fellsway East (paved). It continues west, skirting the south side of the high reservoir and picking up the Mini Rock Circuit Trail. Shortly the two trails come to the Virginia Woods Trail (red-blazed). The Mini Rock Circuit Trail exits right (north) with the Virginia Woods Trail, while the Cross Fells Trail continues west.

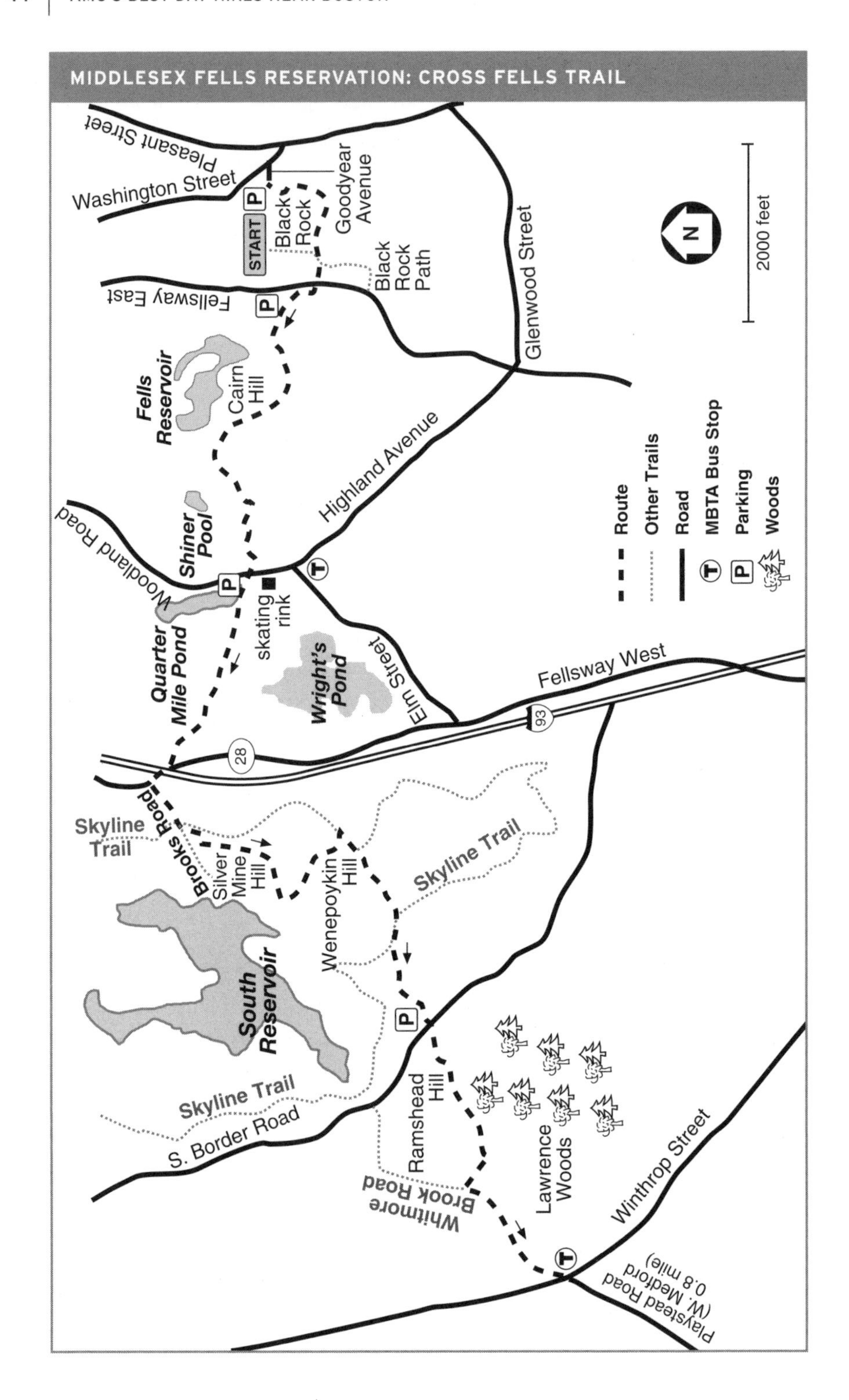
MIDDLESEX FELLS RESERVATION: CROSS FELLS TRAIL
Pleasant Street
Washington Street
START
Black Rock
Goodyear Avenue
Black Rock Path
Fellsway East
Glenwood Street
Fells Reservoir
Cairn Hill
Highland Avenue
Shiner Pool
Woodland Road
skating rink
Quarter Mile Pond
Wright's Pond
Elm Street
Fellsway West
93
28
Brooks Road
Skyline Trail
Silver Mine Hill
Wenepoykin Hill
Skyline Trail
South Reservoir
Skyline Trail
S. Border Road
Ramshead Hill
Lawrence Woods
Whitmore Brook Road
Winthrop Street
Playstead Road (W. Medford 0.8 mile)
N
2000 feet
Route
Other Trails
Road
MBTA Bus Stop
Parking
Woods

The trail crosses several bridle paths before passing south of Shiner Pool. After this pool it rejoins the Rock Circuit Trail and crosses a swampy section. It then leaves this trail and crosses Woodland Road (paved) just north of the skating rink. It next joins the Virginia Woods Trail, passing the southern end of Quarter Mile Pond and heading west over the hills. In 0.3 mile the Virginia Woods Trail exits left (south) to Wright's Pond, while the Cross Fells Trail continues west to Fellsway West (MA 28). The trail follows Fellsway West and the Spot Pond Trail (yellow-blazed) a short distance to an underpass of I-93 then crosses Fellsway West.

The trail follows Brooks Road (dirt) to a junction with the Skyline Trail (white-blazed). Here the Cross Fells Trail turns left (south) to go partway up a short hill with the Skyline Trail. Soon the Cross Fells Trail turns right (west) to follow a ridge above Brooks Road. The trail bends left (south) and picks up a series of bridle paths before turning left (east) into the woods to rejoin the Skyline Trail on the summit of Wenepoykin Hill.

The two trails then head south together to East Dam Road (dirt). Here the Cross Fells Trail continues south downhill to a brook and on to rejoin another section of the Skyline Trail. The two trails continue west until the Cross Fells Trail turns left (southwest) to pick up a group of bridle paths. After crossing South Border Road (paved), the trail climbs Ramshead Hill to the site of the former Lawrence Observation Tower. Descending the hill, the trail follows bridle paths to the reservation's Whitmore Brook entrance on Winthrop Street in Medford, across from Playstead Road (the end of the MBTA Sullivan Square–West Medford bus line). This is the 4.3-mile mark—retrace steps to return to car, or arrange for pickup at Playstead Road.

NATURE NOTES

"Fells" is the English word for hilly, rocky terrain. Both sedimentary and igneous rock can be found at Middlesex Fells.

MORE INFORMATION

Open year-round, dawn to dusk; no fee. For more information, contact DCR Malden, Medford, Stoneham, Melrose, Winchester, 781-322-2851 or 781-662-5230; www.mass.gov/dcr. Trail maps are available on the website and through the AMC.

TRIP 12
MIDDLESEX FELLS RESERVATION: ROCK CIRCUIT TRAIL

LOCATION: Stoneham/Medford/Winchester/Melrose/Malden
RATING: Strenuous
DISTANCE: 4 miles
ESTIMATED TIME: 3.5 hours
OTHER ACTIVITIES: Biking allowed on fire roads and designated mountain bike loop, marked by green blazes in the western area of the Fells
WINTER ACTIVITIES: Cross-country skiing
PUBLIC TRANSPORTATION: MBTA Orange Line to Wellington Station, then MBTA bus 99 to skating rink

This rugged and rocky trail offers the best views in the reservation, including those from White Rock and Melrose Rock.

DIRECTIONS

From I-93 take Exit 33 to MA 28, and travel north to Elm Street. Turn right onto Elm Street and follow to Woodland Road at the rotary.

TRAIL DESCRIPTION

This white-blazed trail affords the best views in the Middlesex Fells. Living up to its name, it is very rocky and offers rewarding but rugged hiking. A convenient approach to this trail is from Woodland Road in Medford, opposite the northern end of the skating rink parking lot (south of New England Memorial Hospital in Stoneham). Follow a woods road east for a short distance to the crest of a hill to pick up the Rock Circuit Trail.

Turning right (south), the trail climbs a nearby ridge overlooking sections of Medford. Here it joins the Virginia Woods Trail (red-blazed) for a few feet, then goes south along the ridge before turning left (east) to another ridge. The trail goes north before turning sharp right (east) to drop into a valley, crossing a bridle path and a brook.

At the brook the trail turns left (north) and soon rejoins the Virginia Woods Trail, again for only a few feet. The Rock Circuit Trail crosses a bridle path and climbs southeast up a ridge. In 0.1 mile the trail turns right (south)

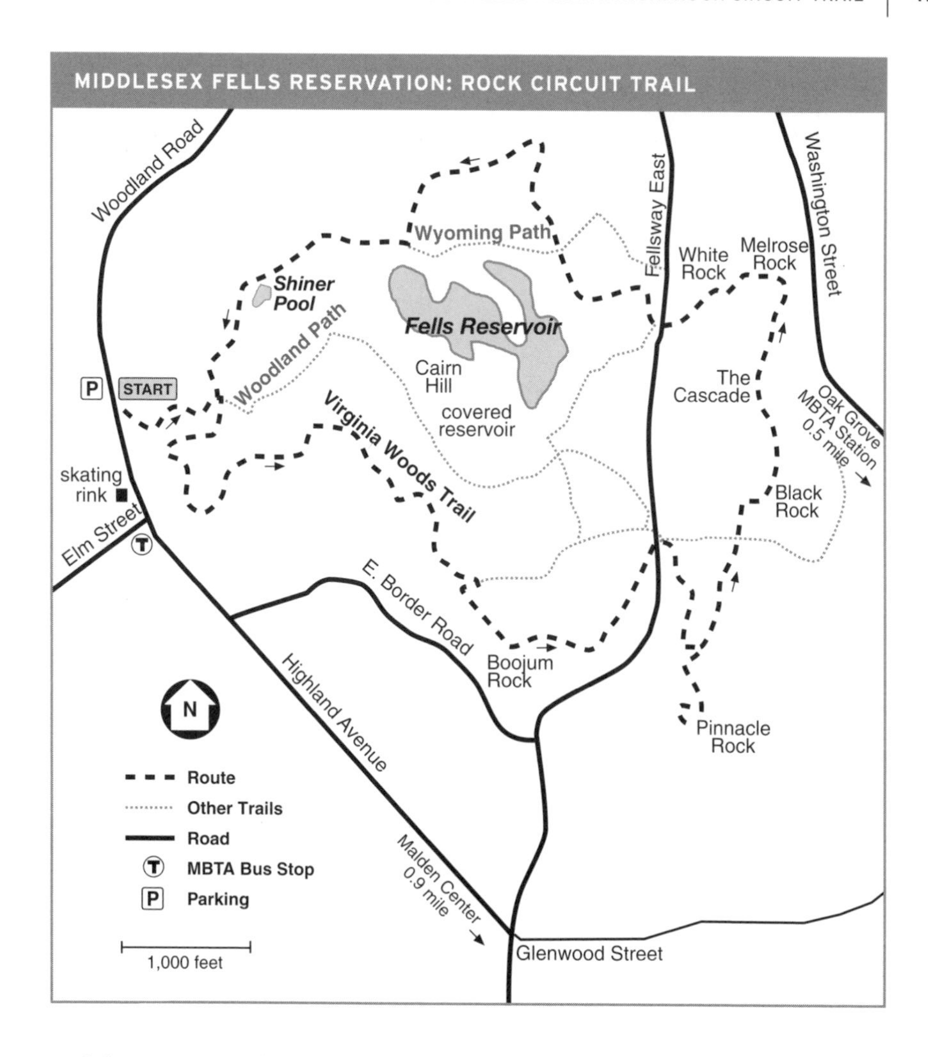

and drops into a valley. The trail then makes a long, gentle climb southeast to Boojum Rock, where it picks up the Mini Rock Circuit Trail (orange-blazed) for 0.1 mile. Leaving fine views of the Boston area, the trail drops sharply and heads east to cross a bridle path and then Fellsway East (paved). It rejoins the Mini Rock Circuit Trail and climbs Pinnacle Rock, from which there are excellent views. At Pinnacle Rock both trails turn north, almost doubling back on themselves, and pass a television tower enclosure, where the Mini Rock Circuit Trail exits.

The Rock Circuit Trail then follows a rough ridge north to Black Rock. At Black Rock, this trail combines first with the Cross Fells Trail (blue-blazed) and then with the Mini Rock Circuit Trail to surmount a fine viewpoint. The three trails continue north a short distance before the Cross Fells Trail turns sharp

Cottontails appear in the most curious places.

right (east) downhill to exit the Fells. The two Rock Circuit Trails continue north along the top of the ridge to White Rock and Melrose Rock with many fine views.

At Melrose Rock the two trails separate, with the Rock Circuit Trail turning left (west) through the woods to recross Fellsway East (paved) and to skirt the eastern end of the high reservoir. The trail crosses Wyoming Path to enter some young tree growth and soon rejoins the Virginia Woods Trail and then the Mini Rock Circuit Trail. It ascends a ridge behind (east of) New England Memorial Hospital, from which there is a fine view north. The Virginia Woods Trail separates here, with the two Rock Circuit Trails turning left from the ridge. Soon the Mini Rock Circuit Trail exits left (south), and the Rock Circuit Trail goes right (west) through a fine pine grove to join the yellow-blazed Spot Pond Trail for 0.2 mile while passing south of New England Memorial Hospital.

After leaving the Spot Pond Trail and crossing several bridle paths, the Rock Circuit Trail passes the northwest shore of Shiner Pool and soon joins the Cross Fells Trail to cross a swampy area. It then leaves the Cross Fells Trail, turning left (south) along a ridge adjacent to Woodland Road to complete the circuit.

NATURE NOTES

"Fells" is the English word for hilly, rocky terrain. Both sedimentary and igneous rock can be found at Middlesex Fells.

MORE INFORMATION

Open year-round, dawn to dusk; no fee. For more information, contact DCR Malden, Medford, Stoneham, Melrose, Winchester, 781-322-2851 or 781-662-5230; www.mass.gov/dcr. Trail maps are available on the website and through the AMC.

TRIP 13
MIDDLESEX FELLS RESERVATION: SKYLINE TRAIL

LOCATION: Stoneham/Medford/Winchester/Melrose/Malden
RATING: Strenuous
DISTANCE: 6.8 miles
ESTIMATED TIME: 5 hours
OTHER ACTIVITIES: Biking allowed on fire roads and designated mountain-bike loop, marked by green blazes in the western area of the Fells
WINTER ACTIVITIES: Cross-country skiing
PUBLIC TRANSPORTATION: MBTA: Take the Orange Line to Wellington Station, then MBTA bus 100 to Roosevelt Circle Rotary; from there walk south to the rotary and follow South Border Road (on the right) less than 0.25 mile to Bellevue Pond

This hike, which loops the western side of the Fells, has some steep ascents to afford great views of Boston.

DIRECTIONS

From I-93 take Exit 33 to MA 28, travel north a short distance around Roosevelt Circle to South Border Road, take a right onto the road, and proceed to the Bellevue Pond parking area on the right.

TRAIL DESCRIPTION

This trail is located in the western section of the Fells. Marked with white blazes, it circles the Winchester Reservoirs as it travels through Medford, Stoneham, and Winchester. A popular starting point is Bellevue Pond, off South Border Road in Medford. Quarry Road (dirt) goes east (right) of Bellevue Pond. The Skyline Trail follows Quarry Road to the first blaze near the northern end of Bellevue Pond.

The trail turns right up Pine Hill, at the top of which is Wright's Tower, with commanding views of Boston, its harbor, and the Blue Hills. The trail continues north along a rocky ridge before turning west to drop into a valley. It climbs the ridge to the west and on top of the second ridge turns north for 0.3 mile, dipping once to cross a notch with a spur of Quarry Road (bridle path). At the northern end of the ridge is a good view north over I-93.

The trail descends northwest, passing the northern end of the next ridge before turning more west and dropping into a valley. It continues west, descending a hill. Near the summit of Wenepoykin Hill the trail turns right (north) and joins the Cross Fells Trail (blue-blazed) for a short distance to the summit. The Skyline Trail follows high land north over several hills, includ-

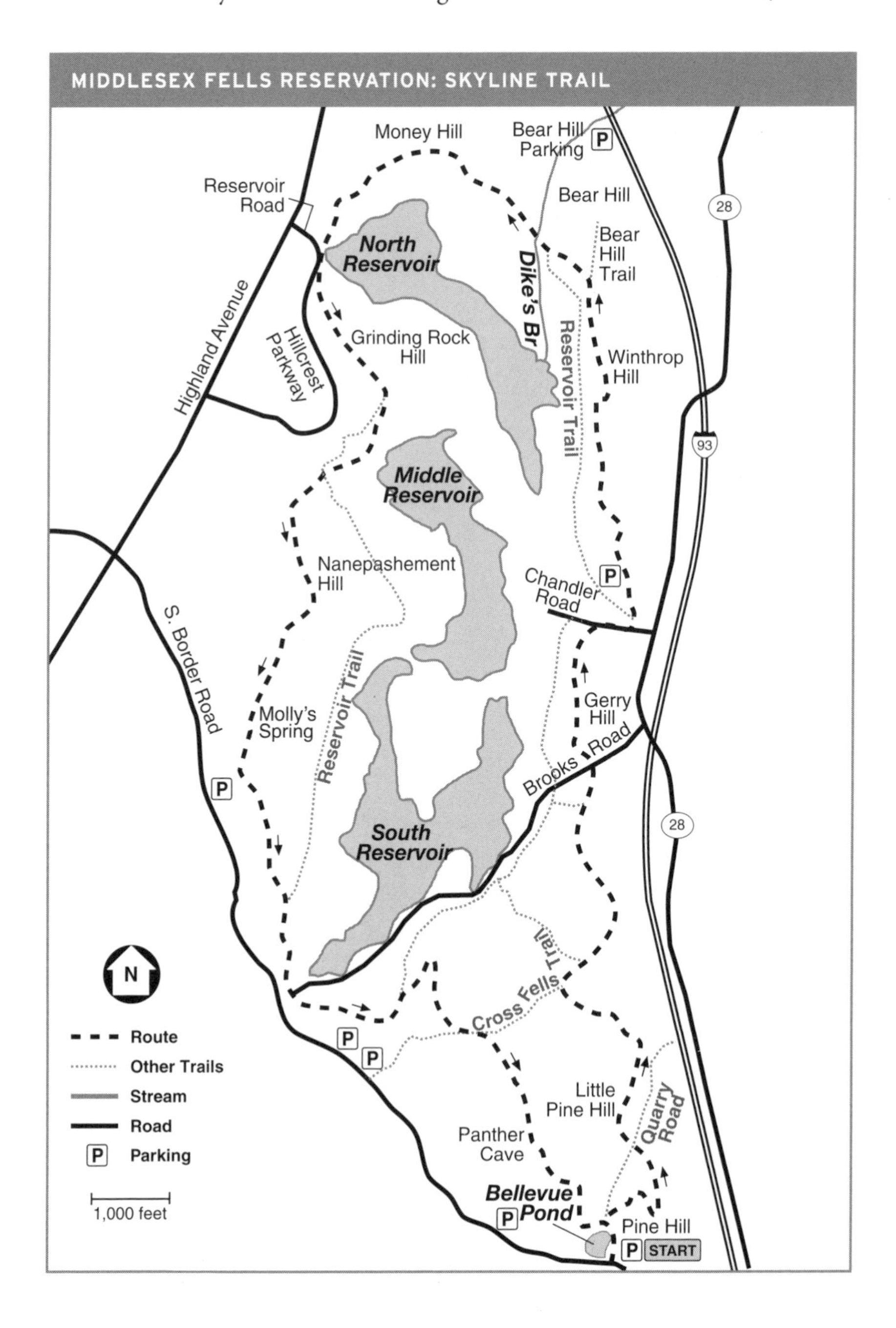

ing Silver Mine Hill. Soon after Silver Mine Hill, the Skyline Trail rejoins the Cross Fells Trail for a short distance as it descends to Brooks Road (dirt). The Skyline Trail continues north over Gerry Hill and on to Chandler Road (dirt) along the Winchester Reservoir fence, which detours the Skyline Trail with the Reservoir Trail (orange-blazed) to the right (east) a short distance and then left (north).

Very shortly the Reservoir Trail exits left (northwest), while the Skyline Trail goes uphill to the Sheepfold picnic area. The trail passes the eastern end of the parking lot, skirts the east side of the picnic area, then crosses a former soapbox derby track on the way north to Winthrop Hill, where there is a fine view of the Winchester North Reservoir. From here it continues along a ridge toward Bear Hill. About 0.2 mile north of Winthrop Hill the Skyline Trail turns sharp left (west) downhill at a trail junction. (Note: Straight ahead—north—uphill is the short Bear Hill Connector Trail, which connects with the Spot Pond Trail at the Bear Hill observation tower.)

The Skyline Trail crosses Dike Road (dirt), where it joins the Reservoir Trail to cross a brook and continue through a former meadow and a pine grove to another dirt road. Here the Reservoir Trail exits left (southwest) on the dirt road, while the Skyline Trail continues straight over Money Hill. On the west slope of Money Hill the two trails remerge and descend, crossing North Border Road (dirt) into a ravine north of the Winchester North Reservoir dam.

The trails cross a brook (leakage from the reservoir), then soon bend left (south) a short distance before zigzagging up the west slope of the ravine to pass north of the old firehouse. They continue to paved Alben Street, on to Reservoir Road, and finally on to Hillcrest Parkway, where there is parking and access to the trail. Both trails very shortly leave the paved roads and go south via the West Dam Path. After crossing a dirt service road, they soon separate. The Reservoir Trail exits right, while the Skyline Trail continues straight over a couple of minor hills. The Skyline Trail crosses the Reservoir Trail and soon climbs steeply up Nanepashemet Hill, where there are limited views.

The Skyline Trail continues south over numerous hills to merge with the Reservoir Trail again at the Winchester South Reservoir standpipe. The two trails continue south, then east around wetland property at the west reservoir dam. The trails almost reach South Border Road before passing over a hill to the Middle Road Path. A dirt road on the right leads shortly to a parking area off South Border Road and an access to the two trails. The trails soon bend left (north) to pick up the East Dam Path. They then separate, with the Reservoir Trail going straight (north) and the Skyline Trail turning right uphill. At the top of the hill the trail bends right along a ridge before turning left to cross Middle

Road (dirt) and soon joins the Cross Fells Trail for a short distance. The Skyline Trail turns right to head for Panther Cave, passing almost directly over the cave before dropping to cross the Red Cross Path and Straight Gully Brook. It then climbs Little Pine Hill on its way to Bellevue Pond, where it completes its circuit.

NATURE NOTES

See "Nature Notes" for Trip 11.

MORE INFORMATION

Open year-round, dawn to dusk; no fee. For more information, contact DCR Malden, Medford, Stoneham, Melrose, Winchester, 781-322-2851 or 781-662-5230; www.mass.gov/dcr. Trail maps are available on the website and through the AMC.

TRIP 14
MIDDLESEX FELLS RESERVATION: RESERVOIR TRAIL

LOCATION: Stoneham/Medford/Winchester/Melrose/Malden
RATING: Moderate (long but not very steep)
DISTANCE: 5.5 miles
ESTIMATED TIME: 3 hours
OTHER ACTIVITIES: Biking allowed on fire roads and designated mountain bike loop, marked by green blazes in the western area of the Fells
WINTER ACTIVITIES: The trail was designed to be a cross-country ski touring trail when snow is sufficient; it has many fine vistas

A very pleasant circuit around the three Winchester reservoirs.

DIRECTIONS

From I-93 take Exit 33 to MA 28 north and exit at Fire Gate 26.

TRAIL DESCRIPTION

Individuals using the trail should be aware that the adjacent waterlands are not for general public access and should observe the nearby No Trespassing signs.

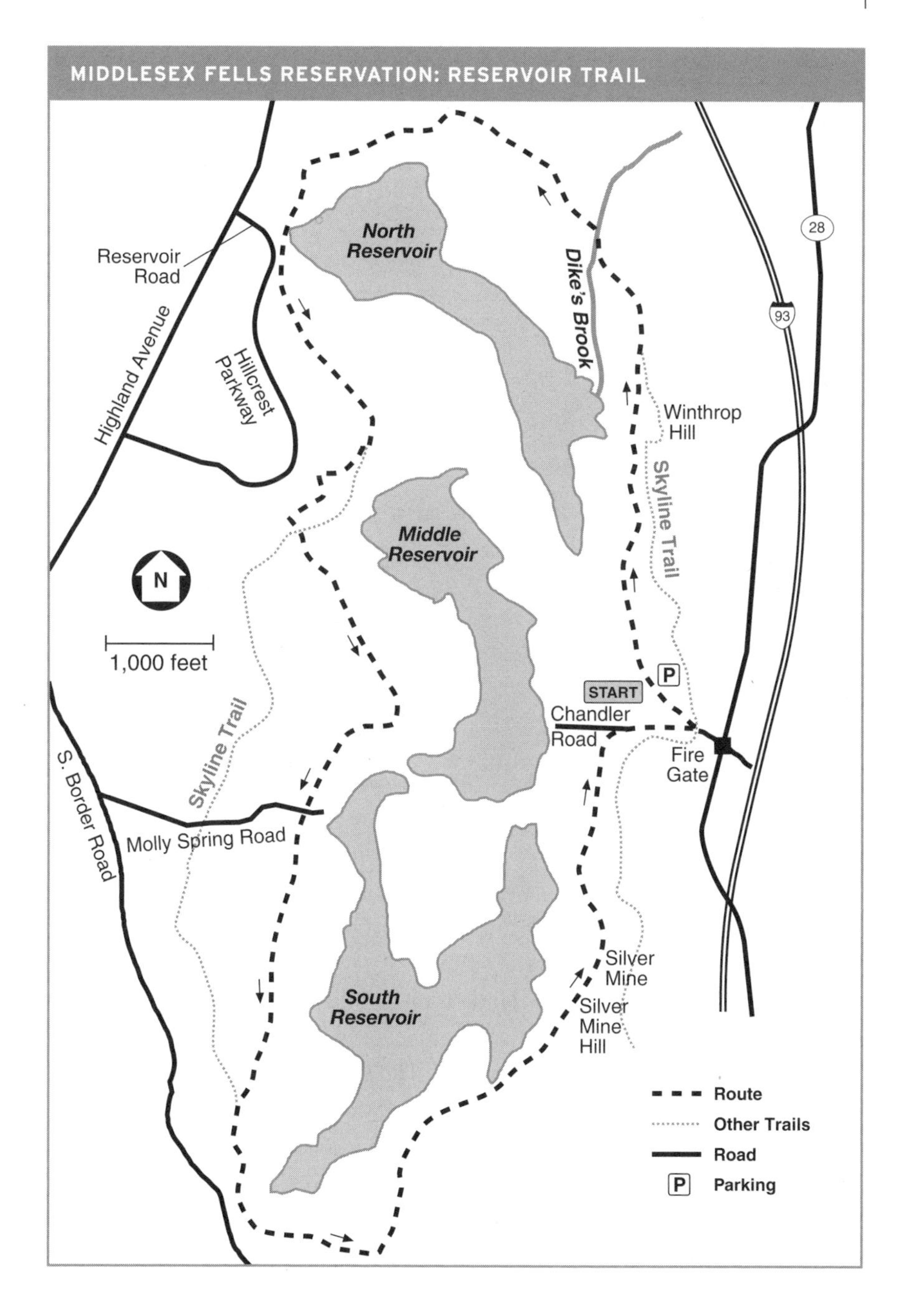

The Reservoir Trail can be joined from several locations. It will be described here starting from the Sheepfold and going counterclockwise. This orange-blazed trail follows closely to the fence on the southern and western boundaries of the Sheepfold picnic area. It leaves the fence, crosses the former

Waterlilies, pickerelweed, and purple loosestrife. Photo by Jerry and Marcy Monkman.

soapbox derby track, and enters the woods on an old bridle path. Soon it leaves the path and winds under Winthrop Hill along gentle slopes to keep between the hill and waterlands property.

North of the municipal waterlands property the trail drops down to Dike Road (dirt). It follows this road north to meet the Skyline Trail (white-blazed) coming down from the side of Bear Hill. Here the Reservoir Trail turns left (west) with the Skyline Trail, goes to Dike Brook, then goes straight ahead through a former meadow and a pine grove to a dirt road. The Skyline Trail goes over Money Hill, while the Reservoir Trail leaves left (southwest) down the road and then climbs to skirt Money Hill to rejoin the Skyline Trail. The two trails descend together to cross North Border Road (dirt) and enter a ravine north of the North Dam.

The trails cross a brook formed by leakage from the reservoir. Shortly the trails bend left (south) a short distance before zigzagging up the west slope of the ravine to pass north of the old firehouse (which has water pumps in the basement) out onto Alben Street (paved) to Reservoir Road/Hillcrest Parkway, where there is parking and access for the two trails. The two trails very shortly leave the paved roads and go south via the West Dam Path. They cross a dirt service road and soon separate. The Skyline Trail goes ahead (south) while the Reservoir Trail goes right (southwest) to skirt a couple of marshes, crosses a brook, and then crosses the Skyline Trail before joining a dirt road southeasterly toward the Middle and South Reservoirs.

At the end of the road, the trail enters a bluff with fine views of the Middle and South Reservoirs and the causeway between them. The trail bends back and drops into a ravine. It crosses a brook and goes over one small hill and then over the shoulder of another hill to a dirt road. From here the trail goes south for nearly a mile, crossing Molly Spring Road (dirt), two brooks, and several stone walls and eventually rejoining the Skyline Trail adjacent to the South Reservoir standpipe. The two trails go south, then east around the wetlands property near the reservoir's West Dam. The trails almost reach South Border Road before going over a hill to the Middle Road Path. (The dirt road to the right leads shortly to parking off South Border Road—an access spot for the two trails.) The two trails go straight, then bend left (north) to pick up the East Dam Path, where they separate. The Skyline Trail turns right (east) up a hill, while the Reservoir Trail goes ahead (north).

As the Reservoir Trail approaches the South Reservoir it leaves the road and heads northeast, not far from East Dam Road (dirt). Adjacent to the small East Dam the trail descends into a ravine, then ascends it and continues parallel to the patrol road going north. After going over Silver Mine Hill, the trail passes close to the sealed shaft of a silver mine. (Note the concrete posts of a former fence around the mine shaft.) The trail continues north with more views of the reservoirs, not far from the patrol road, until it reaches Chandler Road (dirt) with a fence on its north side. The trail goes right (east) along Chandler Road, joins the Skyline Trail, and heads for the Sheepfold to complete its circuit.

NATURE NOTES

See "Nature Notes" from Trip 11.

MORE INFORMATION

Open year-round, dawn to dusk; no fee. For more information, contact DCR Malden, Medford, Stoneham, Melrose, Winchester, 781-322-2851 or 781-662-5230; www.mass.gov/dcr. Trail maps are available on the website and through the AMC.

TRIP 15
GREAT BROOK FARM STATE PARK

LOCATION: Carlisle
RATING: Easy
DISTANCE: 3 miles
ESTIMATED TIME: 1.5 hours
OTHER ACTIVITIES: Birding, horseback riding, paddling
WINTER ACTIVITIES: Trails are flat and well-maintained, excellent for cross-country skiing

More than 10 miles of trail through historic and ecologically rich farmland.

The meadows, ponds, forests, and swamps of Great Brook Farm support a wide variety of wildlife for nature study. Purchased by the state in 1974, Great Brook Farm is also rich in history, and has more than 10 miles of trails. The most remote paths lie at the southern end of the property near Tophet Swamp. Pine Point Loop trail, named for its passage beneath towering white pines, is a shorter ramble around Meadow Pond.

DIRECTIONS

From Route 128, take Exit 29 for Route 2 west. Follow 3.4 miles to the sign for Concord Center (Route 2 turns left here; you should go straight). You are now on Cambridge Turnpike. Follow this 1.7 miles to Concord Center. At Concord Center, go straight to Lowell Road (Lowell Road is at the far end of the green). Follow Lowell Road for 5.7 miles to Carlisle Center. Go around the rotary and continue on Lowell Road for another 1.8 miles. Then turn right onto North Road and go 0.3 mile. The parking area is on the left.

From I-495, take the Route 2A East exit and then follow Route 110 north to Route 225 east. At Carlisle Center go around the rotary and up Lowell Road for another 1.8 miles. Then turn right onto North Road and go 0.3 mile. The parking area is on the left.

TRAIL DESCRIPTION

Exit the parking lot, go left on North Road, and proceed 500 feet to a sign that directs you to the Pine Point Loop Trail on the right. Follow the path for about 600 feet, bearing right as it brings you to Meadow Pond, a shallow body

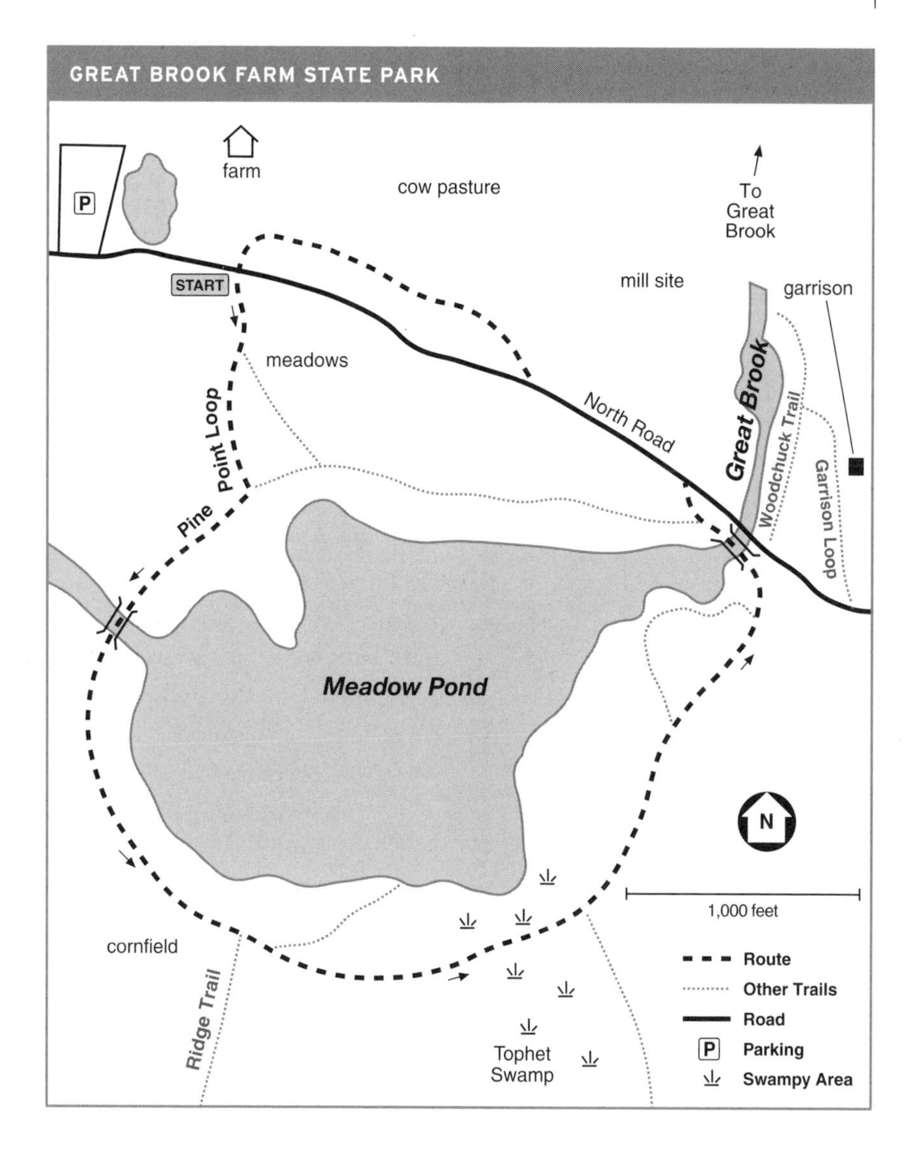

of water with different "fingers" stretching in various directions. The trail is quite wide and flat, making it an excellent place for cross-country skiing. Picnic tables are scattered about the fields and woods, and one table looks like an especially good spot, as it rests on a point of land jutting toward the water.

Stay on the main trail as it passes wetlands first, followed by a cornfield on the right. Listen for the screech of red-tailed hawks that often perch on tree limbs adjacent to the open cornfield. Various side trails on the left will bring you closer to the water if you wish to extend your exploration. After about 1 mile, the trail passes through more low-lying wetlands. Glacial erratics add

A monarch butterfly. Photo by Jerry and Marcy Monkman.

diversity to the scene.

Just before the trail meets North Road, there is a side path on the left that leads to a point of land topped with a large boulder at the shore of the pond. Return to the main trail and follow it to North Road where the waters of Great Brook tumble over a dam and out of the pond. If you follow the Woodchuck Trail across the road and along the stream, it is only 1.25 miles to the site of the old mill on a tiny millpond. At the back end of the pond, the water cascades over a waterfall lined with stones erected by the settlers—try to imagine the work that must have gone into its construction. The pattern of the lichen-covered rocks and the whitewater below make for an interesting scene.

As you retrace your steps toward North Road, notice a small sign for the "garrison," where the pioneers had erected a stone house for protection against the natives. If the approximately 15-foot cellar hole was the entire size of the house, it must have been quite cramped inside. Tight quarters, however, would have been the least of the settlers' worries during a terrifying raid.

Proceed to North Road and follow it 0.5 mile back toward the parking area to complete your loop. Along the way, you will have the pleasure of seeing the farm and pastures on the right. Children enjoy seeing the cows in the fields and the ducks in the pond near the barn. You can top off your trip with a visit to the ice-cream stand at the back of the farm.

NATURE NOTES

Keep an eye out for great blue heron, which can blend in perfectly with the rotting gray tree that stands at the edge of Meadow Pond. Another fascinating bird sometimes seen here is the wood duck. Nesting boxes have been erected on posts in the ponds to help these colorful birds reestablish in New England. The males are especially beautiful, with iridescent greens, purples, and blues, and a white chin patch. Females are a grayish-brown color with a white eye ring. Their habitat includes wooded rivers, ponds, and swamps. They are fast flyers and are quite agile as they fly between trees.

The Native Americans planted corn and other crops in the fertile meadows here. In 1691, John Barett built one of the first cloth-fulling mills in America, later followed by a sawmill and a gristmill erected in the early 1700s. The power of the stream (Great Brook) was also put to work in the 1800s, when mills made such items as wheels, nail kegs, and birch hoops. The mill site can still be seen at the northeastern end of the property just beyond where Great Brook passes under North Road.

MORE INFORMATION

Open dawn to dusk; parking fee. For more information, contact the Department of Conservation and Recreation, 978-369-6312 or www.mass.gov/dcr.

TRIP 16
WACHUSETT RESERVOIR AND RESERVATION

LOCATION: Boylston/West Boylston
RATING: Easy
DISTANCE: Limitless (an 8,000-acre property with forest and a reservoir)
ESTIMATED TIME: 1–4 hours
OTHER ACTIVITIES: Birding, fishing
WINTER ACTIVITIES: Trails are flat and well-maintained, excellent for cross-country skiing and snowshoeing

Approximately 8,000 acres of water and woods, maintained by the Department of Conservation and Recreation, offer tremendous hiking, cross-country skiing, snowshoeing, and wildlife watching.

Wachusett Reservoir was created in 1895 to solve the water needs of the greater Boston area. Today, the reservoir still supplies water to Boston (with the help of Quabbin Reservoir), but it also serves as an important wildlife reservation.

DIRECTIONS

From I-495 take Exit 25 to I-290 west. Drive 7.5 miles on I-290 to Exit 23 for Route 140 north. About 2 miles on Route 140 will bring you to the intersection

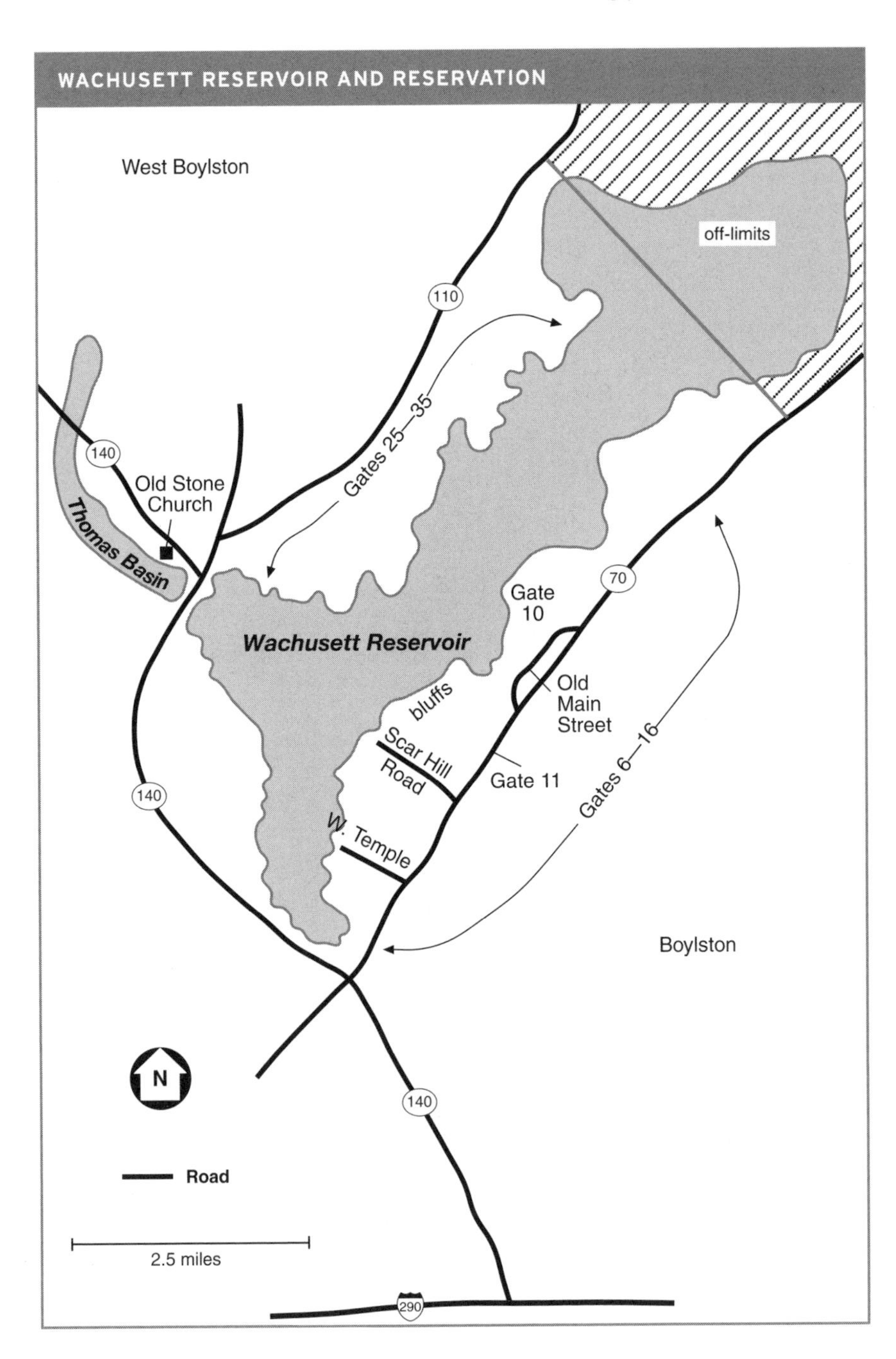

of Route 70 at the southern end of the reservoir. From here you can go another 4 miles on Route 140 to the Old Stone Church or travel north on Route 70 to various gates. Gate 10 can be reached by driving 2.0 miles north on Route 70 and taking a left turn onto a narrow road (Old Main Street). Gate 10 is about 500 yards down on the left.

TRAIL DESCRIPTION

Hiking is allowed in any area that is not posted. The entrances currently open are gates 6 to 16 along Route 70, gates 17 to 24 along Route 140, and gates 25 to 35 along Routes 12 and 110. The Department of Conservation and Recreation is permitting skiing and snowshoeing on portions of the eastern shore along Route 70 (gates 7 to 15) on a trial basis.

The bluffs can be reached by parking on Route 140 (just west of Route 70) and walking along the shoreline, heading to the right. This section of Route 140 also offers good views of the reservoir and gives one an idea of just how large a body of water Wachusett really is.

For history buffs, the place to go is the Old Stone Church, located on the shores of the reservoir just off Route 140 about 200 yards past where it splits from Route 12. (The street name for Route 140 along this section is Beaman Street, where the Thomas Basin section of the reservoir lies.) The stone exterior of the church is all that remains, as it had to be abandoned when the reservoir was created. Even though the interior has been stripped bare, it is still a beautiful structure to visit, and from this spot you can take a nice stroll around Thomas Basin. Large maples and pines line the shoreline path, and waterfowl can often be seen resting in the basin.

NATURE NOTES

The officials who oversee this watershed have seen coyotes, deer, and bobcats. They also do not rule out the possibility that a cougar might roam these woods. Every now and then there are reported cougar sightings in New England, most recently at Quabbin Reservoir. Surely these people are seeing something, and it is possible that the animal was illegally released from captivity, or perhaps the cougar was never really extinct after all. It's fun to speculate, but until one is captured or a high-quality picture is taken along with clearly defined tracks, we can only wonder.

The Department of Conservation and Recreation carefully manages the lands surrounding the reservoir to protect the water quality and enhance the ecological integrity of this valuable natural resource. The deep, clear waters of Wachusett Reservoir offer the fisherman some tremendous angling opportunities for lake trout, brown trout, salmon, and some very large smallmouth bass. No boating is allowed, but shore fishermen can use the same gates open to hikers to reach the reservoir, or they can fish along the southern stretch where Route 140 parallels the shore. Wachusett Reservoir has some special fishing regulations, the most important one being the limited season, from April (if the ice is out) to October.

MORE INFORMATION

Trails are open one hour before sunrise to one hour after sunset; no fee; dogs prohibited. For more information, contact the Massachusetts Department of Conservation and Recreation, which manages this watershed, 978-365-3272; www.mass.gov/dcr.

THE COMMON LOON

The Wachusett shoreline can be walked for miles, and due to the size of this body of water, it attracts a good deal of waterfowl, including an occasional loon. The common loon can be identified by its long pointed bill on a sleek black head with black and white markings on its back. If you are really lucky you might hear its cry, something you will never forget. The loon actually has a number of different cries: At night it tends to emit a mournful wail, while in the daytime you are more apt to hear its tremolo, which sounds like a demented laugh. Both can send shivers up your spine.

Watching a loon is absolutely fascinating, whether it is taking off, flying, or diving. It is a large bird, weighing about nine pounds, and it has difficulty getting into the air. That's why you never see a loon on small bodies of water—it sometimes needs a quarter of a mile to flap its wings and run along the lake's surface to become airborne. But once in the air, the bird is quite at home, traveling at speeds in excess of 60 miles per hour. Equally impressive is the way a loon can dive underwater in search of fish. It uses its wings to propel itself along underwater, and it usually stays beneath the surface for 40 seconds, although it has been known to stay submerged for up to five minutes.

TRIP 17
MOUNT PISGAH CONSERVATION AREA

LOCATION: Northborough
DIFFICULTY: Easy
DISTANCE: 2 miles
ESTIMATED TIME: 1.5 hours
OTHER ACTIVITIES: Birding

Hike along old stone walls to the summit of Mount Pisgah and enjoy views of Hudson and Marlborough.

Mount Pisgah is located in the hilly northwest section of Northborough, adjacent to the Berlin town line. A mix of narrow footpaths and old dirt roads traverses a forest of red oak, white pine, maple, and beech. Stone walls, small streams, and a scenic overlook await your discovery. The Mount Pisgah property abuts other conservation land, so it's a fairly large patch of second- or third-growth forest.

DIRECTIONS

From I-290 take the Church Street Boylston/Northborough exit (Exit 24). At the end of the exit go toward Boylston. After about a hundred feet turn right onto Ball Street. (There will be a sign pointing to Tougas Farm.) Follow Ball Street 1.6 miles to its end. Go left on Green Street for 0.5 mile to where the road forks and bear right onto Smith Road. Travel 0.3 mile to parking area on the right.

TRAIL DESCRIPTION

From the parking area, follow the wide trail heading east, passing beneath tall white pines. A couple minutes down the trail on your left will be a small forest area with young trees, where forest is springing up from what was once a field. Such opportunistic trees as gray birch, poplar, pine cherry, and white pines are the first to become established here, later to be followed by oaks and maples. Look for rabbits in the tangle of undergrowth and in the thick grasses.

Within 0.25 mile step your way over a tiny stream to where the trail splits. Go to the right. Red maple, oaks, and pines line the path, which is quite rocky in places. On the forest floor are blueberry bushes, sheep laurel, and such herbaceous plants as partridge berry, mosses, and princess pine. After walking

another quarter mile the path hits a stone wall and curls to the left, following the stone wall.

The path follows the stone wall for a couple minutes, then breaks to the right at an opening in the wall. The path now heads primarily eastward again. In a quarter mile it intersects with an old logging road called the Pisgah Slope Trail. Turn left on the logging road and follow for about a half mile until you come to a trail on the right. Take this right (marked by orange tape on trees) and go about a quarter mile to a T-intersection and turn left. You are now on the spine of a ridge. Look for a rock to the left embedded with the U.S. Geological Survey marker indicating the summit of Mount Pisgah a few feet off the trail. The vista from the ridge, however, requires about five more minutes of walking to the next T-intersection, where you should turn right and go 20 feet to where the trail forks. Bear left, proceeding about 200 feet to the exposed rock ridge with a view overlooking Hudson and Marlborough to the east.

The walk down from the hilltop only takes about 20 to 25 minutes. To return, make a more direct route down the mountain. From the overlook, return to the last intersection described earlier and instead of going left on the Ridge Top Trail, go straight, and follow the yellow disc markers on the trees. A quarter mile down this path will take you to an intersection with the Pisgah Slope Trail. Stay on the narrow path you have used to descend the hill, leading directly across the Pisgah Slope Trail. The path will lead through a stand of hardwoods where white birch soon become more numerous. It is not uncommon to come across deer and raccoon tracks here. The elusive fisher, a large member of the weasel family, has been spotted here. Fishers are great hunters of squirrels, porcupines, rabbits, mice, and birds.

The trail you are on soon enters into the shade of a pine grove, then merges with the main trail by the stream you crossed on the way up. Turn right here and cross the stream to return to the parking lot.

A climb to the summit of Mount Pisgah gives you the feeling of being in northern New England.

NATURE NOTES

Northborough Conservation Commissioner Sue Bracket stated that an assortment of owls such as great horned and barred owls have been seen here, in addition to hawks, deer, and fox. Massachusetts has both gray fox and red fox, but the northern limit of the gray fox is approximately in the southeastern section of the state, so chances are Mount Pisgah is home only to the red fox.

MORE INFORMATION

Open year-round, dawn to dusk; no fee; no rest rooms; dogs allowed (as long as owners clean up after them). Visit www.town.northborough.ma.us for more information.

TRIP 18
MINUTE MAN NATIONAL HISTORICAL PARK–BATTLE ROAD TRAIL

LOCATION: Concord/Lincoln/Lexington
RATING: Moderate (easy terrain, but long)
DISTANCE: 5 miles round-trip
ESTIMATED TIME: 3 hours (includes time to visit educational sites along the way)
OTHER ACTIVITIES: Biking (note that because the Battle Road Trail is primarily an educational trail, it is not suitable for high speed bicycling), birding
WINTER ACTIVITIES: After a good snowfall, the trails in the park are great for snowshoeing and cross-country skiing
PUBLIC TRANSPORTATION: (It is worth a day's trip to Concord and Minute Man National Historical Park to take the Commuter Rail from Boston, but note there is a 2-mile walk from the Concord Commuter Rail stop to the beginning of this hike.) Take the Fitchburg Commuter Line from North Station or Porter Square Station to the Concord stop. Walk along Sudbury Road to the center of town (Sudbury converges with Main Street) and take a right onto Route 2A. Stay left when, after the Alcott House, the Cambridge Turnpike diverges to the right. You'll pass The Wayside Visitor Center on your right and soon come to Meriam's Corner, where this hike begins.

An historic woodland and meadow trek that doesn't stray far from settled areas but is quaint and pleasant nonetheless, particularly in the fall.

Minute Man National Historical Park is located 22 miles outside of Boston within the towns of Lexington, Lincoln, and Concord. It was created by an act of Congress in 1959 to preserve and interpret the events, ideas, significant historic sites, structures, properties, and landscapes associated with the opening of the American Revolution, which lie along the Battle Road of April 19, 1775. The Battle Road constitutes part of the 5-mile long Battle Road Trail suitable for the whole family to hike back through time. We describe a round-trip hike so you can return to your car or the Commuter Rail in Concord. It takes you from the Meriam House to the Captain William Smith House.

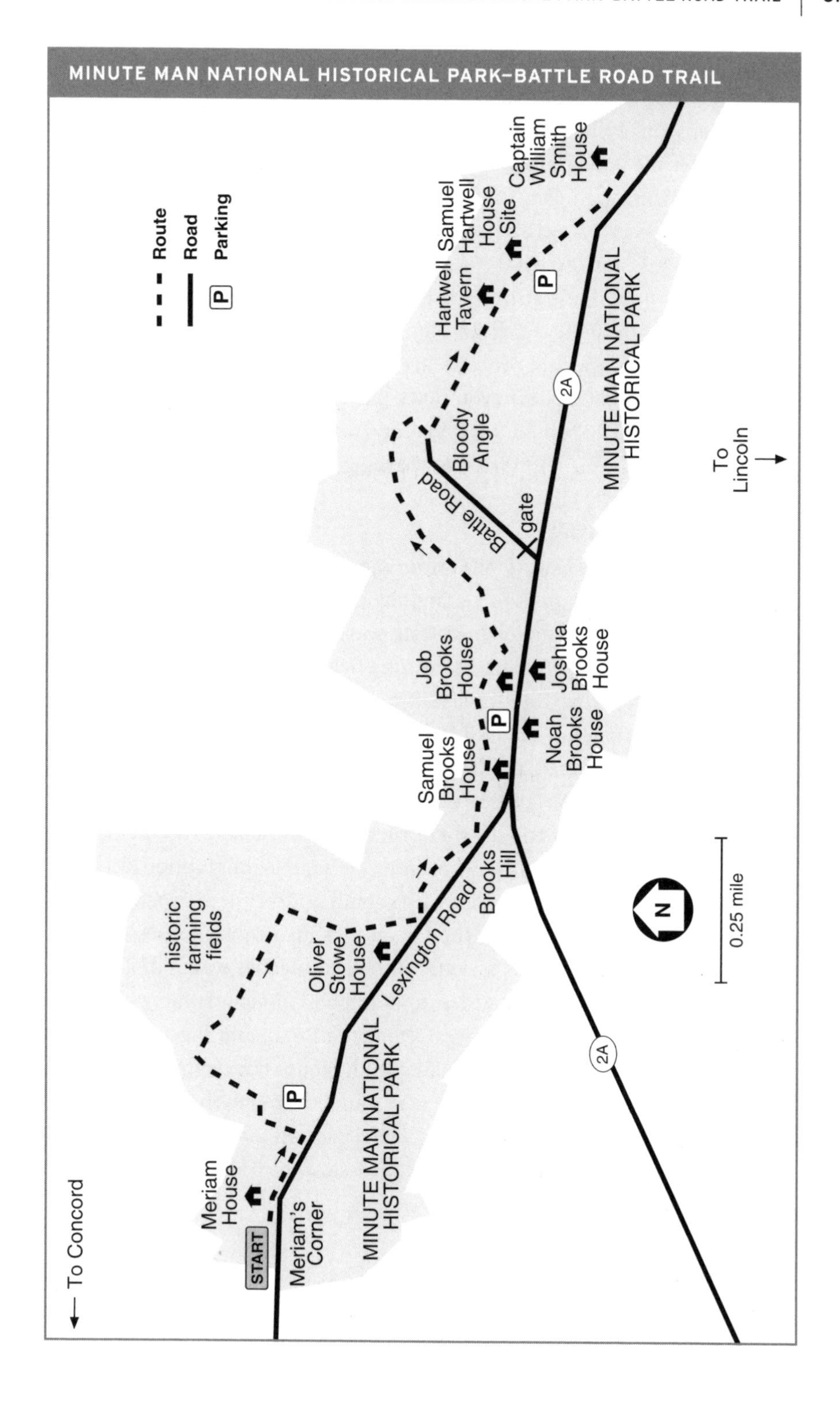
MINUTE MAN NATIONAL HISTORICAL PARK–BATTLE ROAD TRAIL
Route
Road
Parking
To Concord
START
Meriam House
Meriam's Corner
MINUTE MAN NATIONAL HISTORICAL PARK
historic farming fields
Oliver Stowe House
Lexington Road
Brooks Hill
Samuel Brooks House
Noah Brooks House
Job Brooks House
Joshua Brooks House
Battle Road
gate
Bloody Angle
2A
Hartwell Tavern
Samuel Hartwell House Site
Captain William Smith House
MINUTE MAN NATIONAL HISTORICAL PARK
To Lincoln
N
0.25 mile

DIRECTIONS

From the Boston area via Interstate 95/Route 128, take Exit 30B for Route 2A west to Hanscom Field/Concord. Follow Route 2A approximately 0.33 mile. You will enter the park and see signs directing you to the Minute Man Visitor Center located less than 1 mile from I-95/Route 128.

Or, from the west, travel east on Route 2, and look for signs indicating that you have entered Concord. At the Concord traffic circle or rotary, proceed east on Route 2 through the traffic circle and through the next six traffic lights. Before the seventh light, watch for signs indicating Route 2A east. Be sure to stay in your left lane and proceed straight to and then through the traffic light (a Mobil station will be on your left). Once through the light, you will be on Route 2A east. The Minute Man Visitor Center is approximately 2.5 miles down Route 2A on your left. Watch for parking entrance signs.

TRAIL DESCRIPTION

A 5-mile trail connects historic sites from Meriam's Corner in Concord to the eastern boundary of the park in Lexington. Much of the trail follows original remnants of the Battle Road; other sections leave the historic road to follow the route of the Minute Men, traversing farming fields, wetlands, and forests. The theme of this interpretive trail is the Battle of April 19, 1775 that launched the American Revolution, but the trail interprets the broader human story of the people whose lives were altered by the events that took place here, including their relationship with the landscape.

For this 5-mile round trip, begin at Meriam's House and travel east. The nearby historic farming fields have been in the same configuration since the seventeenth century. The trail then turns south and nears the road, passing the historic Brooks houses. After the Job and Joshua Brooks houses, the trail turns northeast and becomes boardwalk over protected wetland. The trail follows the route of the Minute Men up a hill and along a stone wall to the Bloody Angle. Here it converges with the Battle Road, and the section from Hartwell Tavern to the Captain William Smith House travels through beautifully restored historic landscapes. You may wander through the fields on trails as an alternative to the Battle Road, and swing back on the battle road on your return toward the Bloody Angle. From there, follow the trail you came on back to the Meriam House.

NATURE NOTES

By the turn of the eighteenth century, approximately 90 percent of land currently within Minute Man National Historical Park's boundary had been converted to agriculture. Although extensive meadows existed in the area prior to European settlement, acres of forest were cleared to create pasture and cultivated cropland.

Dominant trees include sugar and silver maple, white oak, and American beech. Dominant shrubs at the park are mostly non-native species, including buckthorn and honeysuckle.

The park's varied habitats support a wide variety of terrestrial and freshwater aquatic animals. Common mammals include species typically associated with rural and developed areas, including eastern cottontail, gray squirrel, deer mouse, beaver, red fox, coyote, and white-tailed deer. Less common species, such as bobcat and fisher, also inhabit the area. In addition, at least 70 species of birds, 12 species of fish, and more than 30 species of reptiles and amphibians have been documented at the park.

Fall foliage can be particularly spectacular here, but it can also bring crowds on fall weekends. Winter is quieter, and the park's trails are great for snowshoeing.

Minute Man National Historical Park supports the principles of "Leave No Trace." The national Leave No Trace Program builds awareness, appreciation and respect for our wildlands. For more information, see Appendix E.

MORE INFORMATION

The grounds of the park are open sunrise to sunset, at which time the parking lot gate closes.

As part of the Leave No Trace Program, you must leave what you find in the park and take out all you brought in. For this reason, there are no trash facilities in the park.

Pets are allowed in the park and in all visitor centers; however, they must be on a leash no longer than 6 feet in length at all times. You must clean up after your pet and take the droppings with you.

Visitor centers in the park include the North Bridge, Minute Man, Hartwell Tavern, and Wayside. Some are open only seasonally. For more information, contact the park headquarters at 978-369-6993 or visit www.nps.gov.

TRIP 19
WALDEN POND

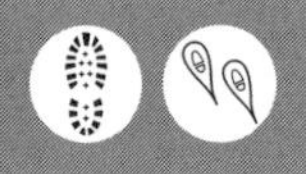

LOCATION: Concord
RATING: Easy
DISTANCE: Approximately 3 miles
ESTIMATED TIME: 1.5 hours
OTHER ACTIVITIES: Birding, fishing, paddling, swimming
WINTER ACTIVITIES: Ice-fishing, snowshoeing
PUBLIC TRANSPORTATION: To get to Concord, take the Fitchburg Commuter Line from North Station or Porter Square (subway) station to the Concord stop, which is near the corner of Thoreau Street and Sudbury Road; walk away from town on Thoreau Street, cross Route 2 (carefully), and Walden Pond State Reservation will soon be on your right; the main entrance to the Pond is approximately 1 mile from the station

Although the pond is not remote and you won't be alone, you somehow feel miles away from civilization. Indeed, you are at the heart of the beginnings of the American conservation movement.

Starting in 1845, Henry David Thoreau lived at Walden Pond for two years, two months, and two days and wrote *Walden* based on this experiment to live "deliberately" and simply in the woods. Today the park is run by the state. It includes the pond, trails, a swimming area, a boat launch, and a replica of Thoreau's cabin. The Thoreau Society runs a shop with further information and gifts.

DIRECTIONS

From the Boston area via Interstate 95/Route 128, take the exit for Route 2. Route 2 turns sharply left (Mobil station and large cell tower masquerading as a flag pole will be on your right). In another quarter mile, turn left onto Route 126. The Walden Pond State Reservation parking lot will be on your left in a quarter mile. Parking fee is $5/day.

TRAIL DESCRIPTION

While in the parking lot, make your way to the gift shop, where you can pick up a trail map showing additional trails in the reservation. This route descrip-

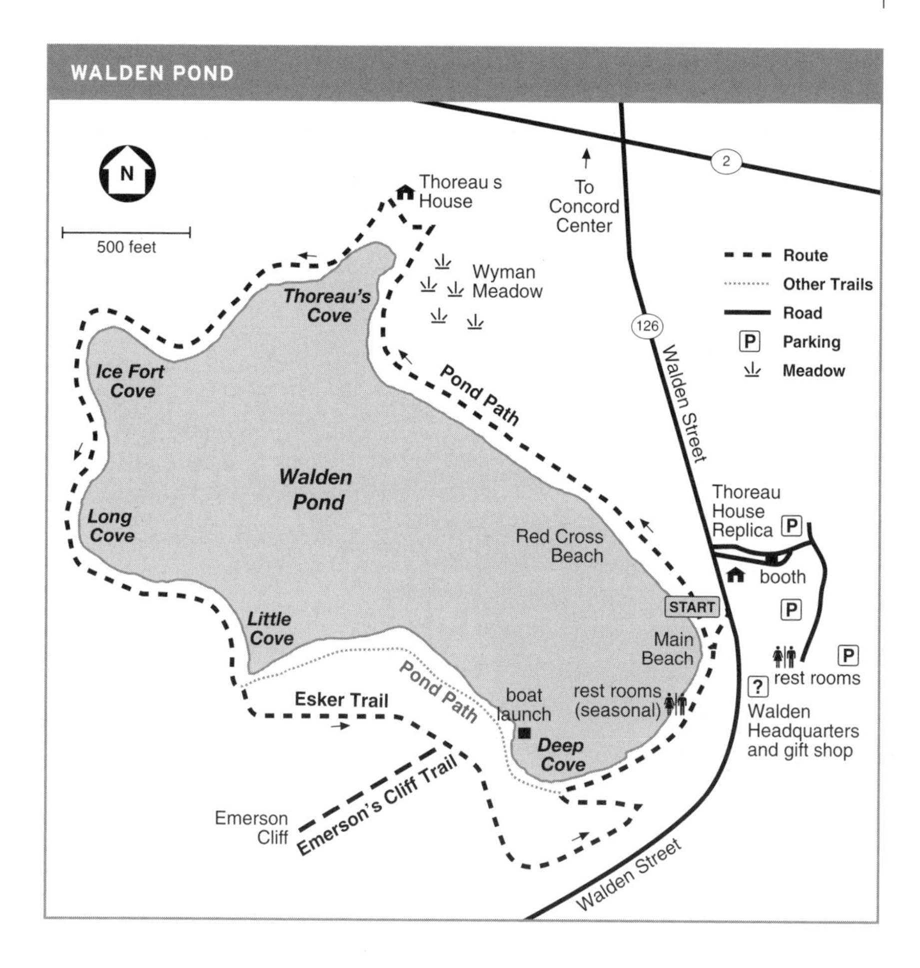

tion takes you around the pond and up to a vantage point from which to view the area.

From the parking lot, cross the road to the ramp down to the pond's beach area. Turn right and walk along Red Cross Beach or the path just above it, but as the beach ends, make sure you are following the path, not the shore. You are now skirting the north shore of the pond on the Pond Path. The path turns right (north) along a cove. This is Thoreau's Cove, and the site of his cabin is just off the main Pond Path here. After this site, the Pond Path turns south and ascends uphill slightly. To the right are train tracks that you might have traveled along if you took the MBTA Commuter Rail from Boston.

The coves on the west ends of the pond are Ice Fort Cove and Long Cove. After Long Cove, Pond Path turns east. At Little Cove, the trail dips southward and there is a side path to the right that leads to Esker Trail. To climb to the overlook, take the side path and turn left onto Esker Trail, which runs parallel and just uphill of Pond Path. Soon, Emerson's Cliff Trail leads to the right and uphill to an overlook. In summer, the view can be obscured by vegetation. Trace your steps back to Esker Trail and turn right onto it, following it to the boat launch ramp. Walk down the ramp to the beach—this is Deep Cove. From here, reconnect to Pond Path. (Or continue following Pond Path to Deep Cove.) Pond Path then leads back to the Main Beach and the ramp back up to the road and parking lot.

NATURE NOTES

When Thoreau lived here, Walden was surrounded by one of the few remaining woodlands in the area—the other lands having been cleared for farming. By the time the state bought the property in 1922, much of this forest had been cut. Now, the woods have grown back and include berry bushes, sumac, pine, hickory, and oak. Thoreau had planted 400 white pines beyond his cabin, but these were leveled in the hurricane of 1938.

Even ducks find peace at Walden Pond's waters.

The wildlife would have been much the same in Thoreau's day: squirrel, chipmunk, rabbit, skunk, raccoon, and red fox. Birds include kingfisher, blackbird, chickadee, and red-tailed hawk. Migratory ducks and geese visit in the spring and fall. The pond is stocked by the state and would otherwise not boast many fish.

The pond itself is a "kettle hole." It was formed more than 12,000 years ago as the glaciers from the last ice age melted. Kettle holes are depressions left by the melting of an ice block (left by a larger glacier) lodged in a deposit of sand and gravel. When the ice block melts within the sand and gravel deposit, a depression is left behind. Kettle holes usually have no streams flowing in or out of them—this is true of Walden Pond.

For decades, the trails and slopes around the pond were eroded by overuse. Over the last two decades, major efforts to quell the erosion and re-vegetate the area were in the works and a visit there today will show their success, but also that restrictions are still warranted. Stay on designated trails and roads or the beach.

MORE INFORMATION

Open sunrise to sunset; no fee; rest rooms; no dogs, fires, camping, bikes, or alcoholic beverages are allowed in the park. For more information, contact the park headquarters at 978-369-3254, or visit www.mass.gov/dcr.

TRIP 20
LINCOLN CONSERVATION LAND (MOUNT MISERY)

LOCATION: Lincoln
RATING: Moderate
DISTANCE: 3 miles
ESTIMATED TIME: 1.5 hours
OTHER ACTIVITIES: Swimming
PUBLIC TRANSPORTATION: Commuter Rail to Lincoln Station

The Mount Misery conservation land provides excellent views of the Sudbury River and Fairhaven Bay while passing through a deeply shaded hemlock forest and a patch of open marsh.

While the throngs of tourists circle Walden Pond in Concord, the woods along the Sudbury River, another haunt of Thoreau's, are relatively free of people. The town of Lincoln offers the hiker more than 60 miles of trails in conservation land, encompassing approximately one-third of this quiet town. With so much land to explore, this walk includes a trail system around Mount Misery that is well marked and diverse in its scenery, wildlife, and terrain.

DIRECTIONS

From Route 128, take Exit 26 onto Route 20 east. Go 0.2 mile on Route 20 and then turn left onto Route 117 west. Follow Route 117 for 6.9 miles to the Lincoln Conservation Land–Mount Misery parking entrance on the right (just 0.7 mile after Route 117 passes the intersection with Route 126).

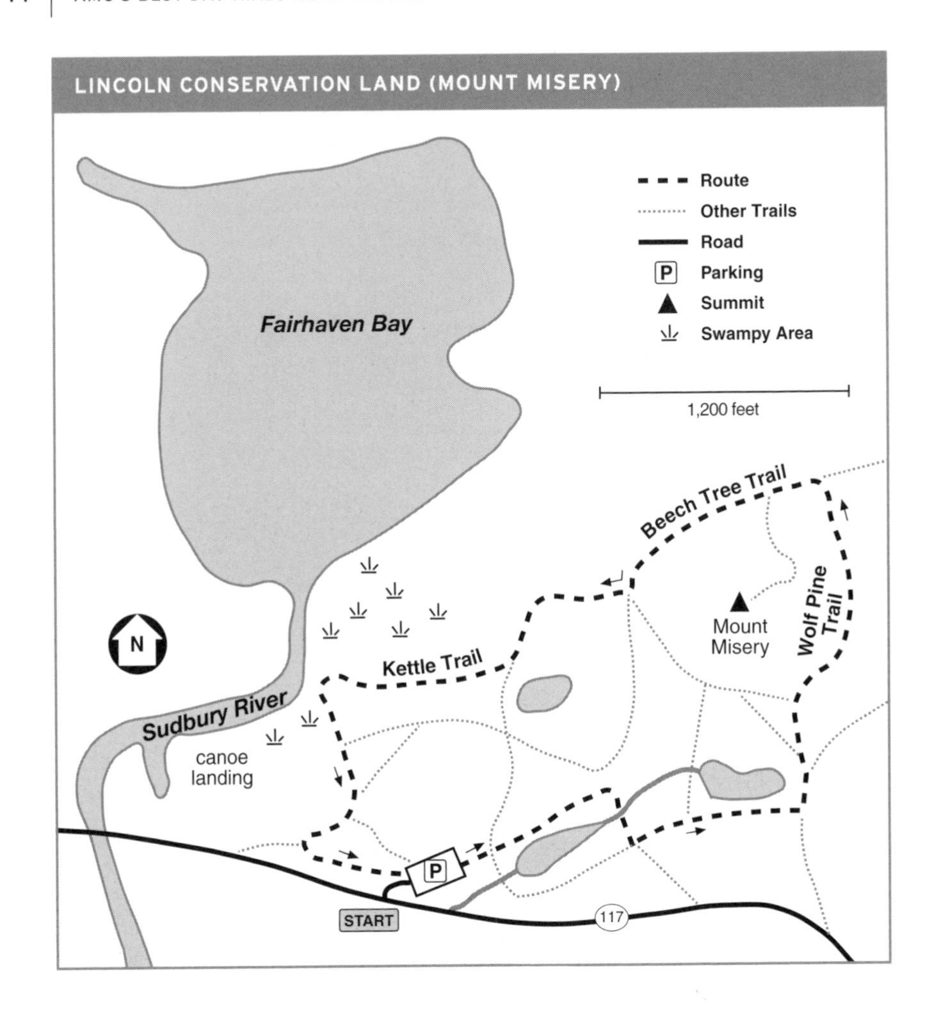

TRAIL DESCRIPTION

The trail begins at a parking lot on Route 117. Enter the woods at the east end of the parking lot. The trails described here are part of the Yellow Disc Trails and are clearly marked by small discs. They circle the eastern end of the property, then loop westward toward the river.

Follow the path as it skirts the edge of a small pond, then turns right, crossing a small stream that feeds the pond. Turn left on Wolf Pine Trail, which passes another pond, and then left again, arriving at the base of Mount Misery. (The "mountain" is really a hill with an elevation of 284 feet.)

Stay to the right on Wolf Pine Trail to circle Mount Misery as you head toward a gently sloping access road that leads to the summit. White-tailed deer are sometimes seen at dusk in the field on the right. The woods on the left are comprised of hemlock, oak, white pine, and an occasional white birch and

A deer emerges from tall grass at Lincoln's Mount Misery.

beech. After walking about 1.5 miles from the parking lot, you will reach the end of Wolf Pine Trail, and you should turn left on Beech Tree Trail. You will soon come to a fork in the trail; the path on the left climbs upward to Mount Misery (only a partial westward view from the summit).

Continue on Beech Tree Trail, and follow the yellow discs onto Kettle Trail (a right turn), which eventually leads to the edge of a broad marsh along the Sudbury River. The trail soon leads to the river itself, where good views are afforded to watch the waterfowl wing their way up and down the river. Follow the yellow discs a short distance farther to complete your loop and return to the parking area.

NATURE NOTES

Mount Misery was so named in the 1780s, according to local lore, when two yoked oxen wandered there and wrapped themselves around a tree. Unable to escape, they perished on the hill.

On Beech Tree Trail, you may notice an old barrel wedged about 50 feet up in a tree. No, this is not the work of a flood! The barrel was placed there by the Lincoln Conservation Commission as a nesting cavity for barred owls. If you look closely during the spring and summer, you might see the fledglings in the nest. Be sure not to linger too long, as this might alarm the mother owl.

Goshawks have also been seen in the area. These hawks are relatively uncommon and feed on birds such as grouse and mammals such as squirrels. It is recognized by its long tail, short wings, and broad white eye-stripe.

MORE INFORMATION

Open dawn to dusk; no fee; dogs allowed. See the instruction sign for the most recent rules. For more information, contact the Lincoln Conservation Committee, Town Offices, Lincoln, MA 01773, 781-259-2612; www.lincolntown.org.

ANYTHING BUT MISERY

From his cabin at Walden Pond, Thoreau preferred to head toward the south-southwest, which would take him along Fairhaven Bay and through the hilly region of Mount Misery. In his essay "Walking" he wrote, "I can easily walk ten, fifteen, twenty, any number of miles, commencing at my own door, without going by any house, without crossing any road except where the fox and the mink do: first along by the river, and then the brook, and then the meadow and the woodside." He would walk every day and wonder how anyone could stay indoors: "I confess that I am astonished at the power of endurance, to say nothing of the moral insensibility of my neighbors who confine themselves to shops and offices the whole day for weeks and months, aye, and years almost together." Thoreau would probably be even more astonished by our society's development and commercialization of open space, but at least the acres around Mount Misery have been saved.

TRIP 21
LINCOLN CONSERVATION LAND (SANDY POND)

LOCATION: Lincoln
RATING: Moderate
DISTANCE: 3.5 miles
ESTIMATED TIME: 2.25 hours
OTHER ACTIVITIES: Biking
WINTER ACTIVITIES: Trails are flat and well-maintained, excellent for cross-country skiing
PUBLIC TRANSPORTATION: Commuter Rail to Lincoln Station

A scenic loop around Sandy Pond in the footsteps of Thoreau.

The Sandy Pond Loop walk offers a long walk on level terrain through mixed woodlands. About twice the size of Walden Pond, Sandy Pond is a public drinking water reservoir, and its trails are not crowded with tourists. Midweek, you will probably have the place to yourself. Much of the walk is at or near the water's edge, allowing you to enjoy the open vistas and scan the pond for ducks and the sky above for hawks. It's a long walk, the kind best done with a good friend rather than young children.

DIRECTIONS

From Route 128, take Exit 28B (Trapelo Road–Lincoln). Follow Trapelo Road 2.6 miles to a stop sign and intersection. Go straight through the intersection onto Sandy Pond Road. Drive 0.4 mile to the entrance to the DeCordova Museum on the right. Follow the entrance road past the sculptures to the signs for the main parking lot and park at the rear.

To reach the property by train, take the commuter rail to Lincoln Station. Walk north on Lincoln Road 1.5 miles and turn left onto Sandy Pond Road. The museum entrance is 0.4 mile ahead on the right.

TRAIL DESCRIPTION

The walk begins at the back end of the main parking lot at the DeCordova Museum. Look for a brown trail sign for Lincoln Conservation Land and follow that trail toward Sandy Pond through woods of oak and maple. (Sandy Pond is also known as Flint's Pond.) In 200 feet, near the pond, the trail intersects with another near an old fireplace with a chimney. Turn right here to begin your loop of the pond. From this point on, almost every turn is to the left as you circle the pond in a counterclockwise direction.

The path takes you past a number of stone walls and through a grove of hemlocks.

The trail forks after a couple minutes' walk; stay left. The trail now begins to skirt wetlands. Another trail soon appears on your left; take this trail to cross the marsh. (If it is too muddy, take the next left to the other side of the

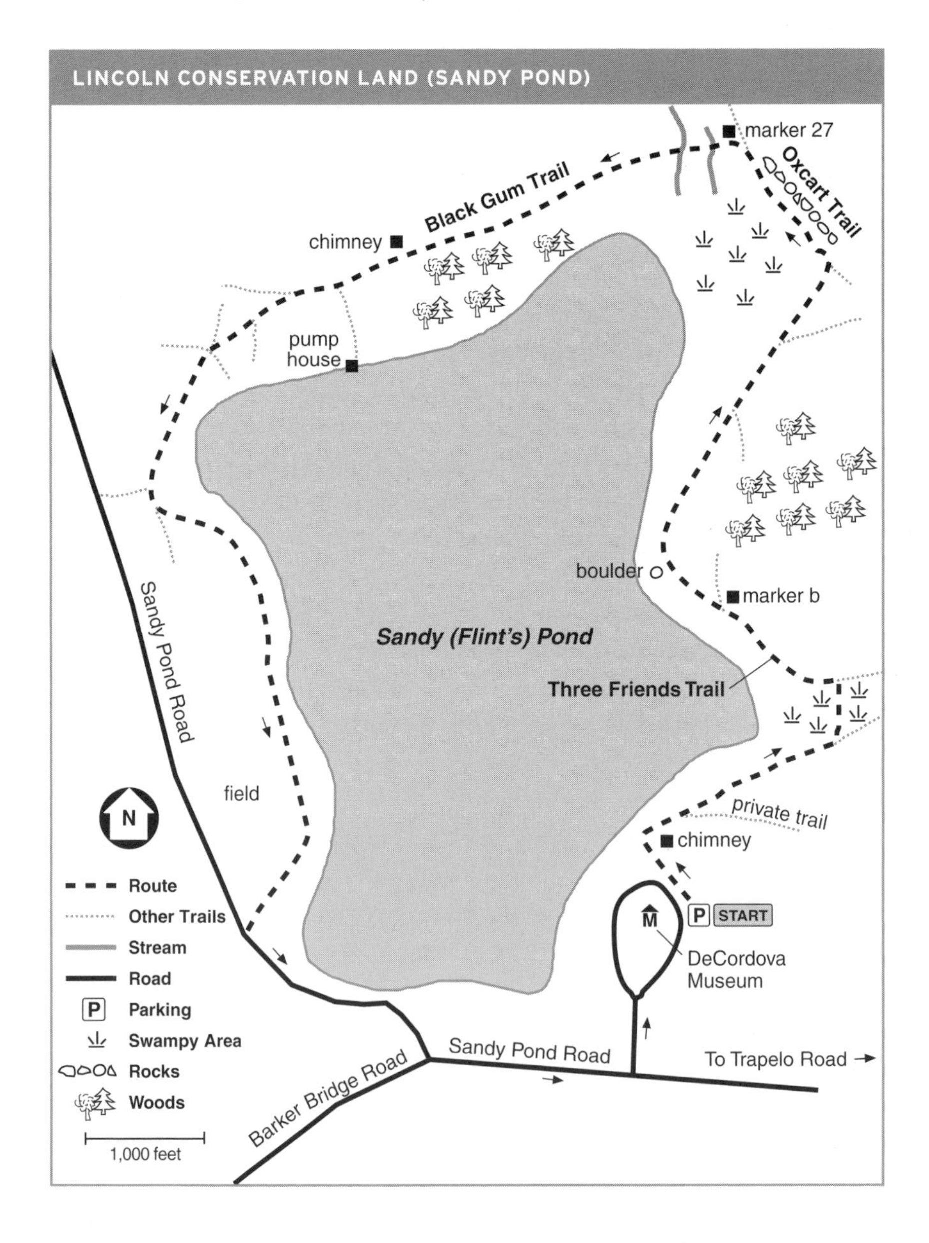

marsh.) The trail then comes to a T-intersection. Bear left again, heading back toward the pond now that you have walked around the marsh.

In about a quarter mile, you'll arrive back at the water's edge, where a small opening in the wooded shore offers a view of the pond. Soon you'll come to a fork in the trail (marker B); bear left. A handful of white birches add contrast to the brown and gray trunks of oaks, pines, and maples that dominate these woods. Farther down the trail you will see a boulder with a sobering plaque describing how a woman fell through the ice and drowned. After pausing at the boulder, proceed down the trail, passing two trails on the right. You will soon begin to skirt more wetlands (you are now about 45 minutes into the walk). Once past the wetlands, the trail comes to another T-intersection. Go left again toward the pond, passing beneath some large oaks. This section of the trail is open to mountain biking and has a stone wall paralleling it on the right. About a half mile down the trail, you will come to a trail heading to the left at marker 27. Take this, again heading closer to the pond. The trail will carry you over two tiny streams on wooden plank bridges, heading in a westward direction.

This section of trail is often used by mountain bikers in warm-weather months and cross-country skiers in winter, and fortunately the trail is wide enough to accommodate people traveling in both directions. After walking about a half mile, pass an old fireplace and chimney on your right; shortly thereafter is a trail on your left that leads to the water's edge near a pumping station. This is a great place to stop, particularly during cold-weather months, when the southern sun hits the shore here and you can rest with your back against the building and overlook the pond. From the pump house, retrace your steps to the main trail and go left. In a few feet, the trail forks; turn left. When it forks again, you should bear right, and you will reach a five-trail intersection. Go straight on the narrow trail with a sign reading Closed to Horseback Riders and Biking. You will soon be traveling parallel to Sandy Pond Road and will hear the traffic through the woods. A trail on the right leads up to the road; continue straight to a fork, where you should bear left toward the pond.

The trail is rocky in places, so your progress will be a bit slower than on the wide trail, but in about 0.75 mile, the trail crosses a field. After you cross the field, the trail leads to Sandy Pond Road; follow it left to return to the DeCordova entrance the parking area. The walk on the road covers about a half mile.

A nearby point of interest is Audubon's Drumlin Farm, which is great if you are hiking with children. It is located on Route 117 in Lincoln, 4.5 miles west of the Route 117 overpass at Route 128. Children will love the farm animals and the live exhibit of wild animals. The property spans 180 acres, and there are trails traversing woods, fields, pastures, and ponds. There is also a gift shop and nature center where programs are held.

NATURE NOTES

Be sure to scan the shoreline for wood ducks, especially late in the day during the fall when they gather in small flocks, preparing for the migration southward. Along with the brilliant coloration of the male, this species is identifiable by its large head, short neck, and long square tail. In spring, the ducks make their nests in hollow trees, and the babies leave the nest within 24 hours of birth, plummeting to the ground or water. With the ducklings so vulnerable, the parents must be secretive in order to guard their young.

At the back part of Sandy Pond, you might glimpse a red fox, which Thoreau especially enjoyed seeing: "His recent tracks still give variety to a winter's walk. I tread in the steps of the fox that has gone before me by some hours, or which perhaps I have started, with such a tiptoe of expectation as if I were on the trail of the Spirit itself which resides in the wood, and expected soon to catch it in its lair. I am curious to know what has determined its graceful curvatures. . . . When I see a fox run across the pond on the snow, with the carelessness of freedom, or at intervals trace his course in the sunshine along the ridge of a hill, I give up to him sun and earth as to their true proprietor."

SAFETY INFORMATION

This trail gets muddy in the spring and after rains, so you may want to return to the parking area by walking down Sandy Pond Road. But if the conditions are good, the trail is the better choice because it keeps you in the woods longer.

MORE INFORMATION

Open year-round, dawn to dusk; no fee; no rest rooms; dogs allowed but prohibited from going in or near the water (public water supply). For more information, contact the Lincoln Conservation Committee, Town Offices, Lincoln, MA 01773, 781-259-2612; www.lincolntown.org.

TRIP 22
BROADMOOR WILDLIFE SANCTUARY

LOCATION: Natick
RATING: Moderate
DISTANCE: 3 miles
ESTIMATED TIME: 1.5–2 hours
OTHER ACTIVITIES: Birding
WINTER ACTIVITIES: Trails are flat and well-maintained, excellent for cross-country skiing and snowshoeing

Broadmoor is a sanctuary rich in both wildlife and history. Walk by the remains of a grist mill that the Native Americans allowed to be owned and operated in the area.

Broadmoor has become a very popular hiking spot because of its diversity of terrain and wildlife. At the nature center building you can pick up a copy of an excellent sanctuary map that details its 9 miles of trails. The trails have color-coded markers, with blue taking you away from the parking lot and yellow leading you back.

In 1651, the entire South Natick area was the scene of an experimental arrangement between Native Americans and the early white settlers. The Reverend John Eliot and a group of "praying Indians" (Christian converts) established a community here that was to be very similar to the white man's style of living. The community was only a partial success, with problems ranging from the imprisonment of the Native Americans during King Philip's War to the cultural difficulties that might be expected. Although Broadmoor has no visible signs of this community, there are remains of the gristmill the Native Americans allowed to be owned and operated here.

A young hiker climbs the Glacial Hill Trail.

DIRECTIONS

From Route 128 take Exit 21 to Route 16 west. Travel 7 miles into South Natick. The parking lot and signs welcoming you to Broadmoor will be on your left. The sanctuary is located on Route 16 (280 Eliot Street), 1.8 miles west of South Natick Center.

TRAIL DESCRIPTION

The most scenic area is at the eastern end of the property, where the Mill Pond–Marsh Trail takes you by the wildlife pond and the mill sites, and the Charles River Trail leads down along the river. Even when the parking area is full, the trails leading to the western end of the property rarely receive more than a few hikers. One such trail is the Indian Brook Trail, which leads to the

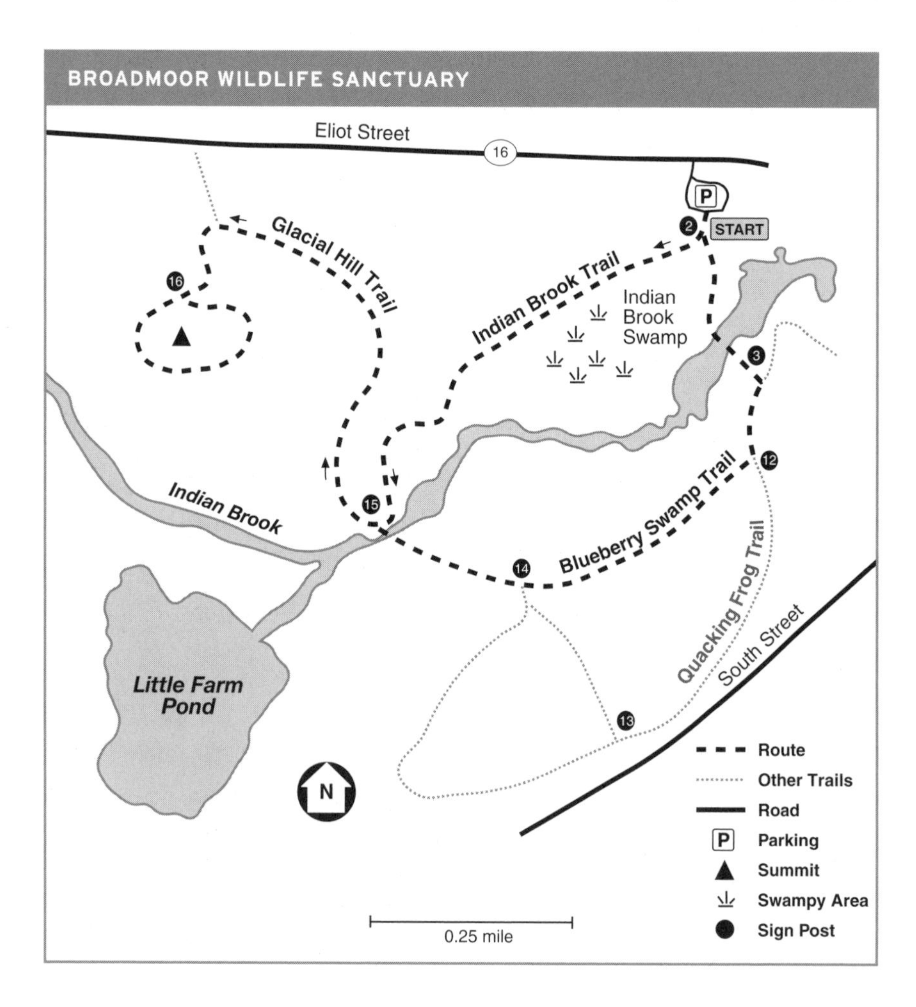

even more secluded Glacial Hill Trail. Begin your walk by registering at the visitor center and then turning right a few feet down the main trail onto Indian Brook Trail. The beginning of Indian Brook Trail passes through a beautiful open field where kestrels, kingbirds, mockingbirds, cedar waxwings, and indigo buntings can be seen in addition to a couple of resident groundhogs. Soon the trail leads into a wooded area of oaks on the right and Indian Brook Swamp on the left.

In 1989, the wetlands here were the scene of an exciting wildlife development—beavers moved into the Indian Brook Swamp. For Charles River watershed lovers, this was big news indeed, as these were apparently the first beavers to inhabit the area in many years. These beavers built their homes by burrowing into the bank rather than building a lodge. They constructed a dam at the junction of Indian Brook Trail and Glacial Hill Trail near signpost 15.

Continue your walk by turning right at signpost 15, which will put you on the Glacial Hill Trail, heading northwest. Glacial Hill Trail winds its way through the oaks for about a mile before reaching the little hill, or drumlin, formed by glaciers. The hill is a doughnut-shaped glacial deposit rising up from the swampy forest below. The trail runs along the top of the hill, forming a small loop before bringing you back to the main path.

From here you can retrace your steps back to the parking lot, or try crossing Indian Brook where Glacial Hill Trail meets Indian Brook Trail. You can then take Blueberry Swamp Trail toward the east. Stay on the Blueberry Swamp Trail by bearing left at signpost 14, which will lead you to the Mill Pond–Marsh Trail. Bear left at signposts 12 and 3 and you will be back at the parking lot.

Another little-known section of the sanctuary is Little Farm Pond, just over the Natick line in Sherborn. To reach this pond drive about a mile or two west on Route 16 from the main parking lot. Turn left onto Lake Street and go about a mile to Farm Road. Turn left onto Farm Road and look for a small parking area on the left side of the road (about 100 yards from the intersection of Lake Street and Farm Road). From here you can hike down the dirt road to the pond and explore some unmarked trails along its west side. This is a special place, quiet and rich with wildlife and unusual plant life such as the carnivorous sundew and pitcher plant.

NATURE NOTES

Wildlife is abundant here, with fairly regular sightings of wood ducks, painted turtles, kingfishers, great blue herons, kestrels, kingbirds, mockingbirds, cedar waxwings, great horned owls, and indigo buntings. This area attracts more than 148 species of birds. Usually unseen but also inhabiting these woods are great horned owls, raccoon, fox, deer, and even river otter. In addition to Indian Brook you can see the small waterfalls, stone foundations of an old sawmill, and the millstones. The hemlock trees not only shade this area, but they also give the stream an enchanting and mysterious look, even on a sunny day. Across South Street, the Charles River Trail follows the river for a half mile, and tupelo trees line the riverbank with the more common pines and oaks.

MORE INFORMATION

Open Tuesday through Sunday and Monday holidays, dawn to dusk; fee for non-members; dogs prohibited. The Nature Center is open Tuesday through Friday, 9 A.M. to 5 P.M.; Saturday, Sunday, and Monday holidays, 10 A.M. to 5 P.M. For more information, contact the Broadmoor Wildlife Sanctuary, 508-655-2296; broadmoor@massaudubon.org.

TRIP 23
NOANET WOODLANDS

LOCATION: Dover
RATING: Moderate
DISTANCE: 3.5 miles
ESTIMATED TIME: 1 hour, 45 minutes
OTHER ACTIVITIES: Biking, birding, fishing, horseback riding
WINTER ACTIVITIES: Trails are flat and well-maintained, excellent for cross-country skiing and snowshoeing

An extensive network of trails leads to a millpond and waterfall and up to modest Noanet Peak.

Diversity of terrain is what makes Noanet so special; swamplands, brooks, mill-ponds, a waterfall, upland forests, and a 387-foot peak can all be found here. These features provide for excellent nature study as well as hiking, jogging, and cross-country skiing on the reservation's extensive trail network. The variety of terrain, coupled with the fact that the property abuts the privately owned Hale Reservation and Powisset Farm, makes this an ideal wildlife refuge.

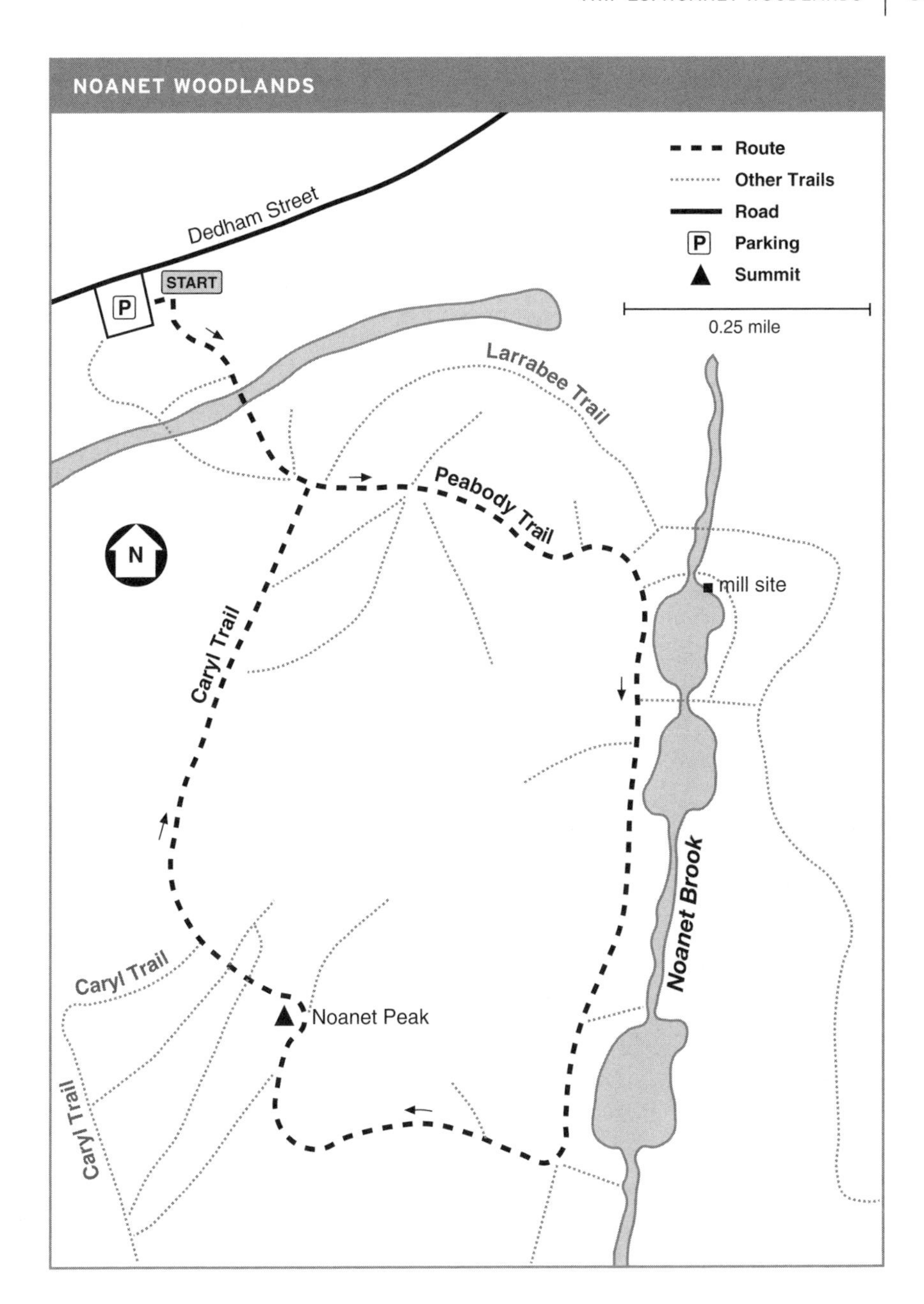

DIRECTIONS

From Route 128, take Exit 17 onto Route 135 west. Drive 0.7 mile. Turn left on South Street just after crossing the Charles River. Go 1.1 miles on South Street and turn left on Chestnut Street. Follow Chestnut Street 0.4 mile to its end and turn right on Dedham Street immediately after crossing the Charles River. Continue 2 miles to the entrance and parking lots on the left at Caryl Park.

From Dover Center, take Dedham Street eastward for 0.6 mile to the park entrance on the right.

TRAIL DESCRIPTION

Noanet Woodlands has so many trails, many unnamed, that it is easy to get lost. The map in this book does not show every trail in the reservation but instead focuses on the trails that lead from the parking lot to Noanet Peak. The main trails have color-coded discs fastened to trees, and this review will mention the appropriate colors for the trails described. (The walk to the ponds is relatively flat, while our walk to the peak gets quite steep in spots.)

From the summit of Noanet Peak you can see all the way to Boston.

To enter Noanet Woodlands, follow the sign pointing to the trail behind the ranger station. Just a few feet away, the trail intersects a dirt road. Go right on this road for about 100 yards. A sign on the left side of the road directs you back into the woods. Take this trail for about a quarter mile until you reach a split in the trail. Bear left, following the main path. You will soon cross a wooden footbridge above a tiny stream. The path then merges with another. Bear left again. After walking for about 100 feet, you will come to a split, where a contributions box has been placed on a post. Go left here. About 20 feet farther the trail splits again. To the left is the Larrabee Trail and to the right is the Peabody Trail. Take the Peabody Trail, which is marked by blue discs. About a quarter mile down the Peabody Trail, you will come to an open area with a trail coming in on the right. Stay straight on the Peabody Trail. A few feet after that the trail forks, and you should continue on the Peabody

Trail by bearing left. The trail now hugs the edge of a ridge.

After about a quarter mile, you will see a sparkling waterfall cascading from the old millpond on the left side of the trail. Continue on the Peabody Trail (blue discs) as it passes between Noanet Brook far on the left and forested slopes to the right. The trail leads in a southerly direction and you should follow it for about 0.4 mile. Just beyond the third pond, you will come to a four-way trail intersection. To reach Noanet Peak, take the unnamed trail on the right, which climbs the hill. After about 50 yards, the trail bears left (the path straight ahead peters out at an area of exposed rock on the hillside). By following this leftward curve, you will circle the peak, rather than make a frontal climb. Yet this trail is still quite steep in spots. Follow this trail for about a half mile, and by bearing to the right at the next intersection, you will reach the summit in only a couple more minutes of walking. The top of the peak grants an excellent view of the Boston skyline and hills to the east. Powisset Peak, part of the nearby Hale Reservation, can also be seen. In the fall, the hilltop is a good place to see migrating hawks wing their way south.

From Noanet Peak, retrace your steps for about 50 feet, then bear right downhill on an unnamed trail that descends the hill to the west. Stay straight on this trail until it meets with the Caryl Trail, marked by the yellow discs (about 0.25 mile from the summit). Bear right on the Caryl Trail. After 0.5 mile, you will pass houses on the left side of the trail, and then it's another 0.5 mile on the Caryl Trail to the parking area.

NATURE NOTES

The waterfall on Peabody Trail was once the site of the Dover Union Iron Company, which operated from 1815 into the 1830s. The Trustees of Reservations, which owns Noanet, says, "Noanet Brook was too small a stream to support the ironworks and the company went out of business." The original dam was destroyed by flooding in 1876 but was reconstructed in 1954 by Amelia Peabody, who later bequeathed the land to the Trustees.

The holding ponds above the dam are a perfect place to sit and have lunch to the sound of falling water and singing birds. Painted turtles, frogs, and bluegills inhabit the various ponds and wetlands. The setting is made complete by the large pines, oaks, maples, and beeches that surround the ponds.

MORE INFORMATION

Open sunrise to sunset; no fee; dogs allowed. For information, contact the Trustees of Reservations, 781-821-2977; seregion@ttor.org; www.thetrustees.org.

TRIP 24
WILSON MOUNTAIN RESERVATION

LOCATION: Dedham
RATING: Easy
DISTANCE: 2 miles
ESTIMATED TIME: 1.5 hours
OTHER ACTIVITIES: Birding

Enjoy a stroll to a hilltop overlook and explore trails adjacent to wetlands.

Thanks are due to all the people who saved Wilson Mountain from development in 1994 and kept it natural. Just 10 miles from Boston, these 200 wooded acres could have easily become the site of a mall or housing lots, but instead, thanks to funds made available through the Open Space Bond Bill, it is now managed by the Department of Conservation and Recreation (DCR) and is open to all. Anyone can walk through the pine groves, admire the view from the hilltop, and traverse along the edges of buttonbush swamps and streams.

The DCR has recently labeled two loop trails: the Red Dot Loop is roughly 0.75 mile long and circles Wilson Mountain at the northeast end of the property, while the Green Dot Trail covers 2 miles heading from north to south. This walk covers a little of both.

DIRECTIONS

From Route 128 take Exit 17 onto Route 135 east and go 0.7 mile into Dedham. Park at the second small lot on the right side of Route 135 (just after Common Street and before a ball field) where a sign welcomes you to the reservation.

TRAIL DESCRIPTION

Begin your walk by following the trail that starts behind the iron gate. Beware of poison ivy in the area, identifiable by its three shiny green leaves with pointed tips. The first part of the walk follows the red dots along the trail. Just 30 feet down the path is a side trail going off to your right leading into lowlands, but you should stay straight on the main trail. About 50 feet later the main trail splits at a granite marker and you should bear right, following the trail that leads uphill into a white pine grove. Rhododendron bushes grow in the shade on your right on the steep hillside. At the next fork in the trail, after

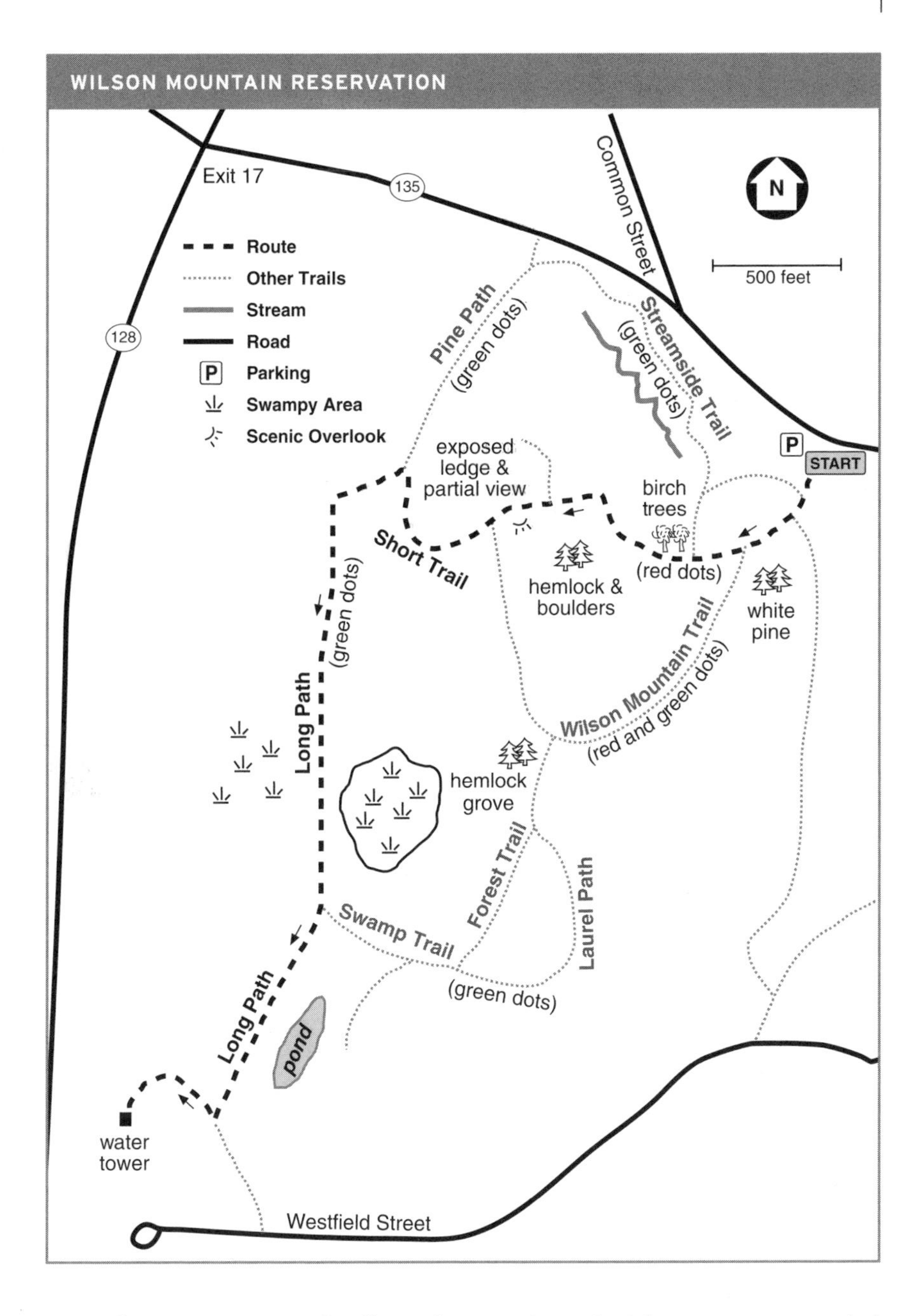

a couple minutes more of walking, bear to the right. The pines are crowded together and consequently they grow tall and thin, with most of the branches near the upper part of the tree where they can receive some sunlight. If a pine is growing in an open field it will have filled out more evenly, with branches even at the lower levels because of unlimited sunshine.

Farther down the trail a side path comes in on the right by some birch trees. Stay straight, following the red dots uphill. On the right, where the hill slopes downward, a few mountain laurel bushes grow in the understory.

As you continue on the trail, the pines give way to mixed woodlands of ash, maple, oak, hemlock, and birch. These trees, some quite large, provide the walker with almost total shade during periods of summer heat. Huge boulders, called glacial erratics because of the way they were haphazardly deposited by the glaciers, litter the forest floor.

The trail soon makes a 90-degree turn to the left, roughly three-quarters of a mile after the start of the walk, and now becomes a more steep ascent up Wilson Mountain. About 50 feet up the trail, it splits; bear left on the path that climbs to the exposed granite ledge. (Children will love climbing on the rocks.) After three minutes of picking your way through rocky terrain, you will arrive at the summit, a nice sunny spot to enjoy the warming rays and a view to the north. There is a partial view of the Boston skyline. The total walk to the summit from the parking lot is an easy 20 minutes. (At this point, if you are hiking with younger children, you may want to retrace your steps back to the parking lot or follow the red dots on the Wilson Mountain Trail back.)

To continue the walk, follow the path behind the rocky summit, staying straight where a side trail comes in from the left. (That side trail leads to more exposed ledge, but there are no good views.) This unmarked trail is called the Short Trail. Oaks and maples dominate this section of woodlands with sassafras growing in the understory. Identified by its mitten-shaped leaves, the sassafras tree rarely grows taller than 30 feet, but there have been individual trees that have reached a height of 80 feet. The branches, leaves, and even the root are all aromatic.

The Short Trial is fairly level for the first 0.25 mile then it starts a gradual descent, and in a couple minutes you will approach an intersection. Turn left here, heading into the southern end of the property, following the Long Path, marked by green dots. Although there are no unusual features or vistas, it's a pleasant walk through mixed woodlands with wetlands on either side of the path. Approximately a half mile down the path is a fork; bear left, no longer following the green dots. After walking another 0.5 mile you will arrive at an intersection. To the right is a water tower and to the left is Westfield Street. From here retrace your steps back to the parking lot to complete a total walk of about an hour and a half. If you wish to vary your return trip, there are three different ways to do so. One option is to follow the green dots all the way back down the Long Path to the Pine Path and then onto the Streamside Path that brings you back to the parking lot (see map). The second option is to take the

Mountain laurel in full bloom. Photo by Jason Thresher.

Swamp Trail to Laurel Path and then follow the Wilson Mountain Trail back to the parking lot. A third option is to retrace your steps back to the Short Trail and just before the Wilson Mountain summit, turn right on the Wilson Mountain Trail and follow the red dots back to the parking lot.

If you still have energy at the end of your hike, try the Streamside Path that leaves from the parking area and follows two small brooks through the woods. Children will enjoy seeing the water and climbing on the rock ledges.

NATURE NOTES

This northern face of the mountain will remind people of the forest more typical of northern New England than Massachusetts. Because this section does not receive the summer sun it is cooler and more moist than the other slopes of the mountain. Yellow birch, white birch, and hemlocks thrive here. Look for delicate pink lady's slippers growing beneath the trees, identified by their drooping slipper-shaped flowers. A member of the orchid family, lady's slippers are protected by law and should never be picked.

Mountain laurel leaves are 3 to 4 inches long, dark green and glossy on the top, and yellow-green underneath. Mature leaves are thick and leathery. The saucer-shaped flowers, which bloom at the end of June, can vary from pink to white or various shades in between. In southern Connecticut, mountain laurel can reach heights of 20 feet, but in northern New England it is rare and much smaller.

Some of the more common birds you are likely to see along the path to Wilson Mountain include tufted titmice (small gray birds with tufted caps at the back of their heads), chickadees (black and white coloring), and nuthatches (usually on tree trunks looking for insects). Another common bird is the flicker. Flickers are about the size of blue jays with a brown back and a black breast crest. They are most easily identified, however, by the white rump seen in flight. While nuthatches usually work their way down a tree, flickers go up the trunk. They make their nests in tree cavities—just one more reason why dead standing timber is so important to birds.

MORE INFORMATION

Open year-round, seven days a week; no fee; no rest rooms; dogs allowed on leash; no mountain biking. For more information, call 617-698-1802 or visit www.mass.gov/dcr.

TRIP 25
KING PHILIP OVERLOOK AND ROCKY NARROWS

LOCATION: Sherborn
RATING: Moderate
DISTANCE: 3 miles
ESTIMATED TIME: 1.5 hours
OTHER ACTIVITIES: Biking, birding, fishing, horseback riding, paddling
WINTER ACTIVITIES: Trails are flat and well-maintained, excellent for cross-country skiing and snowshoeing

Walk or paddle to the rugged hillside slopes of the remote Rocky Narrows on the Charles River.

Rocky Narrows (owned by the Trustees of Reservations) and King Philip Overlook (part of the Sherborn Town Forest) lie adjacent to one another and offer hikers a relatively wild section of woodlands to explore. There is a parking lot on Route 27 in Sherborn large enough to accommodate several cars. The highlight of the walk is the King Philip Overlook, which offers a fantastic view of

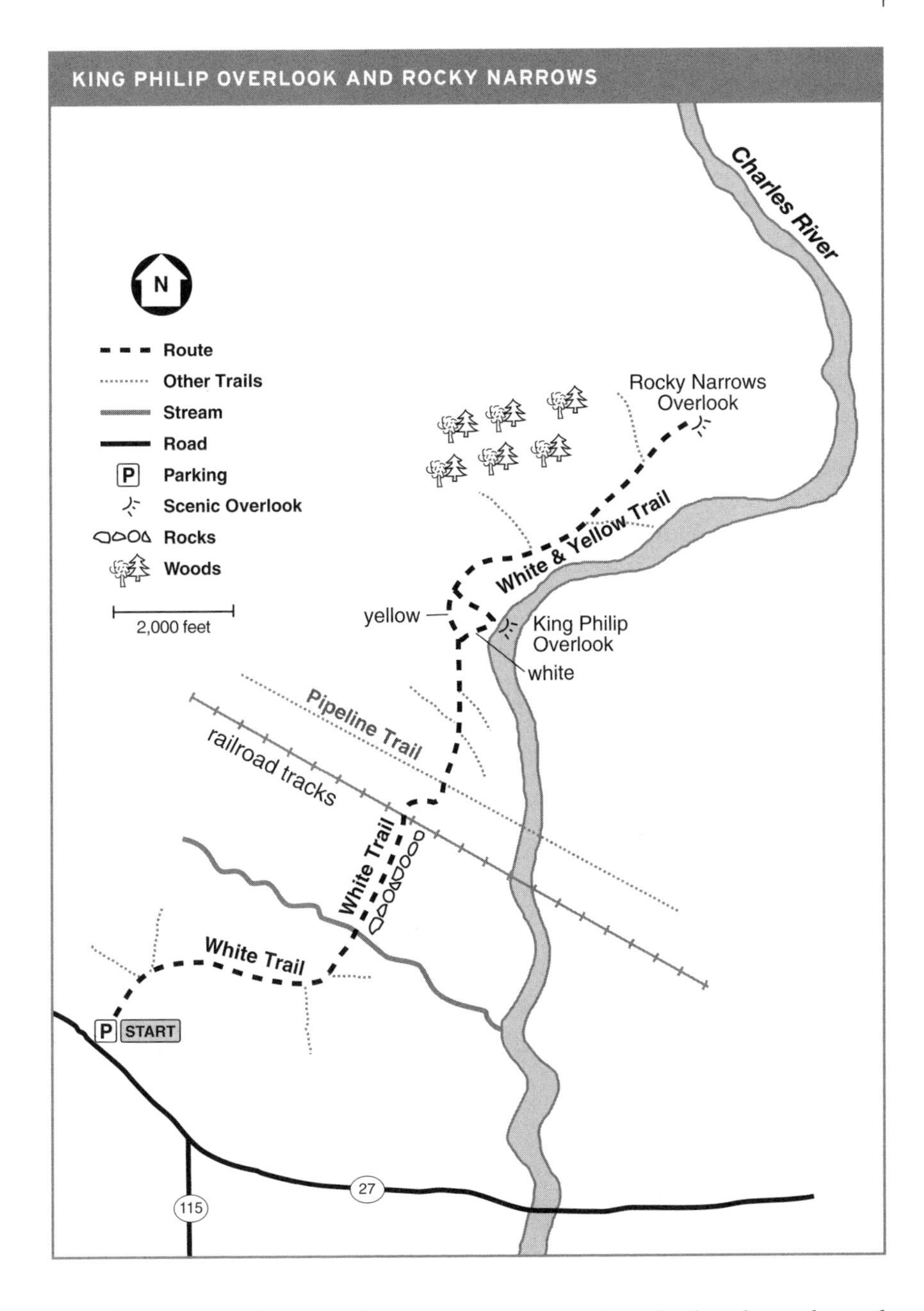

the Charles River. (Some walkers may want to continue farther down the trail for the partial view offered at the Rocky Narrows Overlook.) Hemlock trees cover much of the hills in the reservation, and a walk here feels more reminiscent of northern New England than suburban Boston. This reservation has many unmarked trails. You may get lost, so start your walk well before dark!

DIRECTIONS

From the intersection of Routes 115 and 27, take route 27 north for 0.3 mile to parking area on the right.

TRAIL DESCRIPTION

From the parking lot, follow the trail into woodlands of oak, maple, and white pine. The trail will be marked by white discs and white slashes on trees. Side trails intersect with the white trail at various intervals, so be sure to follow the white marking.

The first natural landmark you reach is a small stream and an earthen bridge, located about 0.75 mile from the parking lot. After 0.25 mile, you reach a set of railroad tracks. (Caution: the tracks are active.) Cross the tracks and turn right. Walk about 20 yards and you see the white-paint markers on your left. Follow this trail uphill into the woods; it crosses a wide trail that follows a pipeline.

About a quarter mile after crossing the railroad tracks, the white trail makes a sharp right turn (the trail directly ahead is the yellow trail). Turn right here. This will lead you to the King Philip Overlook in a couple of minutes.

Many walkers prefer to rest on this beautiful bluff before heading back. Others push on into Rocky Narrows proper to see the hemlock trees and the Rocky Narrows overlook. You can do so by following the white trail directly behind the overlook. A few feet along this trail, it intersects with a trail that has both white and yellow markings; turn right.

After walking about a quarter mile, you will see a split in the trail marked by a tree with two white marks on it. Bear left and follow the white markers for another quarter mile to the Rocky Narrows Overlook. The view here is not nearly as scenic as the King Philip Overlook, offering only a partial vista of a meadow and small part of the Charles River. The terrain, however, is interesting: rugged hills, granite outcrops, and towering hemlocks.

Fantastic views of the Charles await at King Philip Overlook.

Below, the Charles River is constricted by the granite ledges, forming a narrow passageway—hence the name Rocky Narrows. This is a prime canoeing spot, with a good launch site just downstream at the Farm Road/Bridge Street bridge, and another launch site (quite steep) at Route 27. For an afternoon canoe ride, put in at Route 27 and follow it downstream to the South Natick Dam, where you could have a second car waiting. Or, if you are partial to exploring wetlands, launch at Route 109 on the Millis/Medfield border and head downstream through the Great Marsh, then through Rocky Narrows with a take-out on Farm Road/Bridge Street.

Retrace your steps to return to the parking area.

NATURE NOTES

The overlook is a good place to look for hawks soaring above the river. Great blue herons also make their way up and down the river. Their population has increased now that our rivers are cleaner, and because the increasing beaver population in Massachusetts has led to the creation of more ponds with standing timber, the herons' preferred nesting spot.

You will see some of the large hemlocks that make the Rocky Narrows overlook a special place. Hemlocks prefer rocky ridges and ravines, growing to a height of 70 feet in cool, moist spots. To distinguish the hemlock from other evergreen examine its needles closely. The needles are flat with blunt tips and there are usually several needles upside down on the branchlet. They are about 0.25 to 0.5 inch long, shorter in length than spruce and fir. Although they are dark green on the top, turn them over and you will see a silvery underside. Because the needles are acidic, there is often little undergrowth beneath the tree where needles have fallen year after year. Hemlocks have brown cones, about 0.75 inch long, which hang from the tip of the branches. They mature in the fall and stay on the tree until spring. Another way to distinguish the hemlock from fir trees is to look at the crown of the tree: the hemlock will be rounded, while the fir comes to a sharp dense point.

There is also a healthy population of white-tailed deer here; during spring, you might see their tracks in the damp earth of the trail. The tracks are heart-shaped; the narrow part of the track indicates the front of the deer's hoof, showing the way it was traveling. Another large mammal that lives here is the coyote, which can be found throughout the state of Massachusetts. They are very adaptable animals, using whatever food source is available (including house cats), and they are secretive as well, doing most of their hunting at night. A coyote howl in the wee hours of the morning is a sound you won't soon forget.

MORE INFORMATION

Open year-round, dawn to dusk; no fee; no rest rooms; dogs allowed on leash. For more information, contact the Trustees of Reservations, 508-785-0339; seregion@ttor.org; www.thetrustees.org.

ADD A PADDLE TO YOUR OUTING

You can also access the overlook by canoe. The paddle is less than 2 miles round-trip and will put you closer to the shores, where waterfowl and other wildlife abound. To reach the canoe launch from Route 128, take Exit 21 to Route 16 west. Travel 6.3 miles into South Natick and turn left on South Street. Go to the end of South Street (1.8 miles) and turn left on Farm Road. Go 1.2 miles on Farm Road; when you cross the Charles, a canoe launch will be immediately on your left. Paddle upstream about a mile.

FIT FOR A KING

Like so many hilltops in Massachusetts, King Philip Overlook is named for the Native American leader Metacom, whose English-given name was Philip. Beginning in 1675, Philip led an uprising of Wampanoags, Nipmucks, and Narragansetts to try to regain tribal lands from European settlers. Medfield, which lies in front of you as you look off across the river from the overlook, was one of the towns especially hard-hit by the warriors. Many homes were burned and several settlers were killed, but the Indians could not overpower the garrison.

After the Indians withdrew from Medfield, a warrior who had learned English left a note by a burned bridge at the Charles that read: "Know by this paper, that the Indians that thou hast provoked to wrath and anger, will war this twenty-one years if you will: there are many Indians yet, we come three hundred this time. You must consider the Indians lost nothing but their life; you must lose your fair houses and cattle." But the Indians were not strong in number, and there were many more English. The attack on Medfield occurred in February of 1676, and by August of the same year, so many natives had been killed, including Philip, that the war was over. Ironically, Philip was the son of Massasoit, the Wampanoag leader who showed kindness to the Pilgrims during their first disastrous year in Plymouth.

TRIP 26
ROCKY WOODS RESERVATION

LOCATION: Medfield
RATING: Easy to Moderate
DISTANCE: Southern section, 3.5 miles; Cedar Hill, 1 mile; Hemlock Knoll Nature Trail, 1 mile
ESTIMATED TIME: Southern section, 1.5 hours; Cedar Hill, 30 minutes; Hemlock Knoll Nature Trail, 30–40 minutes
OTHER ACTIVITIES: Biking, birding, fishing, horseback riding
WINTER ACTIVITIES: Trails are flat and well-maintained, excellent for cross-country skiing and snowshoeing

Three walks with opportunities to fish, picnic and, in winter, cross-country ski.

Rocky Woods is one of the larger properties owned by the Trustees of Reservations, and it offers a wide choice of year-round recreational activities. (Because it is so large, three walks are described here.) The focal point of the reservation is five-acre Chickering Lake, which has catch-and-release fishing during the warmer months. Picnic tables and grills are scattered about the shoreline.

DIRECTIONS

From the intersection of Routes I-95/128 and 109 (Exit 16B on I-95), take Route 109 west 5.7 miles through Westwood to Hartford Street in Medfield. Take a right (hairpin turn) onto Hartford Street. Follow it 0.6 mile to the entrance and parking lot on the left.

From the intersection of Routes 27 and 109 in Medfield, take Route 109 east. Bear left on Hartford Street 0.6 mile to the entrance on the left.

TRAIL DESCRIPTION

Southern Section. Just after turning off Hartford Street onto the Access Road, you'll find a small parking area on the left and the Loop Trail. Take this wide, well-maintained path of crushed stone for a short distance until its junction with Echo Lake Trail. Continue straight on the main path, which skirts the shallow waters of this small pond. Stop for a moment on the wooden footbridge to look for frogs, turtles, and waterfowl. Then continue back on the main trail, which heads in a southwesterly direction. This trail is excellent for

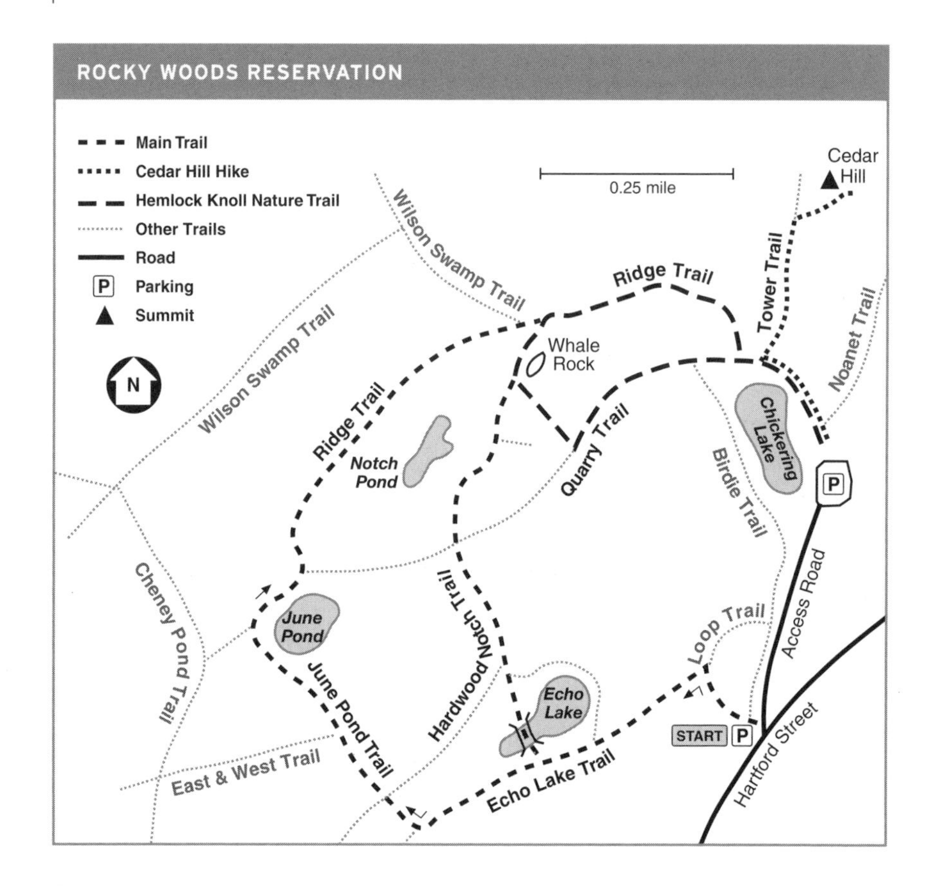

cross-country skiing—there are just enough slopes for excitement, and the trail is wide.

At the next intersection, turn right. This path soon passes by the even smaller June Pond, which is all but dry in midsummer. Just after you spot June Pond, take a right at the next intersection. This is the 0.7-mile Ridge Trail. You will notice that both the trees and the terrain begin to change here. Beech trees and birch trees appear and granite boulders, dropped during the retreat of the glaciers, fill the woods. Now you know the origin of the name Rocky Woods.

Walk along Ridge Trail until you come to Hardwood Notch Trail on the right (a sign will say Intersection 5). Take this right. Soon you will see the giant Whale Rock stretching out like a beached whale along the trail on your left.

Continue down Hardwood Notch Trail, keeping watch for a trail that goes to the left beneath a sign on a tree that says Lookout Point. (The lookout is a narrow view that can be reached after a four- or five-minute walk.) Continuing down Hardwood Notch Trail, pass tiny Notch Pond on your right, then cross the intersection with Quarry Trail. About 400 feet after this intersection, look for a small path on the left that leads back to Echo Lake, where you can cross the footbridge and turn left onto Echo Lake Trail to return to the parking area.

Northern Section—Cedar Hill Hike. Lying north of Chickering Lake, the exposed ridgeline of Cedar Hill can be reached in a short 15-minute hike. There are a number of different views, and there is nothing quite as peaceful as gazing out over the valleys and hills as cool breezes whisper through the cedars.

Access Cedar Hill by taking the Chickering Pond Trail to the Tower Trail. As you walk up Tower Trail, you will see numerous smaller paths leading up to the ridge on the right.

Hemlock Knoll Nature Trail. Hemlock Trail is well-marked and maintained, which makes it a great hike for youngsters. The trail begins at the north side of Chickering Lake and forms a loop in the woods of about one mile.

At the intersection of the Tower Trail and the Ridge Trail, follow the Ridge Trail to begin your walk. One of the most interesting features is the "mini-canyon" at marker 6. The passage was formed during the time of the glaciers, when a stream passed through here.

After about 0.5 mile on the Ridge Trail, turn left on Hardwood Notch Trail. It takes you to the massive Whale Rock, where kids will enjoy climbing. After Whale Rock, the trail begins its return back to Chickering Lake. Turn left directly after Whale Rock; about 400 feet farther, turn left again onto Quarry Trail. On the way back, you will pass the remains of a quarry; in the early 1900s, blocks of stone were cut and hauled out by horses and oxen. Drill marks can still be seen in the rocks. From here, it is a short walk back to the parking lot. Witch hazel, sassafras, shagbark hickory, and dogwood trees can all be seen in the last a quarter mile.

It is interesting to note that the ridge you have just been walking separates the Charles River watershed from the Neponset River watershed. Both of these rivers were used extensively by the Native Americans for travel, and artifacts have been found in numerous sites along their banks.

NATURE NOTES

The name Rocky Woods is appropriate; the land is a series of uneven ridges with many rocky outcrops, including Whale Rock, which looks like the back of a whale rising from the forest floor. The reservation is rich in wildlife, and early morning hikers are often treated to a sighting of a fox, partridge, or a great blue heron wading in one of the ponds.

In addition to the southern hike, Rocky Woods includes the Hemlock Knoll Nature Trail. The Trustees of Reservations sells an excellent 24-page guidebook for the Hemlock Knoll Nature Trail. The trail has 18 numbered markers at various trees, plants, and rocks that correspond with the detail in the guidebook. It is an excellent way for both children and adults to learn about nature.

Take a good look around the shoreline of the lake; you may see a great blue heron hunting there. Kingfishers can also be seen here, and it's thrilling to watch them dive from their perch and into the water to grab a small fish. If you have children, Chickering Lake is a very good spot to fish. Sunfish are relatively easy to catch with worms or other bait. And you never know when the large-mouth bass might be hungry, so bring some lures. All fish must be released.

MORE INFORMATION

Open year-round, sunrise to sunset; fee on weekends and holidays (ranger on duty at these times); no rest rooms; dog walking by permit only. For more information, contact the Trustees of Reservations, 508-785-0339; seregion@ttor.org; www.thetrustees.org.

TRIP 27
NOON HILL RESERVATION

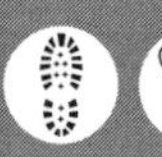

LOCATION: Medfield
RATING: Moderate
DISTANCE: 2 miles
ESTIMATED TIME: 1 hour
OTHER ACTIVITIES: Biking, birding, fishing
WINTER ACTIVITIES: Trails are flat and well-maintained, excellent for cross-country skiing and snowshoeing

Heavily wooded Noon Hill is secluded with a diversity of wildlife. Few people even know of its existence, and as an added bonus, it abuts the Henry L. Shattuck Reservation with an additional 225 acres along the Charles River.

Noon Hill got its name from the early settlers who noted that the sun rose above the hill about noontime. It is said that King Philip (or Metacom), the Native American leader of the Wampanoag tribe, launched his bloody raid on the town of Medfield from here. However, some historians say that on the day

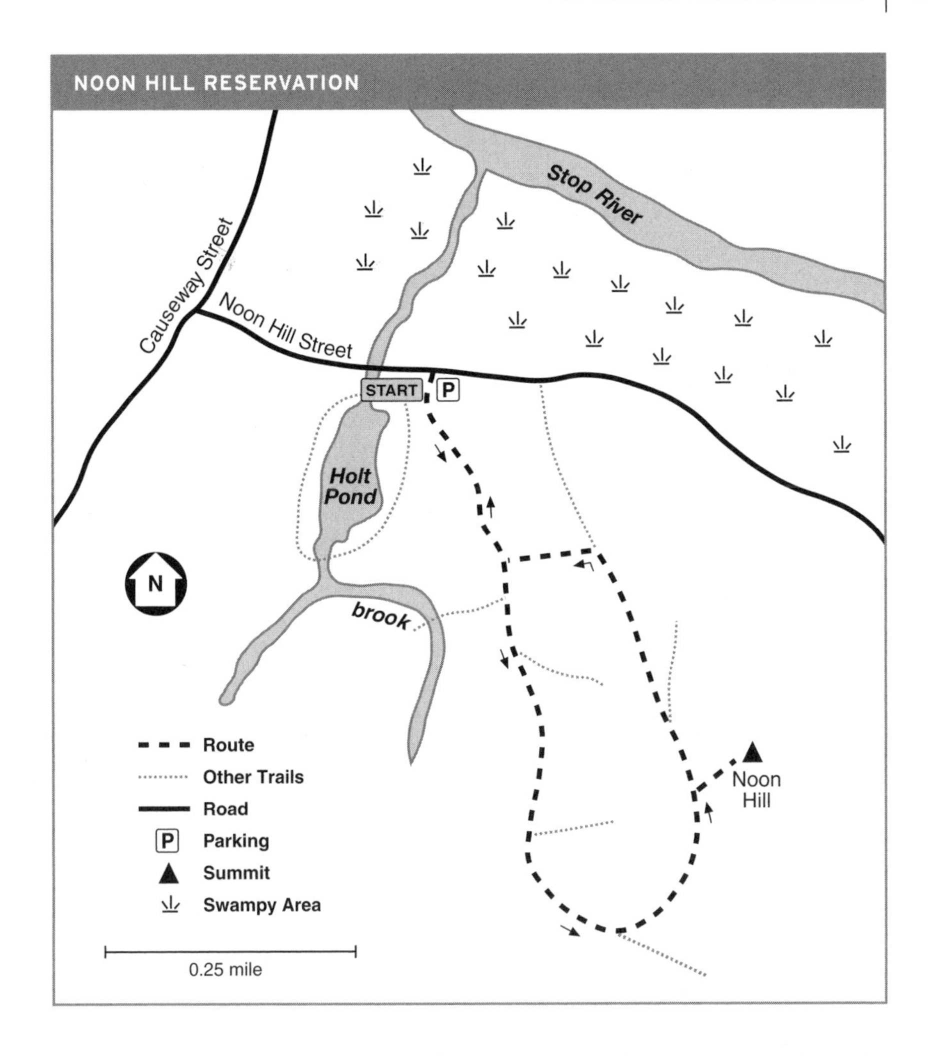

of the actual event in 1676, the raiders were amassed on the west side of the Charles River. No matter where the attack came from, this was probably an important area for the local Native Americans. They preferred to be situated near the confluence of major streams and rivers, and the Stop River makes its entrance into the Charles River below Noon Hill.

DIRECTIONS

From Route 128, take Exit 16 onto Route 109 west. Follow for 7.7 miles (passing through Medfield Center). Turn left onto Causeway Street (just a couple hundred feet after crossing Route 27) and go 1.5 miles. Turn left again on Noon Hill Street. Drive 0.2 mile to a small parking area on the right.

TRAIL DESCRIPTION

The first part of the path is relatively flat and is lined on each side by gray, lichen-covered stone walls. Look for chipmunks and red squirrels running in and out of the rock openings in the wall.

As you continue on the trail you will pass through a low-lying area where a spur of the trail goes to the right. This is not the way to the top, but it is worth a side trip down this path as it leads you to a tiny mountain stream (Holt Brook) that tumbles over granite boulders as it makes its way down to Holt Pond. The path passes over the stream on a bridge made of overlapping stone.

Back on the main trail, you will soon come to another fork in the path; stay to the right to continue toward Noon Hill (do not go left through the stone wall). After about a half mile you will be at the base of the hill. Beech trees and exposed boulders hug the slopes to your left. A small path makes a direct assault on the hill but it's a steep and difficult climb. The main trail circles Noon Hill, allowing for a gentler climb. The trail splits again—stay to the left and you will soon be on the ridge of the hill. The best spot for viewing the countryside

The ruffed grouse (called "partridge" by old New Englanders) stays with us through the winter and always gives me a start when I walk by one. (Thoreau wrote, "whichever side you walk in the woods the partridge bursts away on whirring wings," adding that "this brave bird is not to be scared by winter.")

is an exposed rocky area that lies a few feet off the main trail to the right. The views from the crest look out toward the southeast where you can look down upon Medfield and Walpole in the foreground.

When you descend Noon Hill you can either retrace your path by going left or try a new way by turning right. If you go right, walk about an eighth of a mile just below the ridge crest until the trail splits. Turn left here through an opening in a stone wall. This trail is a bit narrower and marked with white blazes. Proceed down this trail for about a quarter mile and then turn left again, following the white markers. In a quarter mile you will intersect the main trail near the parking area. Turn right to reach your car.

Noon Hill is owned by the Trustees of Reservations. Fishing is allowed on the pond and the trails are open for cross-country skiing (although they are hilly). There is a short, narrow trail around Holt Pond (a man-made pond, probably built around 1764 to power a sawmill). Look for kingfishers perched on branches above the pond.

NATURE NOTES

Prominent bird species in the area include black turkey vultures, ruffed grouse, owls, and kingfishers.

MORE INFORMATION

Open year-round, sunrise to sunset; no fee; no rest rooms; dogs allowed. For more information, contact the Trustees of Reservations, 508-785-0339; www.thetrustees.org.

TRIP 28
BLUE HILLS RESERVATION: PONKAPOAG POND

LOCATION: Canton
RATING: Easy
DISTANCE: 4 miles (around pond)
ESTIMATED TIME: 2 hours
OTHER ACTIVITIES: Fishing, horseback riding, mountain biking, paddling, picnicking, rock climbing, and swimming are all permitted in various parts of the park
WINTER ACTIVITIES: In winter there is alpine skiing at the Blue Hill Ski Area on the western side of Great Blue Hill, ice skating at several ponds and artificial rinks, and cross-country skiing on many of the reservation trails and across the neighboring Ponkapoag Golf Course
PUBLIC TRANSPORTATION: Red Line to Ashmont Station; take the high-speed line to Mattapan; from there take the Canton and Blue Hills bus services to the Trailside Museum and Great Blue Hill on Route 138; For directions from other areas, call 617-698-1802

A short hike to a quaking bog through the Avenue of Maples offers hikers a chance to see diverse and rare plant species.

Due to its location near Route 128, Ponkapoag Pond is a popular hiking, cross-country skiing, and mountain biking destination. If you come here on a weekday, however, the reservation is usually free of people, even after work. The main trail makes a loop of 200-acre Ponkapoag Pond and a unique Atlantic white cedar bog, located on the property's northwest side. The pond attracts all sorts of wildlife, including ospreys and great blue herons.

DIRECTIONS

Take Route 128 to Exit 2 onto Washington Street in Canton. Turn left just before the first set of lights into the golf course parking lot. Signs lead you directly to the reservation. There are three different entrances to this section of the Blue Hills Reservation, which is run by the Department of Conservation and Recreation (DCR). One entrance is on Randolph Street in Canton (which has good parking); another entrance is off Exit 3 from Route 128 (parking is limited); and the most popular entrance is through the DCR/Ponkapoag Golf Course.

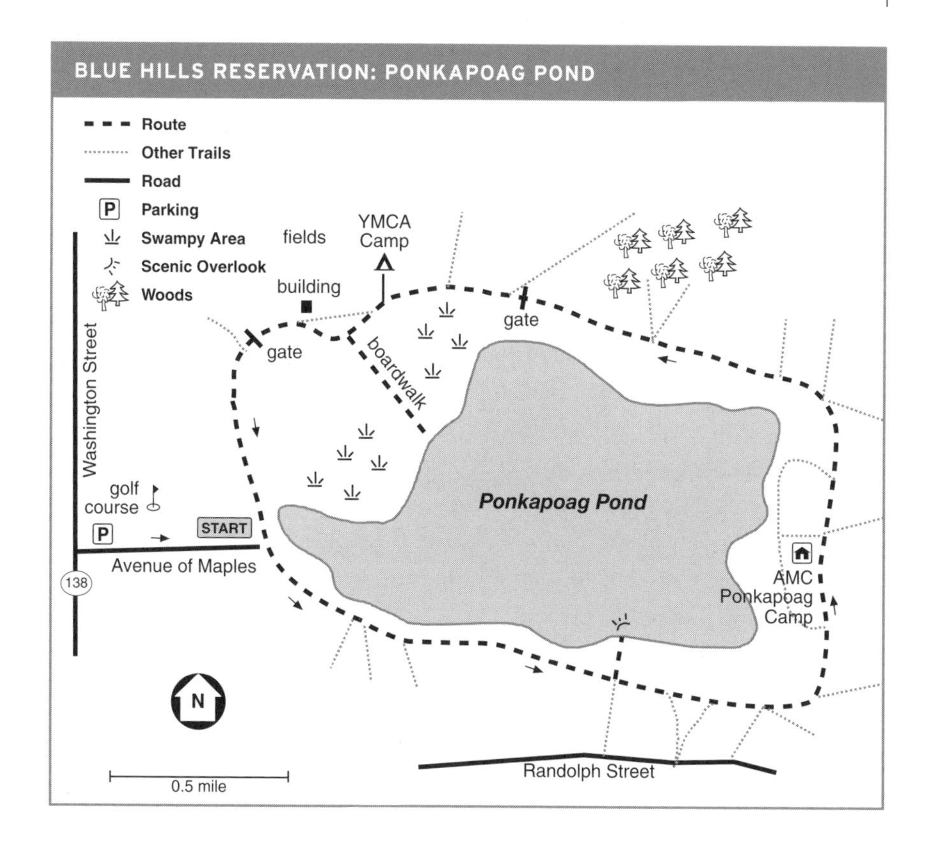

TRAIL DESCRIPTION

From the golf course parking lot, look for a paved road on the right side of the buildings, which passes through the fairways (no cars allowed). It is easy to spot the entrance to this road; just look for the row of stately sugar maples that line it. Appropriately enough, the road is called the Avenue of the Maples. Walk down this road, through the golf course, and to the edge of Ponkapoag Pond. The paved road ends here and a wide, well-maintained dirt road circles the pond. If you go left, you can reach the quaking bog after a short walk of about a half mile, and this is a good ramble if you are with young children. The boardwalk leading into the bog begins opposite a ballfield and some cabins operated by the YMCA.

The following directions take you completely around the pond. At the end of the Avenue of the Maples, go right on the dirt road. The terrain at Ponkapoag is fairly level and most trails are wide, making this a good spot for mountain biking and cross-country skiing, in addition to hiking. The trail hugs the edge of the pond, offering plenty of spots to get to the shoreline. A little more than 0.5 mile down the trail is an open beach area, where there is a nice view of the Blue Hills across the water. The road opposite the beach leads to Randolph Street. This entrance is also known as Fisherman's Landing, because cartop boats can be carried down the path and launched. (The entrance off Randolph Street is right next to Temple Beth David, across the street from Westdale Road. This is a good place to park if you want to bypass the golf course, but it also bypasses the beautiful Avenue of the Maples.)

As the trail passes around the back of the pond, blue diamond markers attached to trees help to keep you on the main path. Cottages managed by the Appalachian Mountain Club are located here, and the side roads can get a bit confusing. The trails going to the left lead to the cabins, so stay to the right. At the third trail juncture, you go down a steep hill where a map is posted. The path is noticeably rougher in this area. Soon the trail intersects with another and you should go left, following the blue markers. Finally you come to a gate where you turn left again. You are now at the north side of the pond. The YMCA Outdoor Center is located a little farther down the trail. The boardwalk to the bog is opposite the ballfield.

Once you are finished exploring the bog, retrace your steps along the boardwalk to the main path by the YMCA Outdoor Center and go left. It's only a short walk (about 0.5 mile) down the main trail to reach the golf course and then the Avenue of the Maples, which will lead to the parking area.

NATURE NOTES

The first mile of the pond trail has rich, moist soil. Trees normally associated with more northern forests can be found here. Yellow birch, hemlock, maples, and beech grow above the ferns below. The trees are quite large, but most of them are probably under a hundred years old. As with most of Massachusetts, early settlers cleared the forests to make pastures and farmland, and used the wood for lumber and fuel. Sadly, there are no significant tracks of virgin forests left in the state and many areas have been harvested more than once. As farming moved westward toward the Mississippi and fossil fuel replaced wood as a heating source, the forests of New England were allowed to make a comeback. Still, we don't have the huge trees that the first explorers had seen. They described the woods as "park-like" because the trees were so massive they blocked out all sunlight from reaching the understory—barely any brush or saplings grew beneath them. In small areas, Native Americans would also burn undergrowth to improve hunting.

Along the trail, look for skunk cabbage, one of the first harbingers of spring. It has large, cabbage-like leaves, and sometimes grows right through late-season snow, melting it with its energy. It has an odor quite similar to a skunk. During

Skunk cabbage. Photo by Jerry and Marcy Monkman.

the summer months the odor of the skunk cabbage along the trail is replaced by the pleasant fragrance of the sweet pepperbush. You can identify the plant by the tiny clusters of white flowers at the end of the branches growing in a dense, slender spike. The plant reaches heights of 10 feet and has narrow green leaves.

The bog adjacent to the pond has been designated a National Environmental Study Area because of its unique ecosystem. A beautiful stand of Atlantic white cedars grows here, along with such carnivorous plants as the unusual pitcher plant. Because the nutrients in the bog soil are relatively sterile, pitcher plants and other carnivorous plants, like the sundew, obtain their nourishment from insects. While many people are familiar with the Venus flytrap (indigenous to the southeastern U.S.), which captures its prey by snapping shut over them, the bog plants of the northeast use a different method of entrapment. The pitcher plant attracts insects into its leaves with scent and colorful veins. Once the insect enters, it has a hard time escaping because tiny hairs in the plant point downward; trapping it and drowning it in the liquid at the bottom of the pitcher, after which the plant's enzymes digest the insect. To identify the plant, look for the pitcher-shaped, reddish-green leaves. It is between one to two feet tall. In the summer it will have a large, solitary, purplish-red flower on a leafless stalk.

The boardwalk is quite narrow and starts out through a dense jungle of swamp maples and other trees before it reaches the white cedars; finally penetrating the more open area of the bog, which is dominated by leather leaf. In the summer you will see the pink flowers (about a half inch wide) of sheep laurel. The sheep laurel grows between one and three feet tall, and looks similar to the more common mountain laurel plants. It thrives in bog areas, and is expanding its range at Ponkapoag as the size of the bog area expands. Each year, the pond becomes shallower as vegetation closes its ring around the pond. There are no underground streams and few springs to replenish and oxygenate the water. Sphagnum moss flourishes in the stagnant water of the bog, and as it dies it fills the pond.

Great blue heron frequent the pond, which is not surprising, due to the abundance of warm-water fish. Both the heron and anglers try their skill for largemouth bass and pickerel, but the heron tend to fish for those under five inches. Shore-bound anglers have the best chance of catching fish in the spring when the fish look for warm, shallow water to either spawn or feed. Osprey occasionally stop at the Ponkapoag, so be sure to bring binoculars. They are migrating birds, and spring and fall offer the best opportunities to catch a glimpse. The sight of an osprey diving from the sky to snatch a fish is a scene you will never forget. The osprey skims low over the water and grabs fish with its talons. Winged blackbirds also descend upon the pond, and in the springtime you can see the red-shouldered males arrive first in huge flocks. They explore the entire shoreline as they wait for female birds. Mosquitoes also inhabit the reservation—so come prepared.

MORE INFORMATION

Open year-round, dawn to dusk; no fee; no rest rooms; dogs allowed on leash. For more information, contact Massachusetts Department of Conservation and Recreation/Blue Hills at 617-698-1802 or visit www.mass.gov/dcr.

The AMC's Ponkapoag Camp, on the east shore of Ponkapoag Pond, has cabins available for rent. Reservations are required; contact the AMC's Boston headquarters at 617-523-0655 or visit www.outdoors.org/lodging for more information.

TRIP 29
BLUE HILLS RESERVATION: OBSERVATION TOWER LOOP

LOCATION: Canton
RATING: Moderate
DISTANCE: 2 miles
ESTIMATED TIME: 1.5 hours
OTHER ACTIVITIES: Fishing, horseback riding, mountain biking, paddling, picnicking, rock climbing, and swimming are all permitted in various parts of the park
WINTER ACTIVITIES: In winter there is alpine skiing at the Blue Hill Ski Area on the western side of Great Blue Hill, ice skating at several ponds and artificial rinks, and cross-country skiing on many of the reservation trails and across the neighboring Ponkapoag Golf Course
PUBLIC TRANSPORTATION: Red Line to Ashmont Station; take the high-speed line to Mattapan; from there take the Canton and Blue Hills bus services to the Trailside Museum and Great Blue Hill on Route 138; For directions from other areas, call 617-698-1802

A hike to the observation tower takes you through a variety of woodland terrain and affords a tremendous view at the top.

The trails here are popular on the weekends, so plan accordingly. If you are hiking with young children you might want to go only part way up the hill or reverse the walk and go up the gentler incline first. Another option is to walk up the Summit Road, which is closed to traffic (see map).

DIRECTIONS

From Route 128, take Exit 2B (Route 138 north) and go 1 mile to parking lot on the right, adjacent to the Trailside Museum.

TRAIL DESCRIPTION

Begin your hike from the trailhead that starts at the parking lots just to the right of the Trailside Museum (as you face it from the street). There is a signboard, and red dots on trees mark the trail. This is the most direct route to the summit, and it rises steeply in some places. In some sections logs are imbedded in the ground to serve as stairs. White pine, maple, beech, oak, and hickory shade the path. On your right are the open slopes of the Blue Hill Ski Area.

About fifteen minutes into the hike you will cross a narrow trail and then cross the paved Summit Road. Proceed through an area of red pine. They can be distinguished from the more common white pine because their needles are thicker and a bit longer, and the bark of the red pine is lighter with a rusty hue.

Continue to follow the red dots and at about the 25- or 30-minute mark you

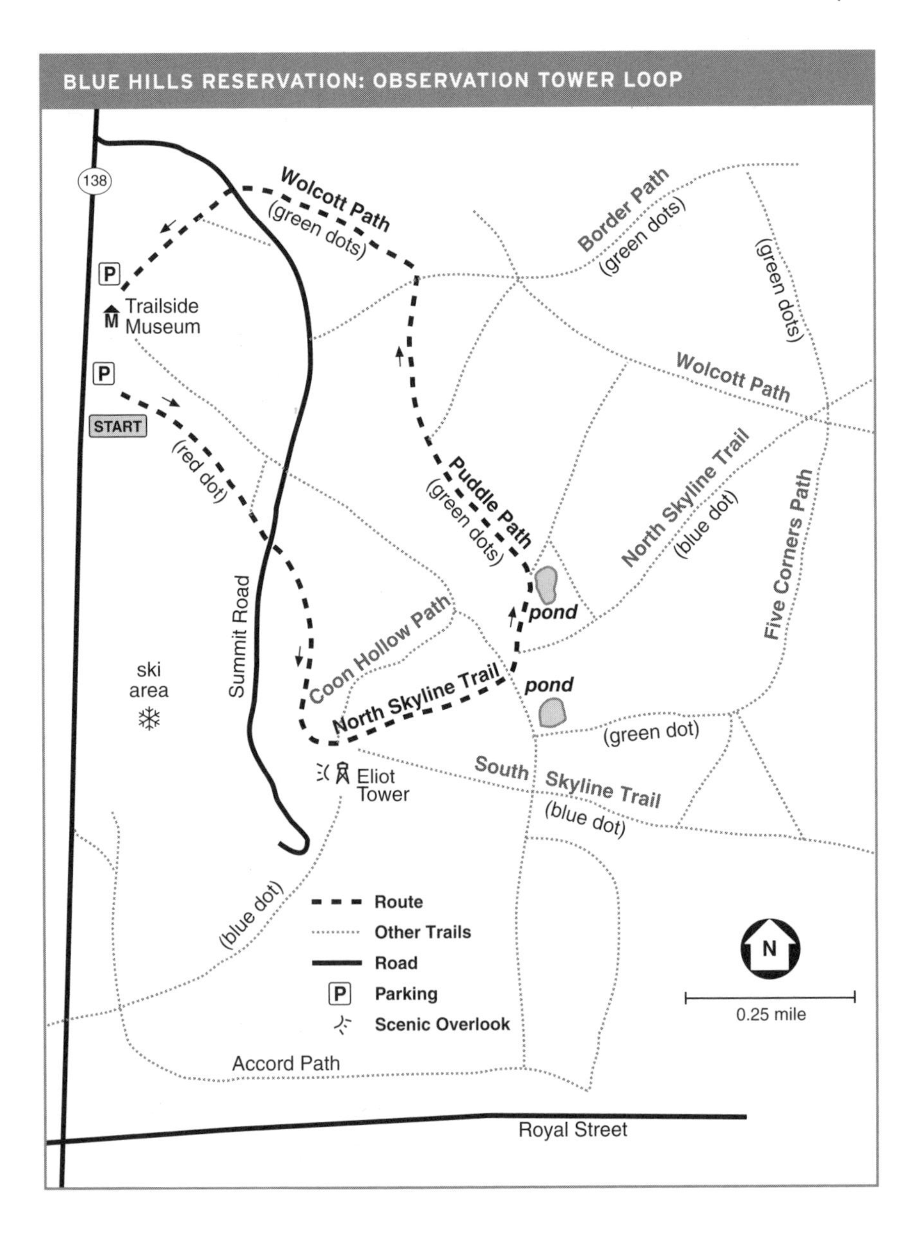

will arrive at the stone observation tower. The tower is called the Eliot Tower after famed landscape architect and lover of open spaces, Charles Eliot. (There are two picnic benches beneath the shelter of the tower structure.) Low-bush blueberries grow in sunny spots, and in autumn their scarlet leaves contrast nicely with the gray bedrock.

Although the most direct route back to the parking area is on another section of the red dot trail called the Coon Hollow Path, you may want a more gradual descent in a northwesterly direction. Follow the North Skyline Trail (so marked on a granite post), which begins near the back of the tower. The trail is marked by blue dots, but be aware that the South Skyline Trail is also marked by blue dots. As you descend on the North Skyline Trail you will have partial views of the surrounding hills, which will give you an appreciation for just how large the reservation is. The footing on the trail can be a bit tricky because of the many small rocks and steepness.

A young red fox surveys the terrain. Photo by D. R. Santoro.

After ten minutes of hiking you will reach an intersection. Take the second left onto a trail called the Puddle Path, which is marked by both blue and green dots. (Do not take the first hard left on the unmarked trail going uphill.) In 30 feet the blue dot trail goes to the right but you should stay straight on the Puddle Path, following the green dots. In a couple minutes you will come to a fork in the trail. Go left, continuing to follow the green dots.

The Puddle Path is a wide trail passing through an area of handsome beech trees. Even in the dead of winter the lower branches of the beech trees still are covered with paper-thin tan leaves, which do not fall off until new growth begins in the spring. In ten minutes you will pass an unmarked trail on the right, and in five more minutes you will begin to notice hemlock seedlings followed by a large hemlock with sweeping branches on the right. The hemlock needles are only about a quarter inch long and have rounded edges. More hemlocks shade the path ahead before the trail comes to a T-intersection. Turn left here on the wide Wolcott Path, ignoring the narrow trail also on the left just before the T-intersection. In five minutes the trail crosses the Summit Road and in another three or four minutes you will arrive back at the parking lot and the museum.

Outside the Trailside Museum is a water-filled pool and pen, which is the home to two otters. Spend some time here, as the otters put on quite a show, sliding down the chute, diving beneath the water, and rolling on the surface. Next to the otter pen are other pens for injured wildlife, such as deer, turkey, hawks, and owls. Inside the Trailside Museum there are interpretive exhibits such as a wigwam and live animals including a timber rattlesnake, a copperhead, and snapping turtle.

Be sure to make repeat visits to the reservation to travel the trails to the east of the Great Blue Hill. You might want to consider making an all-day hike with a friend, leaving one car at the opposite end of the reservation. The Skyline Trail (see Trip 32) is approximately 14 miles long, and some hikers use this as a training ground to get in shape before they climb the White Mountains of New Hampshire. Several great views can be seen from the Skyline Trail. (The entrance off Chickatabet Street was recommended by park rangers as a less traveled section of the reservation.)

NATURE NOTES

This hike has exposed ledges of granite to pick your way over, and children love the challenge of "mountain climbing." This is a great place to introduce children to mountainous hikes, without taxing their endurance. Be sure to stop every now and then after the first ten minutes of climbing both to catch your breath and to admire the view of the Boston skyline over your shoulder. The birch trees growing in this rocky soil are mostly gray birch, which are among the first trees to colonize an area of poor soil or a section of land where a fire has destroyed a more mature forest.

The summit of Blue Hill is 635 feet and provides for sweeping vistas of Boston and the ocean beyond. But it is the trees and hilltops in the foreground that will capture your attention. From this vantage point it's interesting to see the patterns of tree species, particularly in the fall when the rusty-colored oaks dominate with patches of hemlock and white pine scattered about the hills.

During the spring and fall migration of hawks, the summit of Blue Hill provides a good vantage point to watch them wing their way. Early September is usually the best time for a successful hawk watch. Go on days when the wind is out of the north or west, as this helps propel the hawks (mostly broadwings) on their southerly journey.

MORE INFORMATION

Open year-round, dawn until to dusk; no fee; dogs allowed on leash. For more information, contact DCR/Blue Hills, 617-698-1802 or visit www.mass.gov/dcr. The Trailside Museum is open Wednesday–Sunday 10 A.M. to 5 P.M; admission fee; call 617-333-0690 or visit www.massaudubon.org.

TRIP 30
BLUE HILLS RESERVATION: GREAT BLUE HILL GREEN LOOP

LOCATION: Milton/Canton/Randolph/Braintree/Dedham/Quincy
RATING: Moderate
DISTANCE: 2.8 miles
ESTIMATED TIME: 2.5 hours
OTHER ACTIVITIES: Fishing, horseback riding, mountain biking, paddling, picnicking, rock climbing, and swimming are all permitted in various parts of the park
WINTER ACTIVITIES: In winter there is alpine skiing at the Blue Hill Ski Area on the western side of Great Blue Hill, ice skating at several ponds and artificial rinks, and cross-country skiing on many of the reservation trails and across the neighboring Ponkapoag Golf Course
PUBLIC TRANSPORTATION: Take the MBTA Red Line to Ashmont station and take the high speed line to Mattapan; from there take the Canton and Blue Hills bus service to the Trailside Museum

This 2.8-mile loop meanders through the Great Blue Hill section of the reservation. It generally follows the cols between the hills, never ascending to any of the summits.

DIRECTIONS

From Route 128, take Exit 2B (Route 138 north) and go 1 mile to parking lot on the right, adjacent to the Trailside Museum.

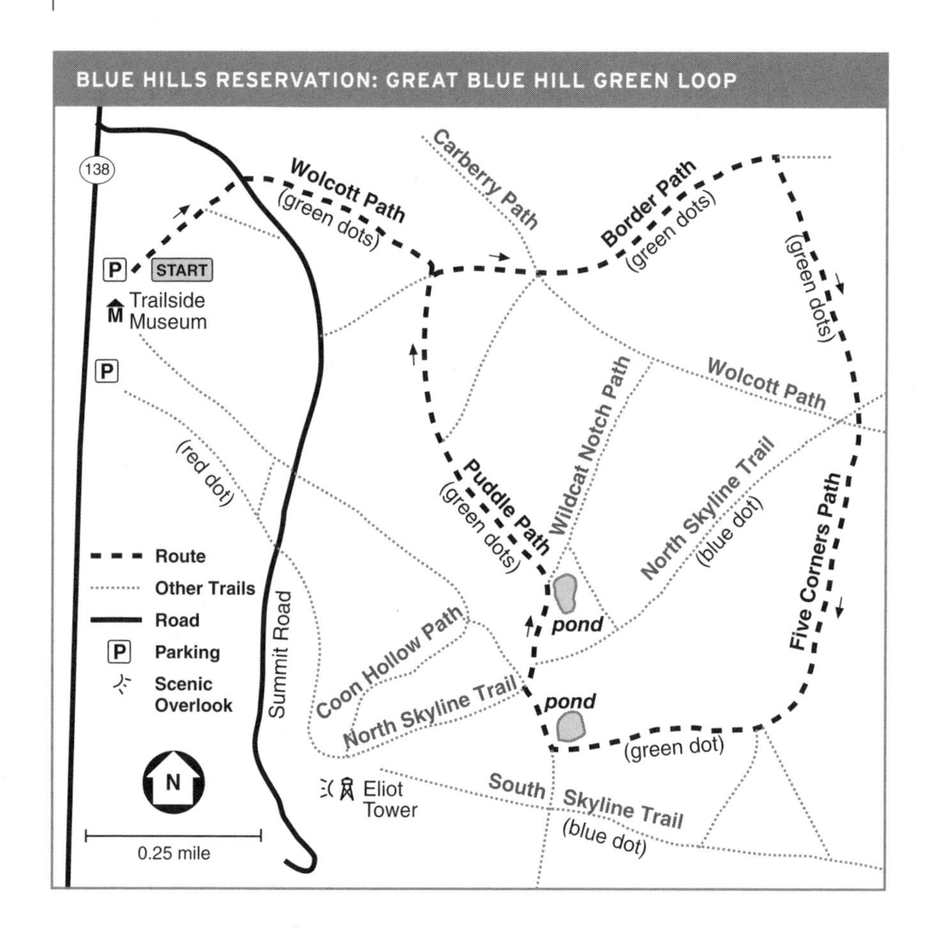

TRAIL DESCRIPTION

This trail begins at the north parking lot at the Trailside Museum. Heading northeast, it soon reaches paved Summit Road, where it turns right and immediately bears left onto a dirt road (Wolcott Path), which heads east through a stand of tall white pines. At marker 1085 the loop proper begins, with the return trail coming in from the right. Continue straight on the road for a few hundred feet to marker 1100, where the trail turns left onto Border Path and runs northeast along the edge of some wetlands.

At marker 1135 the trail turns right and heads southeast through the col between Wolcott Hill on the right and Hemenway Hill on the left. At marker 1141 it crosses a dirt road and the Skyline Trail. Continuing southward on Five Corners Path, the trail circles Wolcott hill and turns north through Wildcat Notch on Wildcat Notch Path, which separates Wolcott Hill from Great Blue Hill. It passes two small swamps, and just after the second, the trail turns left and heads northwest to the dirt road (Wolcott Path) where the loop began. Turn left onto the dirt road to return to the parking lot.

Climbing the rocky slope of Blue Hill.

NATURE NOTES

The larger, northern section of Blue Hills Reservation includes a stretch of the Neponset River and the adjoining wetlands of Fowl Meadow; a series of wooded summits, the largest of which are Great Blue Hill (635 feet) and Chickatawbut Hill (517 feet); Houghtons Pond and several smaller ponds; and the Quincy Quarries Historic Site, now a popular rock-climbing locale.

MORE INFORMATION

The Mass Audubon Society operates two educational facilities within the reservation. The Trailside Museum on MA 138, 0.5 mile north of I-93, is open to the public (617-333-0690 or visit www.massaudubon.org). The Trailside Museum is open Wednesday –Sunday 10 A.M. to 5 P.M. Trail information and maps are available at the Trailside Museum as well as at the reservation headquarters on 695 Hillside Street, Milton, MA 02186, behind the state police station. The Chickatawbut Hill Education Center offers workshops and programs for organized groups by reservation only.

Blue Hills Reservation is open from dawn until dusk. For more information, visit www.mass.gov/dcr.

TRIP 31
BLUE HILLS RESERVATION: HOUGHTONS POND YELLOW LOOP

LOCATION: Milton/Canton/Randolph/Braintree/Dedham/Quincy
RATING: Easy
DISTANCE: 1 mile
ESTIMATED TIME: 1 hour
OTHER ACTIVITIES: Fishing, horseback riding, mountain biking, paddling, picnicking, rock climbing, and swimming are all permitted in various parts of the park
WINTER ACTIVITIES: In winter there is alpine skiing at the Blue Hill Ski Area on the western side of Great Blue Hill, ice skating at several ponds and artificial rinks, and cross-country skiing on many of the reservation trails and across the neighboring Ponkapoag Golf Course
PUBLIC TRANSPORTATION: Take the MBTA Red Line to Ashmont station and take the high speed line to Mattapan; from there take the Canton and Blue Hills bus service to Blue Hill River Road, then cross the road and walk one mile East on Hillside Street

This easy, 1-mile trail is a popular walk for families with small children.

DIRECTIONS
Take I-93 to Exit 3 (Houghtons Pond). Turn right onto Hillside Street and then a quick right into the parking lot.

TRAIL DESCRIPTION
The trailhead is at the main parking lot for the Houghtons Pond swimming area. The trail proceeds to the left (east) past the beach, bearing right just after the bathhouse. It joins a dirt road for a short distance around the eastern end of the pond, and then turns right off the road just before reaching a playground. The trail continues along the southern edge of the pond, crosses the pond's outlet at the western end, and heads north past a field and playground. It then travels through a small swamp and bears left (east) up a hill past a pavilion to the starting point.

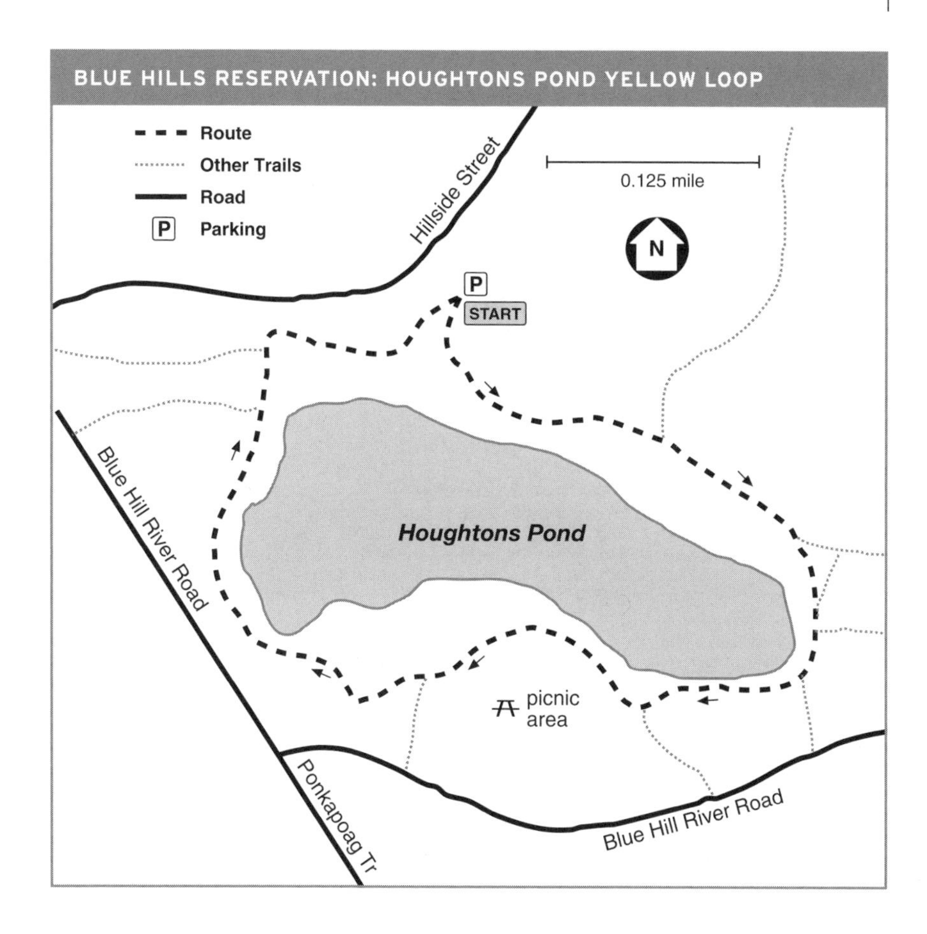

NATURE NOTES

The Massachusetts tribe of Native Americans lived by the Blue Hills, and the word Massachusetts means "people of the great hill." The area was ideally situated for Native Americans because of its close proximity to the ocean and the Neponset River, its high vantage points, and the quarry materials (brown volcanic rock or hornfels) used to make tools and weapons. Later, the granite hills at the east end of the reservation were quarried for their granite. In 1825, a large-scale quarry produced granite for buildings, monuments, and fortifications across the nation. The top of Blue Hill also was the scene of one of the first weather observatories in the country, when in 1885 meteorologist Abbott Lawrence Rotch established his wind-swept outpost to conduct weather-related experiments.

The reservation has both large wildlife, such as deer, fox, coyote, and raccoon, and the smaller wildlife that we sometime overlook: insects, salamanders, and common birds.

MORE INFORMATION

The Mass Audubon Society operates two educational facilities within the reservation. The Trailside Museum on MA 138, 0.5 mile north of I-93, is open to the public (617-333-0690 or visit www.massaudubon.org). Trail information and maps are available at the Trailside Museum as well as at the reservation headquarters on 695 Hillside Street, Milton, MA 02186, behind the state police station. The Chickatawbut Hill Education Center offers workshops and programs for organized groups by reservation only.

Blue Hills Reservation is open from dawn until dusk. For more information, visit www.mass.gov/dcr.

TRIP 32
BLUE HILLS RESERVATION: SKYLINE TRAIL

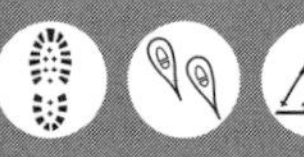

LOCATION: Milton/Canton/Randolph/Braintree/Dedham/Quincy
RATING: Strenuous
DISTANCE: 9 miles
ESTIMATED TIME: 6 hours
OTHER ACTIVITIES: Fishing, horseback riding, mountain biking, paddling, picnicking, rock climbing, and swimming are all permitted in various parts of the park
WINTER ACTIVITIES: In winter there is alpine skiing at the Blue Hill Ski Area on the western side of Great Blue Hill, ice skating at several ponds and artificial rinks, and cross-country skiing on many of the reservation trails and across the neighboring Ponkapoag Golf Course
PUBLIC TRANSPORTATION: Take the MBTA Red Line to Ashmont station and take the high speed line to Mattapan; from there take the Canton and Blue Hills bus service to Blue Hill River Road, then cross the road and walk one mile East on Hillside Street

This trail, marked by blue rectangular blazes, is the longest in the Blue Hills Reservation, extending from Fowl Meadow in Canton east to Shea Rink on Willard Street in Quincy.

DIRECTIONS

Take I-93 to Exit 3 (Houghtons Pond). Turn right onto Hillside Street.

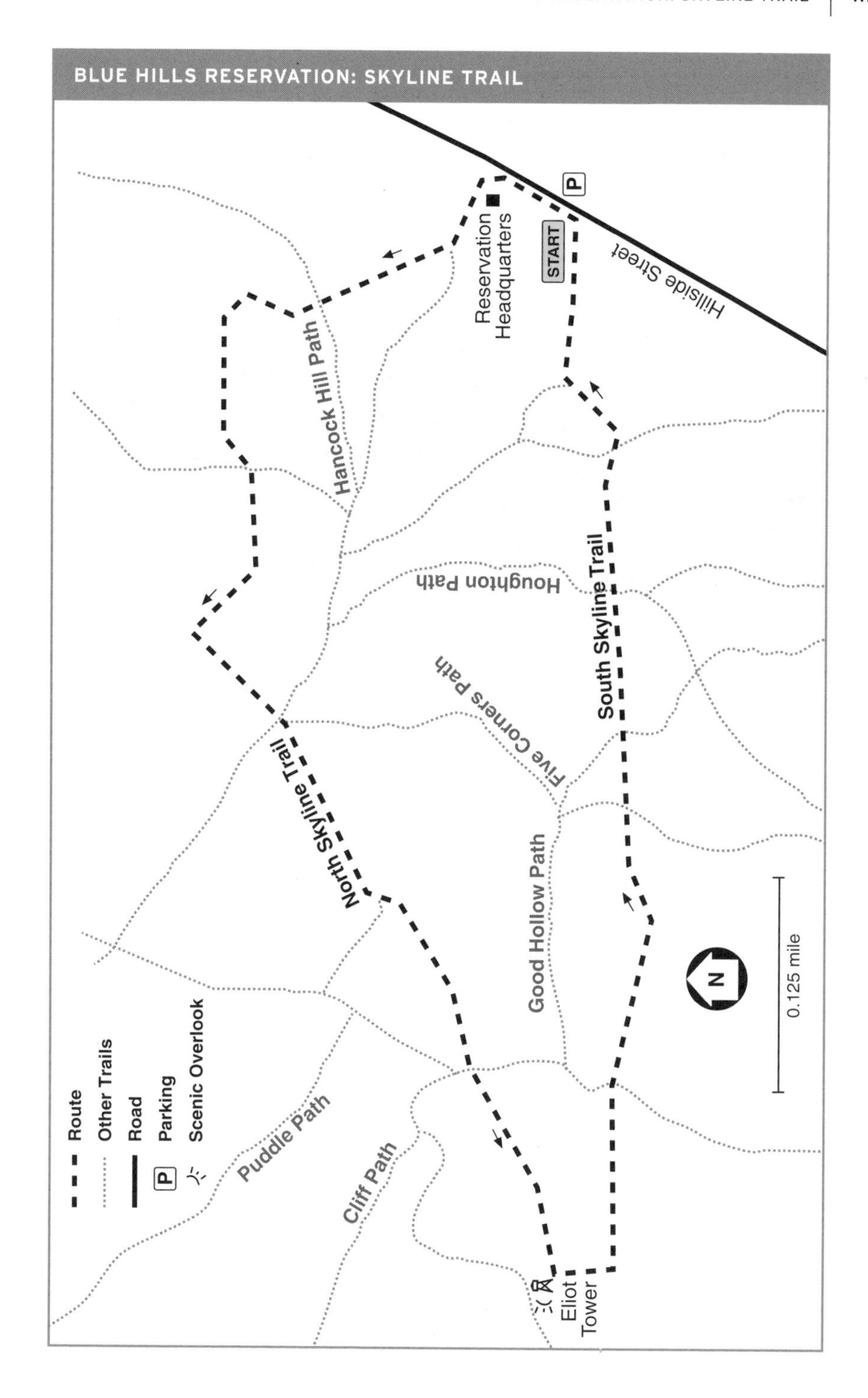
BLUE HILLS RESERVATION: SKYLINE TRAIL
Route
Other Trails
Road
Parking
Scenic Overlook
P
START
Reservation Headquarters
Hillside Street
Hancock Hill Path
Houghton Path
South Skyline Trail
Five Corners Path
North Skyline Trail
Good Hollow Path
Puddle Path
Cliff Path
Eliot Tower
N
0.125 mile

A view of the Boston skyline awaits at the summit of Blue Hill.

TRAIL DESCRIPTION

The trail can be accessed from any one of four major streets: 1) MA 138, at a parking lot on the west side about 0.5 mile south of the Trailside Museum. 2) Hillside Street, at the reservation headquarters. 3) Randolph Avenue (MA 28), where the closest parking is about 0.25 mile south of the trail crossing. 4) Willard Street at the trail terminus at Shea Rink.

You should choose your route based on whether you can get a car pick-up at some point on the trail, or if you need to return to your car. For a complete route map of this lengthy trail, see the AMC's *Massachusetts Trail Guide*, 8th ed. map 4: Blue Hills Reservation (the Skyline Trail is in blue).

A recommended route that includes the summit of Great Blue Hill (and is mapped here) starts at the reservation headquarters on Hillside Street and takes advantage of the north and south spurs of the Skyline Trail to create a loop hike. From the headquarters, hike northeast to Hancock Hill, turn east and cross Breakneck Ledge Path at marker 1162. Continue east and cross Five Corners Path at marker 1141. Pass markers 1117 and 1092 and start your ascent up the Great Blue Hill. You'll reach the tower and observatory at marker 1063, where the trail turns south and the South Skyline Trail enters from the left. To return on the South Skyline Trail, turn left at marker 1066 and continue following the blue blazes back to the headquarters.

NATURE NOTES

See "Nature Notes" for Trip 31.

MORE INFORMATION

The Mass Audubon Society operates two educational facilities within the reservation. The Trailside Museum on MA 138, 0.5 mile north of I-93, is open to the public (617-333-0690 or visit www.massaudubon.org). Trail information and maps are available at the Trailside Museum as well as at the reservation headquarters on 695 Hillside Street, Milton, MA 02186, behind the state police station. The Chickatawbut Hill Education Center offers workshops and programs for organized groups by reservation only.

The AMC's Ponkapoag Camp, on the east shore of Ponkapoag Pond, has cabins available for rent. Reservations are required; contact the AMC's Boston headquarters at 617-523-0655 or visit www.outdoors.org/lodging for information.

Blue Hills Reservation is open from dawn until dusk. For more information, visit www.mass.gov/dcr.

TRIP 33
GREAT ESKER PARK

LOCATION: Weymouth
RATING: Easy
DISTANCE: 1.5 miles
ESTIMATED TIME: 1 hour
OTHER ACTIVITIES: Birding
PUBLIC TRANSPORTATION: Take the Commuter Rail to Weymouth to the 220 bus

The esker runs parallel to a salt marsh, making it interesting for exploring, and offers an excellent opportunity to see a wide variety of birds.

With a little imagination a walk on top of the glacial esker at Great Esker Park can be compared to walking on the back of a giant snake. Formed by glacial deposits during the last Ice Age (12,000 years ago), the mile and a quarter long esker rises above the woodlands and the marsh, reaching a height of 90 feet.

(The esker could have been lost to development, but the town of Weymouth acquired the acreage in 1966 from the federal government, which owned the area, using it as a buffer zone to an ammunition depot located on the other side of the Weymouth Back River.)

Two walks are described here: the first goes through an area south of the parking lot (which can have wet spots at high tide), and the second is a short half-hour walk that goes through the northern portion the park.

DIRECTIONS

From Route 3 take Exit 285 (Route 18). At the first traffic light turn left onto Middle Street. At the end of Middle Street (2.9 miles) turn left onto Commercial Street and proceed 0.4 mile to the first traffic light. Turn right onto Green Street and go 0.6 mile to the triangular divider. Bear right on Elva Road and go uphill 0.2 mile to end and park in the large lot.

TRAIL DESCRIPTION

From the parking area follow the paved road (closed to vehicles) that begins to the right of the maintenance buildings and climbs the esker. In three minutes you reach the top at an intersection with another paved road that follows the contours of the esker. (Eskers are shaped when rivers within the retreating glaciers fill with debris left behind as the glacier melts.) Turn left here and walk along the top of the esker in a northerly direction passing beneath oaks (red oaks have bristle-tipped lobes and white oaks have rounded lobes) and maples. In the understory are gray birch and staghorn sumac. The staghorn sumac gets its name from the velvet covering its stems that looks like the velvet on a stag's antlers. It is non-poisonous and especially colorful in autumn when the leaves are a dark crimson. In roughly 200 feet you will come to a sign for the Reversing Falls; turn right at a dirt trail. The trail leads down off the esker toward the salt marsh, and after three or four minutes of walking you arrive at another sign (for Twin Oaks). Bear right toward the reversing falls.

Walk along the edge of the marsh and look through the trees to spot birds feeding in the marsh grass. Park ranger Mike Doyle reports that he often sees wood ducks, snowy egrets, great egrets, and even an occasional little blue heron in the marsh.

The trail climbs a smaller esker and at the top of the ridge turns right. There are good views of the marsh from both sides of the trail, and if you look to your left you will see an osprey pole used by these magnificent birds as a nesting platform.

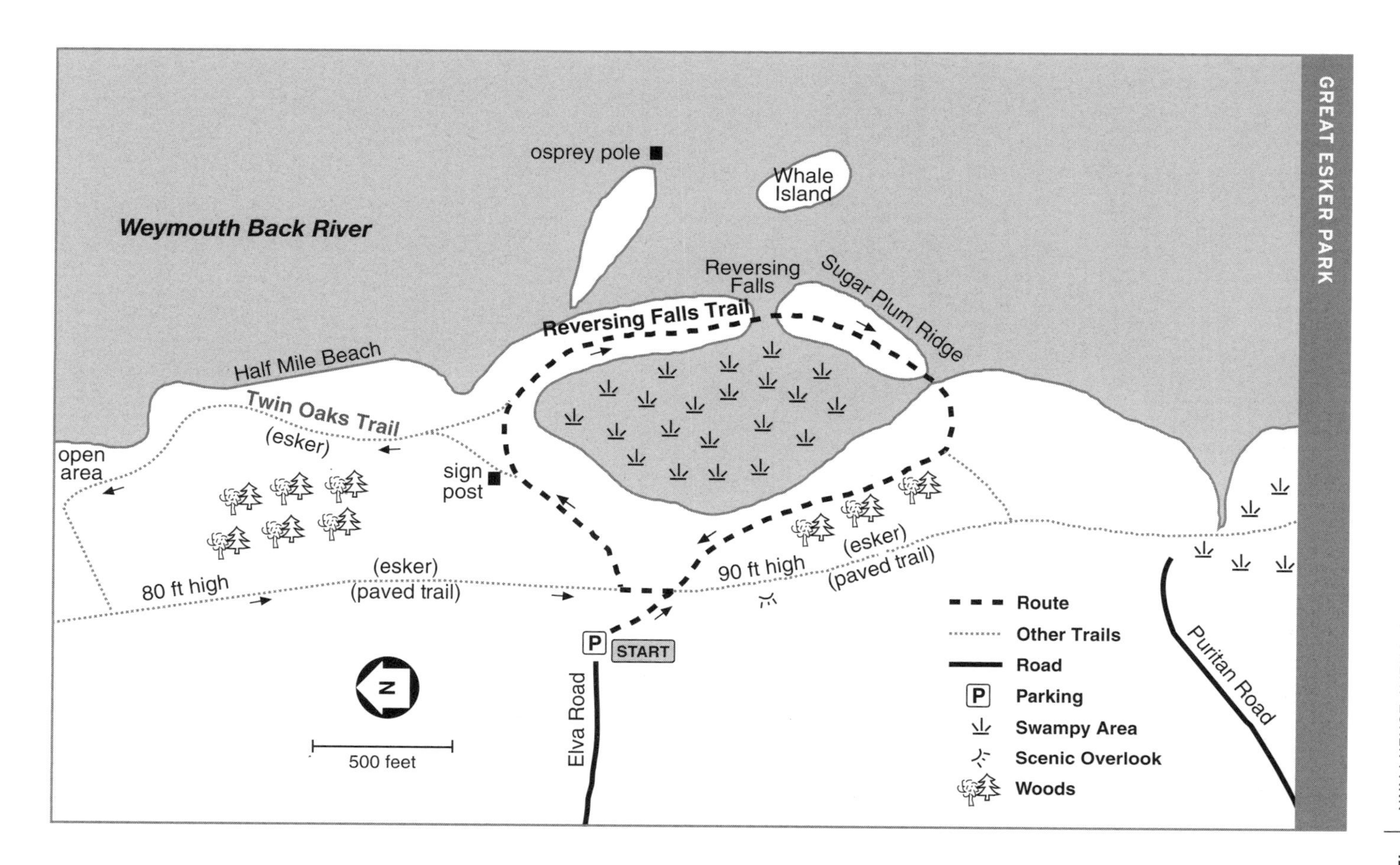
GREAT ESKER PARK
Weymouth Back River
osprey pole
Whale Island
Reversing Falls
Sugar Plum Ridge
Reversing Falls Trail
Half Mile Beach
Twin Oaks Trail
(esker)
open area
sign post
80 ft high
(esker)
(paved trail)
90 ft high
(esker)
(paved trail)
P
START
Elva Road
Puritan Road
N
500 feet
Route
Other Trails
Road
Parking
Swampy Area
Scenic Overlook
Woods

Puffy, ball-like flowers dot the buttonbrush shrub. Photo by John Hayes.

After another quarter mile of walking you will descend the hill and arrive at Reversing Falls—not exactly Niagara (or even a waterfall for that matter), but a passageway between two sections of the marsh where the water rushes in at high tide and exits at low tide. (Look for hermit crabs and other marine life in the estuary.) A series of stepping stones crosses the passage, making it possible to pick your way across at low tide. At high tide you may have to remove your shoes and carefully wade across. On the other side of the passage, follow the narrow trail that passes over Sugar Plum Ridge, offering nice views of the Weymouth Back River and Whale Island. Look for the pure white coloring of mute swans floating out on the water.

Low-bush blueberries are scattered about the woods beneath the oaks. At the end of Sugar Plum Ridge, cross a low-lying area (where you need to remove your shoes at high tide) and follow the trail straight into the woods, bypassing a side trail on your left. In a couple minutes bear to the right, passing beneath a power line. Then at the next fork stay right (if you go straight it leads directly to the paved trail on top of the esker). You will be walking through a grove of beech trees with smooth gray trunks then passing beneath the power lines again. (The esker will be on your left.) After walking about three-quarters of a mile the trail swings left, and climbs the esker to the top where it intersects the paved road. You are at the spot where the paved road from the parking lot meets the paved road on top of the esker. There is a partial view of the Boston skyline from the top of the esker if you turn left and follow the top of the esker south for five minutes.

You can extend your walk an additional half hour by following the top paved road on top of the esker in a northerly direction. Retrace your original steps along the paved road then go right on the wide trail, which will bring you to the Twin Oaks sign. Follow the arrow toward Twin Oaks, climbing up the hill. In a couple minutes you will arrive at an intersection where you should bear left. Follow this trail for five minutes, first passing some birch trees and then by the edge of the salt marsh. (Take time to explore the shoreline, examining the driftwood and shells.) In about ten minutes you will arrive at an open area. Cross the open area (comprised of wood chips and grass) and follow a dirt road to the left that brings you back to the paved road on top of the esker. To return to your car just go left on the paved road for about three-quarters of a mile. There will be a bench for resting along the way, offering a fine view of the salt marsh. Wildflowers line the paved road here, making it a good place to see butterflies, particularly in the fall when the monarchs are passing through.

NATURE NOTES

The salt marsh and estuary at Great Esker is quite large and is a critical link in the food chain, second only to rain forests as productive habitats. More than 30 species of fish can be found here including flounder, bluefish, striped bass, eel, herring, and smelt. Many young fish and invertebrates grow up here, finding shelter in the dense grasses. Beneath the water's surface, oysters and shrimp feed on top of the mud while sea cucumbers and worms live beneath the mud. Crabs use the tides to their advantage, burrowing in the mud at low tide for protection and scavenging along the bottom at high tide. In the spring there is an annual herring run up the Weymouth Back River and into Whitman Pond where the fish spawn in the fresh water. And in the last couple of years as Boston Harbor has become cleaner, seals have been seen in the Weymouth Back River in the springtime.

There have been a breeding pair of osprey here since 1992, and many young ospreys have been a raised at the site. "The osprey," said ranger Doyle, "catch fish in the Back River and upstream at Whitman's Pond. You can expect to see the osprey arriving about the same time as the herring run."

MORE INFORMATION

Open year-round, seven days a week; no fee; no rest rooms; dogs allowed on leash. Contact Weymouth Recreation Department, 1393 Pleasant Street, East Weymouth, MA 02189; 781-335-8299; www.weymouth.ma.us/rec.

TRIP 34
WORLD'S END RESERVATION

LOCATION: Hingham
RATING: Moderate
DISTANCE: 4.5 miles
ESTIMATED TIME: 3 hours
OTHER ACTIVITIES: Biking, birding, fishing
WINTER ACTIVITIES: Trails are flat and well-maintained, excellent for cross-country skiing and snowshoeing
PUBLIC TRANSPORTATION: From Quincy Center Red Line station, take the 220 bus

Tremendous views, rolling fields along the ocean's edge, and an impressive assortment of flora and fauna make for a beautiful walk.

World's End is a peninsula that juts out from the mainland separating Hingham Harbor from the mouth of the Weir River, providing magnificent views in every direction. (It is unknown who named World's End or why, but I assume it got its name because it is a peninsula.) The rolling, open terrain will make you feel like you're on the landscaped grounds of some English estate. Best of all, World's End is a prime spot for viewing migratory birds.

DIRECTIONS

From Route 3, take Exit 14 to Route 228 north. Go 6.6 miles to Route 3A and turn left. Proceed on 3A for 0.9 mile, then take a right on Summer Street and proceed for 0.3 mile. Cross Rockland Street at the light and follow Martin's Lane 0.7 mile to the entrance and parking area.

Public Transportation. Take the Red Line to Quincy Center; exit the station and board the 220 Hingham Depot via Washington Street bus; exit at North Street and Otis Street. From here, it is a 1-mile walk to the World's End Reservation (start walking northeasterly; Otis Street joins with Summer Street).

TRAIL DESCRIPTION

After entering the reservation, take the trail to the left, which leads to the reservation's two smooth hills. Just a short way up the path is a sweeping view of Boston Harbor, with the skyline of the city of Boston rising in the distance. The path then climbs Planter's Hill, which is the highest point on the reserva-

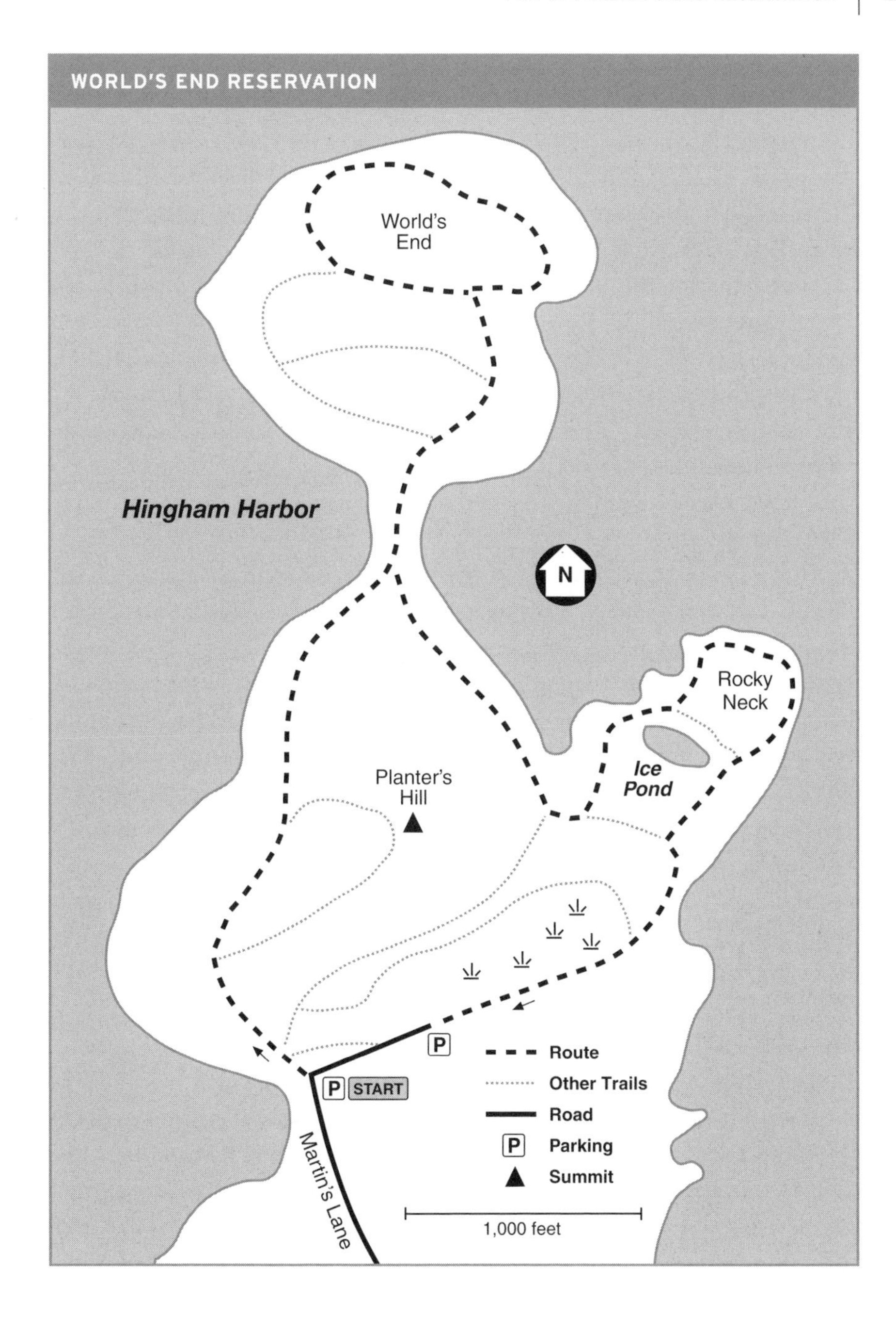

tion at 120 feet. Along the way, there is an occasional bench placed at some of the more strategic points for capturing the magnificent views.

After climbing to a tremendous viewpoint at the top of Planter's Hill, the trail begins its descent to the sandbar that links the Planter's Hill drumlin to the main World's End drumlin. Early settlers built this causeway, known as the "bar," to allow travel between the two islands during high tide.

Crossing the causeway allows you easy access to the rocky beach; it's a perfect spot for children to explore. As you climb the outer hill, look back toward Planter's Hill and admire the unique topography. The outer island has two connecting roads that loop around this island's two highest mounds.

After exploring this area, cross the sandy causeway again, then bear left onto a road that leads to Rocky Neck. Through the trees on the left, you can see the jagged cliffs of Rocky Neck, which stand in contrast to the smooth hills you have just explored. Bear left at the next fork in the trail, and then take the first left after that. As you enter Rocky Neck, the open landscape changes to a more intimate area of woods where the trail is often shaded. You will soon come to the edge of a cliff that rises 50 feet above the water. This makes a fine place to sit and rest.

After walking the perimeter of Rocky Neck, the trail soon intersects with another. I usually turn left here and pass by the northeastern end of the marsh. Just as you reach an area of hemlock trees on a knoll (about a quarter mile down the path), there is a trail through a field on the right—this leads to the boardwalk that passes through tall cattails and marsh grass. You can hear the birds in the reeds, but it's impossible to see them. However, just up ahead is a rock ledge that offers a sweeping view of the marsh. The ledge can easily be climbed from the rear, and it's a great place to sit and watch a few minutes of marsh life unfold.

From here, it's only a short walk to the parking lot by continuing on this foot trail, or by returning to the cart path by the hemlocks and going right (southwest). World's End is not a secret spot, and on warm weekend afternoons the parking lot can fill up.

NATURE NOTES

All the regular small mammals of New England are represented here, including the red fox. Foxes are known as smart or sly because they are extremely suspicious animals that rely on their strong sense of smell to avoid humans. And yet, they have learned to live in close proximity to us by making nocturnal forays to hunt for mice, moles, and other small rodents. The red fox can now be found all over North America, except for several western states (Washington, Oregon, California, Nevada, Arizona, and New Mexico).

The paths leading through the open meadows were designed by famed landscape architect Frederick Law Olmsted in 1890 as part of a proposed development, which fortunately never came to be. However, the winding roads and the stately rows of trees that line them are here for all to enjoy. Prior to

Olmsted's plan, the area had been stripped for timber and only three elm trees remained on all of World's End. The tree-planting program that followed Olmsted's plan transformed the bare drumlins into a diverse landscape with a wide variety of trees, including imported English oaks.

Since that proposed planned community, World's End has escaped development a number of times. The property was considered for projects ranging from the site of a nuclear generator to development of public housing. It was even considered as a site for the United Nations! In 1967 the local citizens raised the necessary money for the Trustees of Reservations to purchase the property.

Small clumps of woodlands, primarily comprised of eastern red cedar and such tall hardwoods as maple and oak, provide habitat for a variety of small animals the hawks were hunting. Lichen-covered stone walls are visible in some spots, reminding you of the area's former agricultural days. Also visible along the woods and in the meadows is poison ivy—learn to recognize the plant's three-leaf stems, and give it a wide berth.

Cottontail rabbits thrive in this combination of fields, shrubs, and small patches of woods. They were once much more common in New England when farmlands, rather than forests and developed areas, dominated the region.

The Ice Pond lies on the eastern arm of the reservation, which seems quite out of place on this rocky point. The Ice Pond was built by farmers in 1909 as a nearby source of ice in the winter. Today, the pond attracts wildlife. Mallards are common along with wide-ranging fowl that often flocks with black ducks. They are surface feeders that eat aquatic vegetation and an occasional insect or mollusk. The males have green heads with white neck bands and rusty breasts. Females are a mottled brown, and both sexes have a distinctive blue rectangle at the hind area of their wings. When you surprise a mallard, it often lets out a loud quack and takes off nearly vertically.

This little pond adds to the enchanting character of Rocky Neck. And if it's springtime, flowering trees, such as the apple tree (whose blossoms have such a sweet smell), will be in bloom. Every season is a good one at World's End; in the summer there are often cool ocean breezes, in the fall the foliage is alive with color, and in the winter the cross-country skiing is superb when there is enough snow to cover the gentle slopes. Sea ducks are also seen more frequently in the winter.

MORE INFORMATION

Open year-round, 8 A.M. to sunset; fee for non-members; dogs allowed on leash; picnicking and swimming prohibited. For more information, contact the Trustees of Reservations, 781-740-6665; www.thetrustees.org.

TRIP 35
WHITNEY AND THAYER WOODS

LOCATION: Hingham
RATING: Easy
DISTANCE: 3 miles
ESTIMATED TIME: 1.75 hours
OTHER ACTIVITIES: Biking, birding
WINTER ACTIVITIES: Trails are flat and well maintained, excellent for cross-country skiing and snowshoeing

Hike and cross-country ski these well-maintained yet removed woodland trails.

Quiet woodland trails, and plenty of them, are the primary features of this large reservation that straddles the towns of Cohasset and Hingham. A large stand of giant rhododendrons and azaleas located on the southern border of the property provide an attractive contrast to the thickly forested hills and glacial boulders. This ramble makes a loop of the eastern portion of the property leading you through the rhododendrons and azaleas.

DIRECTIONS

From Route 3 take Exit 14 to Route 228 north. Follow Route 228 north for 6.6 miles, then go right (southeast) on Route 3A. Follow Route 3A 2.1 miles to the parking area on right across from Sohier Street.

TRAIL DESCRIPTION

From the parking area follow the wide gravel road near the signboard and beneath the telephone wires that leads into the woods. Follow the trail through pines and hardwoods for about three minutes then turn right on the first trail you come to. This is approximately named Boulder Lane, after the many glacial erratics that were deposited by the retreating glaciers.

This is a good section of trail to see the holly tree's shiny green foliage in the understory of the larger oaks, pines, and maples. About three-quarters of a mile into your walk you will see Bigelow Boulder on your right. This boulder weighs about 200 tons. Another couple minutes down the trail is a second boulder, which has little nooks and crannies in the jumble of rocks around it.

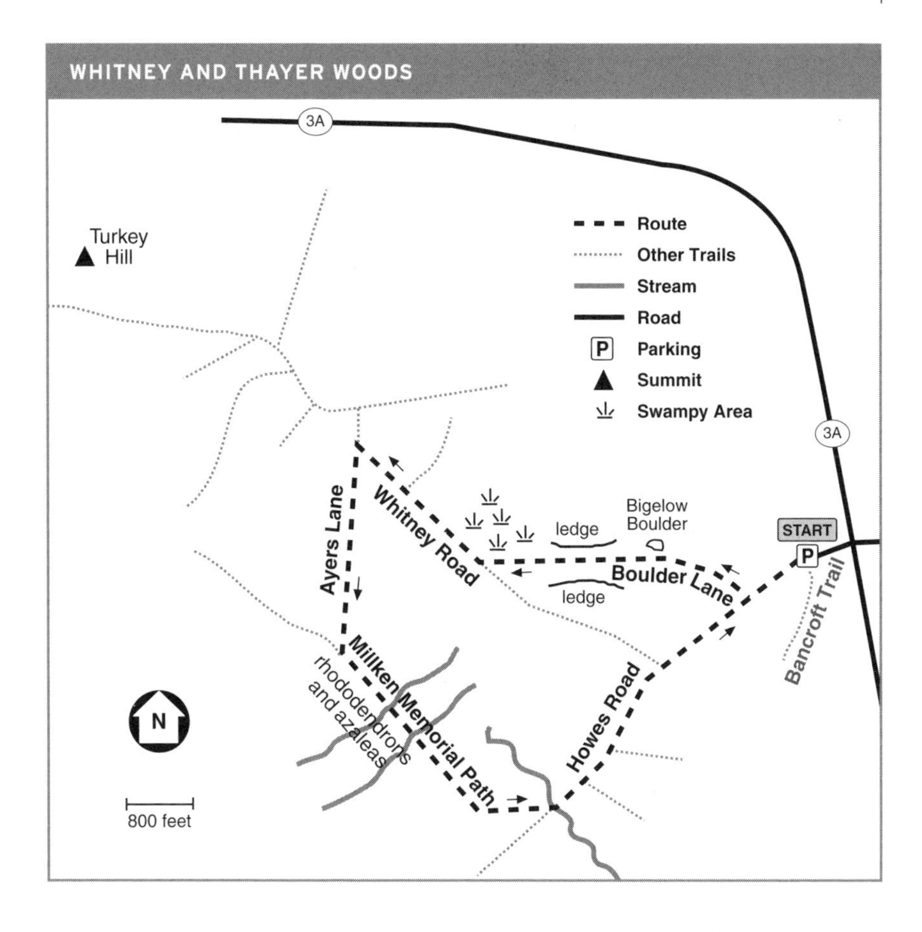

The trail passes a scattering of beech trees that brighten up the forest with their light gray trunks. Even in winter they add a touch of color because the papery golden-brown leaves on the lower limbs often stay on the tree until new growth pushes them off in the spring. Large outcroppings of rock line the trail on the right and left before the trail crosses through a small swamp and arrives at the intersection with Whitney Road, about 1.25 miles into your walk. Stay to the right at the intersection and continue walking for another 0.5 mile. You will come to another intersection. Turn left here onto Ayers Lane.

We often look straight ahead while hiking, but it's a good idea to look down to see what's growing on the forest floor. On this section of trail you might spot sarsaparilla, partridgeberry, and club mosses. Farther down this trail brings you to an intersection at the Milliken Memorial Path. Turn left here to complete your loop back toward the parking lot. Rhododendrons and azaleas line the path, with hollies and hemlock trees growing nearby. All of this greenery crowding the path gives it a mysterious and enchanting feel, even in winter. But in late spring and early summer the scene is truly magnificent when the pinks and whites of thousands of flowers from the azaleas and rhododendrons brighten the woods.

Old stone walls crisscross the woods, indicating the area was once used for pasture or farming—hard to believe with some large white pines towering overhead. Settlers called their annual harvest of stones "New England potatoes," because the frost pushed up stones at such a great rate. If you look closely at stone walls they yield clues: Walls with lots of little stones mixed with the bigger ones means that adjacent land was probably cultivated, but if there are only large rocks in the wall the land was probably used for grazing livestock or mowing for hay.

The Milliken Memorial Path narrows in some spots, and the rhododendrons along the trail's edge give it a tunnel appearance. During wet periods this trail can be very muddy, and there are a couple of small streams to pick your way across. After walking about a mile down the trail you come to an intersection; bear left as the Milliken Memorial Path turns into Howes Road, which crosses over a stream on a bridge. Stay on the main trail, passing by various entrances to the narrower Bancroft Trail. After going about a half mile you arrive at a point where Whitney Road comes in on the left, but continue straight ahead. Within a couple minutes you come to a chain barrier that looks like private property, but is still part of the reservation. Step over the chain and pass a private residence on the right. The trail, which turns into a gravel road, will lead you back to the parking lot in 0.5 mile.

If you are interested in a longer walk on your next visit, explore Turkey Hill at the northwest end of the property (see the map). From the summit there is a nice view of Cohasset Harbor. Adjacent to Turkey Hill is a relatively new Trustees property, Weir River Farm. This 75-acre property includes a combination of hayfields and woodlands. Both Turkey Hill and Weir River Farm can be accessed from Turkey Hill Lane.

Try visiting World's End Reseravtion and Whitney/Thayer on the same day if you are driving from a long distance. World's End is a very special Trustees property: two glacial drumlins jutting into Boston Harbor. Old carriage roads laid out by Frederick Law Olmsted, a noted landscape architect, wind through the hilly terrain with great water views.

NATURE NOTES

Coyotes probably roam these woods, but seeing one is difficult because they are stealthy, nocturnal animals. They moved into the state in the 1950s and their population has been slowly expanding. Coyotes can now be found throughout the state of Massachusetts and their numbers continue to grow because their predator, the wolf, has been exterminated. Coyotes are very adaptable and have found a ready food source of mice, carrion, birds, rabbits, domestic animals (such as ducks and geese and even cats), and berries.

Rhododendrons grow up to 30 feet and sometimes the branches from several different trees interlace them and form an impenetrable jungle. Their evergreen leaves are large and leathery, sometimes reaching a length of 10 inches. Flowers are often white or pink and grow in showy clusters. The bark is reddish brown, and the new twigs are green. While rhododendron flourishes in southern New England it is very rare in the northern states.

The Bigelow Boulder lies adjacent to a woodland path at Whitney and Thayer.

The native American holly found here could be the northernmost stand in the U.S. The hollies are easiest to see in the forest during the winter, because their prickly evergreen leaves are still on the tree. The distinctive red fruits are also on the tree in the winter, if not first consumed by wildlife such as songbirds, wild turkey, and bobwhite.

MORE INFORMATION

Open year-round, dawn to dusk; no fee, but donations accepted; no rest rooms; dogs allowed on leash. For more information, call 781-740-7233, visit www.thetrustees.org, or email seregion@ttor.org.

TRIP 36
NORTH HILL MARSH WILDLIFE SANCTUARY

LOCATION: Duxbury
RATING: Moderate
DISTANCE: 3.5 miles
ESTIMATED TIME: 1.5 hours
OTHER ACTIVITIES: Birding
WINTER ACTIVITIES: Trails are well maintained for snowshoeing

Take a hefty walk around a large freshwater pond that is teeming with birds and waterfowl.

The pond at North Hill Marsh attracts all sorts of birds and waterfowl, such as ring-necked and black ducks, mute swans, buffleheads, hooded mergansers, herons, kingfishers, and egrets. Wood ducks find this a good place to nest because of the dead timber standing in the pond and the many nesting boxes that have been erected. Recently, there have been a number of sightings of osprey near the pond, and a nesting platform has been erected to induce the osprey to nest here.

DIRECTIONS

From Route 3A in Duxbury, take Mayflower Street 1.3 miles. The parking lot will be on your right.

From Route 3 south, take Exit 11 (Congress Street) and head toward Duxbury. About 100 feet from the exit, turn at the first right onto Lincoln Street. Follow Lincoln Street about 0.8 mile and bear left onto Mayflower Street. Follow Mayflower Street 0.3 mile and bear left where the road forks to stay on Mayflower. The parking lot is about 0.5 mile down Mayflower Street, on the left.

TRAIL DESCRIPTION

If you bring young children, limit your walk to the Yellow Loop Trail, which is about 1 mile in length and clearly marked by yellow markings on trees. The trail starts at the parking lot and leads to the south shore of the pond before turning back to Mayflower Street, just a short distance from where you parked your car.

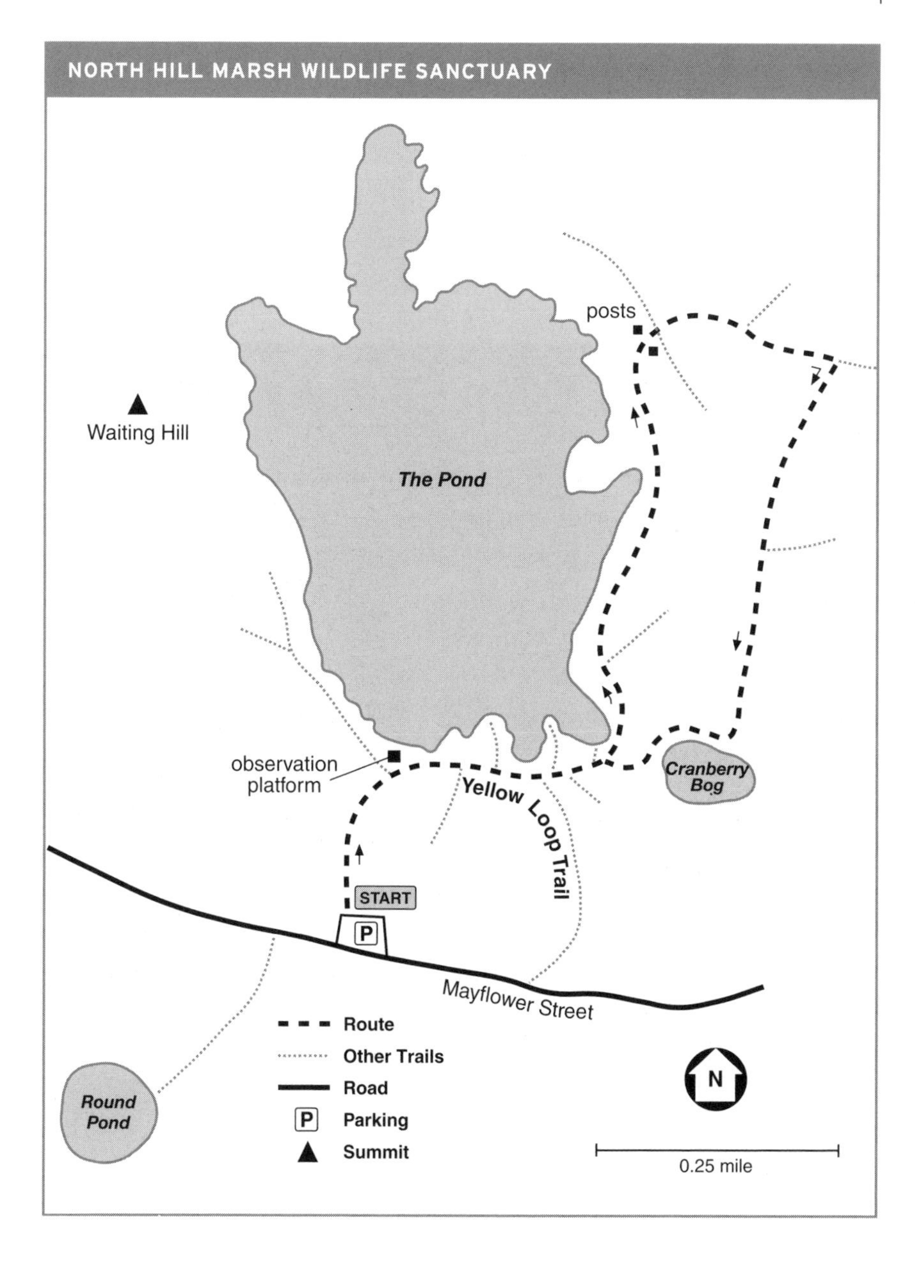

There are several miles of secluded (and confusing) nature trails, split between the east and west sides of the pond. Trails on the west side will take you to a small hill called Waiting Hill, which supposedly got its name when the wives of fishermen and merchants would look off the hill and scan the ocean for returning ships. (Today the woods obstruct the views.)

Our walk is on the east side of the pond, where we follow the trails that make a wide loop of the area. The first part of the outing hugs the pond's shoreline, and the return portion passes through a pine-oak forest and then goes on to a scenic cranberry bog.

Start your walk from the signboard at the parking lot and follow the Yellow Loop Trail down to the pond. An observation platform has been erected near the water; from there follow the yellow markings on the hilly trail. You

will pass a trail to the right marked by red discs, followed by a trail to the left that ends at the pond's edge. A short way farther down, bear left at the next intersection, off the Yellow Loop Trail, and follow the path that stays near the water's edge. Stay straight on this path, passing a trail on the left that ends at the pond, a trail on the right, then another on the left. Take the next trail on the left that goes downhill through a low-lying area (just 0.125 mile west of the open cranberry bog). This path parallels the eastern side of the pond. Stay on it, ignoring a couple of trails to the right.

After you have walked about 45 minutes from the parking area (about 1.75 miles), the trail passes between two posts. A few feet later, the woods open up a bit at the site of an old sand pit, which is now covered with pine seedlings. At the back side of this small opening is a four-way intersection. Go straight through the intersection, and continue to bear right wherever the trail splits, bringing you back toward the south end of the pond, near the parking lot. About 0.75 mile into your return, you will arrive at the cranberry bog, where the sun is quite welcome after so much time in the shaded woods.

The main pond lies just over the crest of the hill (on the right, as you face the cranberry bog where you first arrived). Follow the path along to the right, and you will soon be back on the trail you started on, where you can retrace your steps back to the parking area.

Total walking time is about an hour and thirty-five minutes, but allow plenty of time because it's easy to get lost on the unmarked trails on your first visit.

NATURE NOTES

The deadwood standing in the pond offers nesting birds a bit of protection from raccoons. (The man-made boxes with the small holes are for tree swallows and the boxes with larger holes are for wood ducks.) The timber is also excellent cover for such warm-water fish species as pickerel and largemouth bass.

The woods here are home to great horned owls. They do their hunting at night, but sometimes people spot them perched on a limb of a tall white pine. If you are lucky enough to see one, it's a sight you won't forget. They swoop into their nests bringing mice, squirrels, rabbits, and skunks to their young.

MORE INFORMATION

Open daily, dawn to dusk; fee for non-members, dogs prohibited. For more information, call Mass Audubon at 781-837-9400 or visit www.massaudubon.org.

A great blue heron feeding. Photo by Jerry and Marcy Monkman.

TRIP 37
CAMP TITICUT RESERVATION

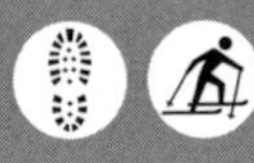

LOCATION: Bridgewater
RATING: Easy
DISTANCE: 1.5 miles
ESTIMATED TIME: 1 hour
OTHER ACTIVITIES: Paddling
WINTER ACTIVITIES: Trails are flat and well-maintained, excellent for cross-country skiing

Camp Titicut Reservation is a small but scenic conservation area situated along the banks of the Taunton River.

The name Titicut is derived from the Wampanoag Indian name for the Taunton River, "Seip-teih-tuk-qut," which means "the long waterway used by all." A Wampanoag village was once situated next to the river for access to the waterway and because the river was low enough to wade across at one point. Later, in the early 1800s, the Titicut area was the site of shipbuilding activities, and a number of schooners were built here and floated down the river during the high water of springtime.

DIRECTIONS

From I-495 exit onto Route 28 North. Go 2.7 miles to Plymouth Street on the left. Follow Plymouth Street 1.7 miles to where it turns into Green Street and then follow Green Street 0.3 mile to Beech Street on the left. Follow Beech Street for 0.2 mile and park at entrance gate on the left.

From Route 24 exit onto Route 44 and go 2.8 miles east to Richmond Street. Turn left onto Richmond Street and follow 2.4 miles to its end. Turn left onto Green Street and proceed 0.1 mile, then turn left onto Beech Street. Follow Beech Street for 0.2 mile and park at entrance gate on the left.

TRAIL DESCRIPTION

Begin your walk by following the dirt road by the gate and entrance sign. White pines line the road before it leads you to an open field. Notice the opportunistic trees such as pine, cedar, and poplar that are beginning to reclaim the field. They are all sun-loving species and fairly quick growers that establish themselves in disturbed areas that receive sunlight. Look for rabbit, deer, and

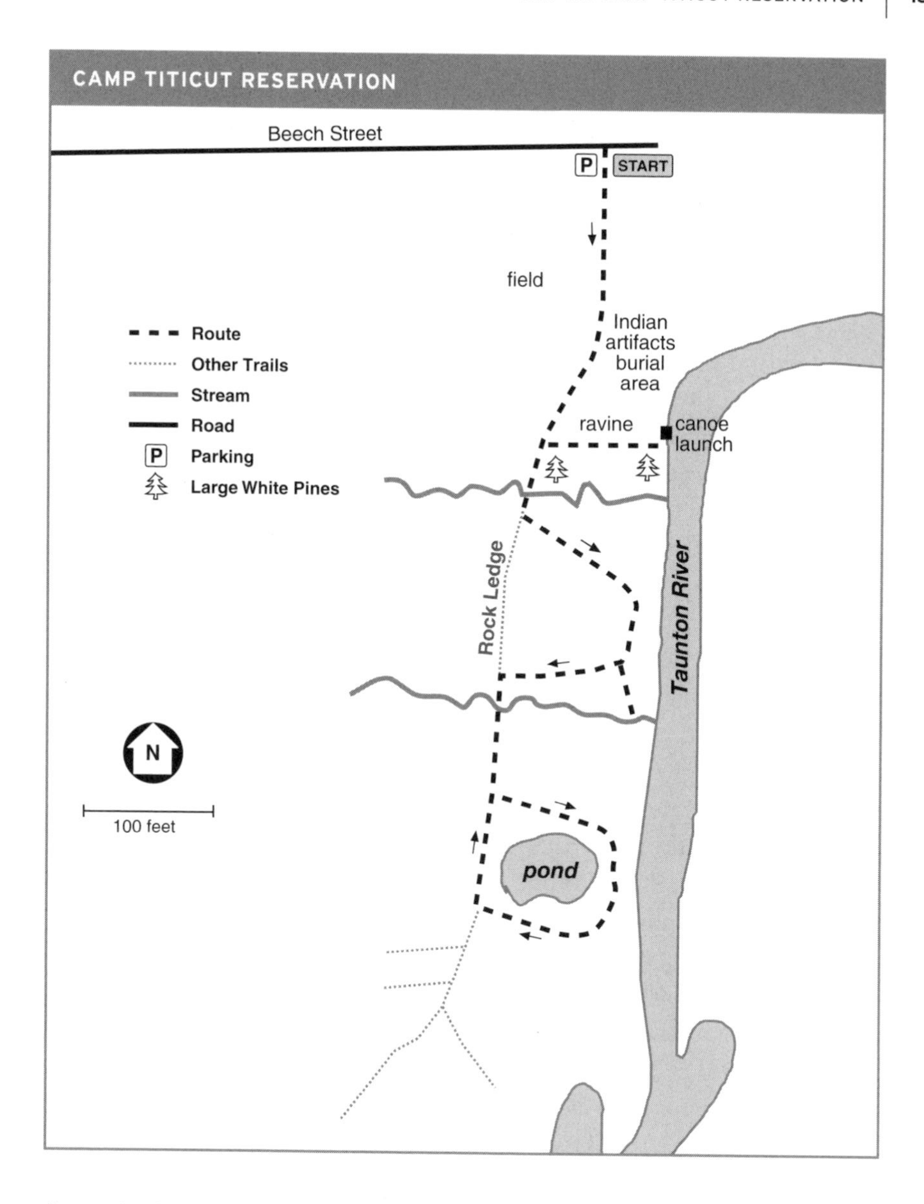

fox in the field, and scan the treeline for hawks and owls.

Just beyond the field, only a five-minute walk from your car, you will see a ravine and trail on your left that leads to the river. There are two enormous white pines growing at the right side of the ravine. Large pines like these attracted the attention of shipbuilders, who used the timber for ship masts. The size of these pines is somewhat unusual as most older growth trees have either been logged or cleared by farmers. Be sure to search the base of the tree for pellets from owls that perch in pines such as these.

Take a moment to watch the slow brown waters of the Taunton River flow by. Great blue heron, wood ducks, green-backed herons, and night herons are sometimes seen along the shoreline, as are a variety of other ducks. The mud along the river may hold the tracks of mink, raccoon, and otter that prowl the shoreline for food. Raccoons are primarily nocturnal creatures so the best time to see one is in the late afternoon or evening when they begin to prowl about. They are quite at home on the Taunton River, searching for crayfish, frogs, snakes, turtle and birds eggs, grubs, and crickets. Baby raccoons are born in the spring and generally stay with the mother that first year. Many birdwatchers have mixed emotions about raccoons; while they are fascinating creatures and they play an important roll in the natural world, they can wreak havoc on birds by stealing eggs.

This section of the Taunton River has a good buffer of open space along its banks and the entire upper portion of the river offers a peaceful float. You can launch canoes from this site, but you will have to drag them the short distance from the entrance gate to the shore. The river has a rich history. In the eighteenth century one of the major sea ports in the world was located in the town of Taunton, even though it is about fifteen miles from the ocean. Because the river is tidal all the way to Taunton, large ships could come up the river when it rose with the high tide. In fact if you canoe down the river today, you can see the tidal effect at Taunton: during high tide the water is forced back upstream, and the river actually goes "backward" at a slow pace.

On the ridge to the left of the ravine is a spot where Indian artifacts and a burial area was found. Clay pottery, arrow heads, and human remains were found here, ranging in age from several thousand to several hundred years old. The area appealed to Native Americans because the river served as both a transportation route and a source of food, where herring could be gathered and ducks, muskrat, and other birds and animals hunted. The slopes along the river were high enough to allow protection from spring flooding and provide shelter from cold northwest winds, while streams in the area provided drinking water. Southeastern New England once had among the highest concentration of Native Americans found anywhere and Taunton was the land of the Wampanoag. Massasoit, who helped the Pilgrims survive their first winter, was the sachem of the tribe and his son, Metacom (Philip), later fought to regain the tribal land from the English. Much of the action during King Philip's War took place on the banks of the Taunton River.

After examining the river and shoreline, walk back up the ravine and continue south on the main trail. You will pass over a tiny stream that trickles into the river. Beech trees line the streambed, and in winter the beige paper-thin leaves of the trees cling stubbornly to branches, creating a handsome contrast to the snow. Beech trees have smooth gray trunks, and have been likened to the legs of an elephant. The beech nut is consumed by many birds and animals, and up north it is a favorite mast crop of the black bear. Just beyond the stream the trail splits. Bear left. You will pass a cellar hole largely hidden by vegetation on your right.

This is a beautiful trail, especially the section that hugs the ridge alongside the river. Take a moment to admire a couple of mountain laurel bushes growing beneath the beech trees. They are an understory plant, preferring shade from the sun, and can be identified by shiny green leaves that stay on the plant all winter.

Follow the trail west, paralleling the stream, to where you will intersect with the main trail. Turn left here, cross over the stream, and then a couple minutes farther down the trail turn left again. You will soon see a small pond on your right. The trail curls around the pond and then reconnects with the main trail. By turning right on the main trail you can reach your car in about twenty minutes. The total walk in an easy one-hour stroll, which most children should be able to handle without difficulty.

NATURE NOTES

Deer are quite populous in Eastern Massachusetts because many towns have hunting restrictions and natural predators such as the wolf and mountain lion have been eliminated. Whenever you explore areas where deer live be sure to take precaution against deer ticks, which carry Lyme disease. Never wear short pants in grassy areas or fields, and pull your socks up over the bottom of your trousers. When you get home, give yourself a "tick check" and be sure to see your doctor if you develop a rash that is shaped like a bull's eye, one of the early warning signs.

MORE INFORMATION

Open year-round, sunrise to sunset; no fee; no rest rooms; dogs allowed on leash. For more information about Camp Titicut Reservation, visit the Natural Resources Trust of Bridgewater at www.nrtb.org or call 508-697-7317.

TRIP 38
MOOSE HILL WILDLIFE SANCTUARY

LOCATION: Sharon
RATING: Moderate
DISTANCE: Bluff Head, 2.5 miles; Eastern section, 1.75 miles
ESTIMATED TIME: Bluff Head, 1.5–2 hours; Eastern section, 1 hour
OTHER ACTIVITIES: Birding
PUBLIC TRANSPORTATION: Take the Commuter Rail to the Sharon Station

Moose Hill Wildlife Sanctuary covers 1,435 acres of quiet trails and secluded hilltops.

Moose Hill Wildlife Sanctuary in Sharon has one of the best views in the region. The stunted cedar trees and the sheer rock walls give the illusion that this is a hilltop in Maine, New Hampshire, or Vermont. And for a view this good, the trail to the top is surprisingly gentle.

The sanctuary has varied topography, much of which was once farmland, now reverted back to forest. More than 400 species of wildflowers grow here, and due to the high elevations found in the sanctuary there are yellow and white birches to add to the feeling of being in the North Country. There are no moose here, but the origin of the sanctuary's name is from the moose that were said to inhabit the area in the late 1700s and early 1800s.

DIRECTIONS

Take I-95 south to Exit 10, and take a left off the ramp. At the intersection, take a right onto Route 27 north toward Walpole. Follow Route 27 for 0.5 mile. Take a left onto Moose Hill Street and travel 1.5 miles uphill. Parking is on the left.

Take I-95 north to Exit 8, and take a right off the exit ramp onto Main Street. Travel approximately 1 mile. Turn left onto Moose Hill Street and drive 1.5 miles; parking is on the right.

TRAIL DESCRIPTION

Bluff Head. To begin your walk up to Bluff Head, cross Moose Hill Street from the parking area and look for the stone pillars that mark the entrance to the Billings/Boardwalk Loop Trail (the stone pillars are exactly opposite the intersection of Moose Hill Street and Moose Hill Parkway). The trail follows

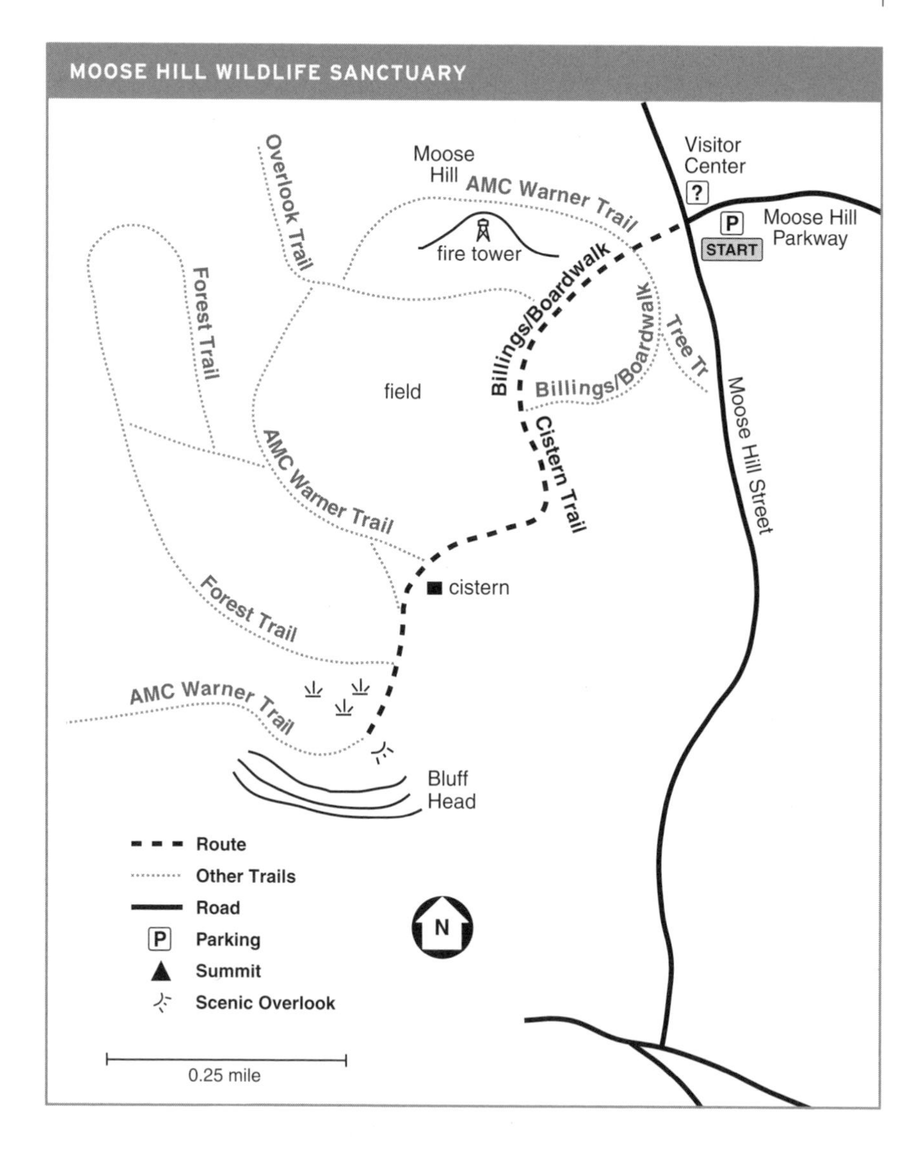

a wide grassy road that's easy on the legs. Mobility-impaired people can enjoy the first half mile of this outing before the trail narrows and begins its ascent of the bluff. Stone walls and large sugar maples line the trail, making it a visual treat. Stay on the Billings/Boardwalk Loop Trail as it curves to the left. Soon you will pass the old Billings barn on the right and two enormous maples on the left. A short way down the Billings/Boardwalk Loop Trail is a circular opening in the woods where an assortment of trees are labeled, providing the perfect classroom for a young naturalist interested in identifying white pine, Colorado blue spruce, white birch, hickory, red oak, red pine, sassafras, and northern white cedar. After studying the trees, continue down the trail (look over your shoulder to see the blue spruce framed against the sky). Soon you enter another open area of low-lying plants and bushes; there are unusual species of wildflowers present at Moose Hill as well as 27 species of ferns. Spring is the time to see the best show of colors.

The trail soon intersects with another; go right on Cistern Trail, marked with a C on a post. Here the hiking gets harder: Exposed roots on this narrow trail seem to grab at your boots. A maple, oak, and pine forest surrounds the trail. On the left you will pass a huge round cistern dug into the earth and lined with stones. The trail now becomes part of the AMC Warner Trail, which is a 34-mile trail going from Canton, Massachusetts, to Diamond Hill in Cumberland, Rhode Island. Just beyond the cistern is an impressive stand of beech trees on the left and a swampy area on the right.

Here is where the trail starts its gradual climb to the bluff. But the designers of the trail knew what they were doing when they picked this route to the summit: It never gets steep and is a relatively easy walk to the top. Just as you begin your final steps to the summit you see the gnarled and wind-swept branches of the eastern red cedars that dot the hilltop. These trees can be distinguished from the white cedars by their needlelike leaves with bluish green berries. These hard fruits are eaten by birds.

The granite ledge at Bluff Head offers sweeping views to the south and west. Gillette Stadium, home of the New England Patriots, can be seen just a few miles off. This is one of the nicest hilltops in eastern Massachusetts; it's the perfect place to sit, gaze off in the distance, and let your mind wander. No traffic sounds can be heard, only the breeze as it whispers through the trees. There are a number of outcrops along this hilltop ridge offering vista changes.

When you are ready to head home, retrace your steps back to the parking lot. More-ambitious hikers can try the Forest Trail, which makes a long loop at the northern end of the property (see map).

Eastern Section. On another trip, you may want to try the less-traveled eastern end of the property. Coyote have been seen here, and I think it's only a matter of time before more are spotted as this is a secluded area of the sanctuary. A trail leaves the parking lot and follows Moose Hill Street southward a few feet and turns left (eastward) into the forest, first descending through an oak-pine woodland. (The trail is marked by an A on the map and is actually part of the Warner Trail.) After about a ten-minute walk the path follows a bubbling brook. Swamp maples soon mix in with the other trees as the trail veers to the southeast.

Some people prefer to go on to Hobbs Hill at the junction of the Warner,

A male green frog peeps out from among the lily pads. Photo by John Hayes.

Hobbs Hill, and Kettle Trails (see map), but I usually make a shorter outing to see the flowering shrubs along the Kettle Trail. The Kettle Trail leads you back toward the parking lot. Turn right off the Warner Trail at the junction.

The Kettle Trail got its name for the many kettle hole depressions formed by huge blocks of ice left by the glaciers roughly 12,000 years ago. It is rugged in spots, hugging the ridges that are called eskers. The eskers formed when streams, flowing beneath the glacial ice sheets, deposited sediments along the stream bed that now make up the thin ridgeline.

The trail continues back toward the parking lot, passing through a stand of hemlocks and then by a lush green field on the left.

NATURE NOTES

Wildflowers abound here—pink lady's slipper, jack-in-the-pulpits, and maple leaf viburnum, to name just a few. But the highlight of this trip is the beautiful basin filled with mountain laurel and rhododendrons. If you happen to hike through here in early summer, you just might hit the peak of the bloom.

Seeing plants with dazzling displays of color in a wild, natural setting is much more impressive to me than the same plants growing around the foundation of a home.

Look for red and gray squirrels scrambling on their branches. Other animals in the sanctuary include skunk, opossum, fox, raccoon, and deer. All are nocturnal, so your best bet at catching a glimpse of them is at dawn or dusk. The bird life is varied and easier to see. Some of the birds present are warblers, nuthatches, scarlet tanagers, northern orioles, bluebirds, woodpeckers, and a wide assortment of hawks, such as kestrels, red-tailed hawks, and broad-winged hawks. (While sitting atop 600-foot Bluff Head during the autumn, you might be able to see a hawk riding a thermal on its migration.)

MORE INFORMATION

Open Tuesday through Sunday 8 A.M. to 6 P.M. (closed Mondays); fee for nonmembers of the Massachusetts Audubon Society. Sanctuary programs range from children's programs to birdathons and guided field trips. For more information, call 781-784-5691 or visit www.massaudubon.org.

TRIP 39
F. GILBERT HILLS STATE FOREST: BLUE TRIANGLE LOOP

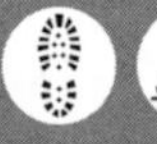

LOCATION: Wrentham/Foxboro
RATING: Easy
DISTANCE: 1.5 miles
ESTIMATED TIME: 45 minutes
OTHER ACTIVITIES: Biking, birding
WINTER ACTIVITIES: Trails are flat and well-maintained, excellent for cross-country skiing

A number of rocky ridges, swamps, and secluded ponds provide the hiker with diverse scenery.

The sprawling F. Gilbert Hills State Forest has a wide assortment of trees such as red pine, spruce, tupelo, and dogwood, as well as abundant wildlife including deer, pheasant, grouse, and fox. The Civilian Conservation Corps was active here during the 1930s, hacking out many of the roads, planting red pines,

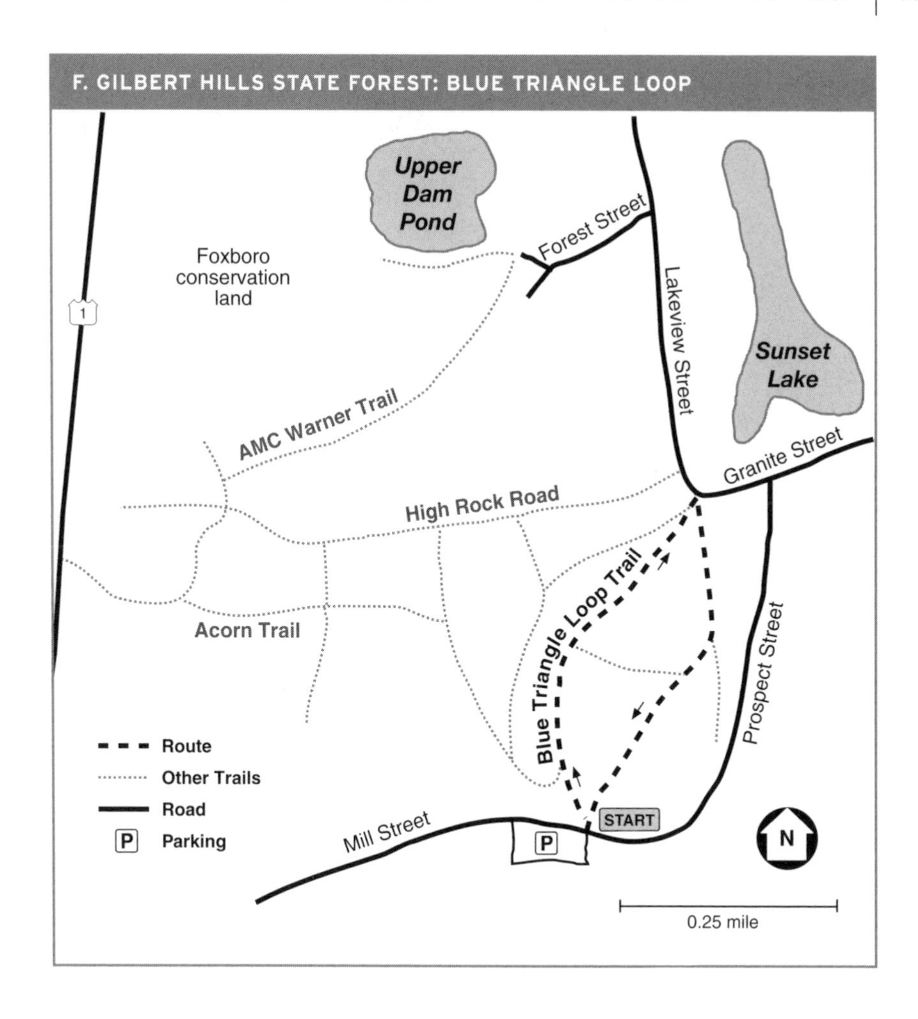

and digging water holes to provide a ready source of water in case of forest fire. Seventeen of these stone-lined water holes can still be seen, with most of them situated along High Rock Road.

There are miles of trails to explore, including a portion of the 34-mile AMC Warner Trail, which runs from Canton, Massachusetts, to Cumberland, Rhode Island. The trail is dedicated to Charles Henry Warner, who with fellow hiker John Hudson conceived the idea of a woodland trail that linked the Boston area to Rhode Island. At age 83, Mr. Warner actually walked 25 miles of the trail!

DIRECTIONS

From I-95 take Exit 7 and follow Route 140 north about 1.7 miles to Foxboro Center. At Foxboro Center go almost all the way around the rotary and take South Street for a mile and a half, then turn right onto Mill Street. Go 0.5 mile

A turtle crosses the Blue Triangle Loop Trail.

on Mill Street to the entrance. Parking is across the street from the Forest Fire Station and the forest administration building.

TRAIL DESCRIPTION

Our outing follows the Blue Triangle Loop Trail, which is well marked with blue triangular signs. It begins by heading from the parking lot through an area of white pines and oaks, where a scattering of spruce and large boulders add contrast to the forest. The trail bears right where it narrows, and eventually passes by a crumbling stone wall, with its various shades of green moss mottled on the gray stone beneath. Just past the intersection with the stone wall is a muddy spot where two logs, cut lengthwise, act as a bridge to help keep your feet dry.

The trail soon intersects with Granite Street, where you walk right about 15 feet before the blue triangles direct you back into the woods to the right. A bit of the Wolf Meadow Swamp can be seen on the right as the trail heads through a thick stand of hemlock. At the intersection of Pine Hill Trail, stay to the right, and then follow the blue markers that soon lead you to the left along a smaller, hilly trail that winds through pine trees. This trail brings you back to the parking lot after about a ten-minute walk. Many of the other, longer trails are popular with mountain bikers and also provide a challenge for cross-country skiers due to the many hills.

NATURE NOTES

Be on the lookout for ruffed grouse, which often stay perfectly still until you approach too closely, and then explode into the air in rapid flight. You might also see a pheasant. Ring-necked pheasants were first introduced in the U.S. from Asia in 1881. They have a distinctive white ring around their necks, and their feathers have hues of green, purple, and red. There are few purebred pheasants left as the ring-necked and the English pheasant have been bred together extensively.

In the fall and winter, pheasants congregate together, but in the spring the males go off to establish their harems, crowing regularly to attract the hens. The hens lay an average of twelve to thirteen eggs, and the male goes on its way, leaving all the parenting to the female.

Owls also make their home at F. Gilbert Hills, probably preferring to roost in the thick cover of Wolf Meadow Swamp. The barred owl is a nocturnal predator with an incredible sense of hearing, able to detect the scurrying of mice as they forage along the forest floor. With a silent approach the owl can swoop through the woods, snatch a mouse, and then return to its perch as quietly as it approached.

MORE INFORMATION

For more information, visit the Massachusetts Department of Conservation and Recreation site for this property at www.mass.gov/dcr.

TRIP 40
WHEATON FARM CONSERVATION AREA

LOCATION: Easton
RATING: Easy
DISTANCE: 2.5 miles
ESTIMATED TIME: 1.5 hours
OTHER ACTIVITIES: Birding, fishing, paddling
WINTER ACTIVITIES: Trails are flat and well-maintained, excellent for cross-country skiing

A relatively easy ramble through level terrain that features a white pine forest, shallow ponds, and open fields.

Wheaton Farm is the largest conservation area in Easton and is a great place for walking with children or cross-country skiing in the winter. Some of the property is still actively farmed, but the majority of acres serves to protect the source of Easton's public water supply.

DIRECTIONS

From I-495 take Exit 9 (Bay Road) and go north toward Easton. Watch your odometer carefully and travel 3.2 miles. On the right side of Bay Street look for the Wheaton Farm sign by a brown barn, and on the left side of Bay Street look for a beautiful old Federal-style house set behind evergreens. The entrance road to Wheaton Farm will be just after this house on the left. Turn into the road and follow to the parking area.

(From the intersection of Route 106 and Bay Street in Easton, take Bay Street to the south and follow 1.2 miles to the entrance road on your right.)

TRAIL DESCRIPTION

To begin your walk from the parking area, take the trail to your left as you face the woods. (The trail is alongside a wooden fence and cuts behind the pumping station.) There is a gentle descent as you walk a few feet into the woods, then the trail crosses an earthen dike, separated by two shallow ponds. The dike is a good spot to look for wood ducks, muskrat, and other wildlife that makes its home on fresh water.

When you cross the dike, turn left where a trail intersects the one you are on. You will enter a forest almost totally comprised of white pines, some of them quite large. The pines block out most of the sun. In summer the pine needles make for a soft cushion on the trail, and there's nothing quite like the scent of green pine needles.

After a half mile you'll intersect another trail on your left. Turn left here, following the trail past a small concrete building housing a well. Continue along the edge of the water. On your left will be a large dead tree. Hawks often use such trees as perches because they offer views, unobstructed by foliage, of the forest floor. Woodpeckers peck at the rotting wood for insects, and animals such as raccoons will use the hollow areas of such trees for shelter.

The trail loops around to the right, heading back the way you came. It takes about three-quarters of a mile to return to the trail intersection by the dike. Extend your walk by walking straight through the intersection heading north. There will be a small field on the right, so be sure to approach quietly in case there is a deer feeding. Often deer will wait by the edge of open space until dusk falls.

Along the trail a few pitch pines mix in with the white pines that dominate the woods of Wheaton Farm. Notice how the pitch pine's bark is more furrowed than the white pine. Other differences between the two are that the pitch pine needles are more rigid, its cones more rounded, and the overall size of the tree is smaller than the white pine. By walking about five minutes down

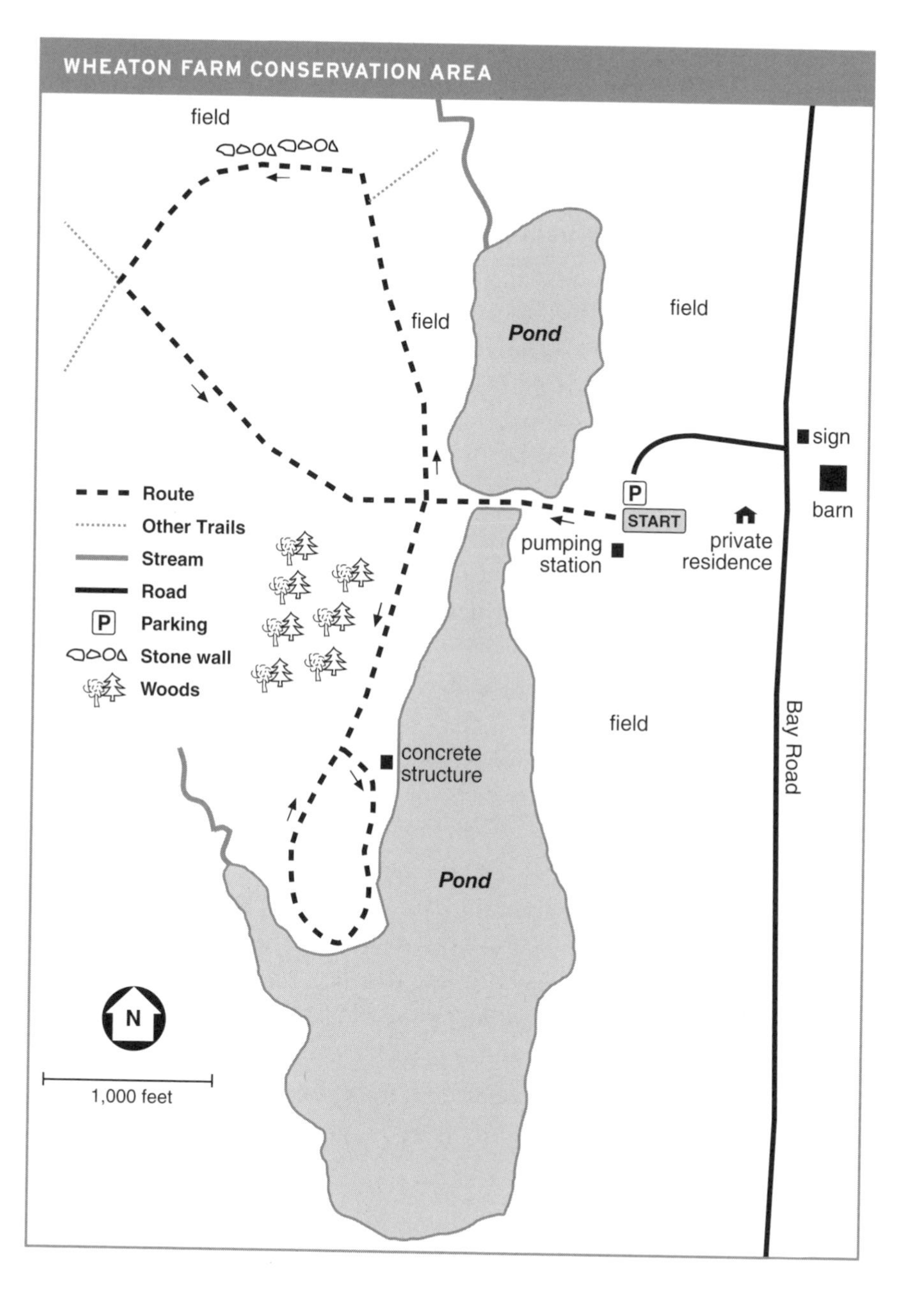

the trail you will reach another field, this one a bit larger than the last. For a look at the stream that feeds the pond, you can backtrack about 20 feet and there will be a small path on the east side that cuts into the woods and leads to a red-maple swamp. Look for the tracks of raccoon, mink, muskrat, and otter in the mud along the streambed.

Continue your walk from the larger field by turning left and following the trail that runs parallel to the stone wall. Chipmunks like to burrow beneath the rocks, and often you will see them running along top of the wall then disappear into one of their holes. You may want to also scan the trees for signs of opossum, which are often seen here.

After about a quarter mile this trail will bring you to a four-way intersection where you should turn left. Keep walking back to the main intersection by the pond near the beginning of your walk. (Local residents say the ponds have good bass fishing.) Cross the dike to return to the parking area.

Before leaving, be sure to take a brief walk along the edge of the fields. This is prime habitat for bluebirds and kestrels.

NATURE NOTES

This is a great place to see great blue herons. The shallow waters provide good hunting grounds for the birds, which stalk the pond for fish and frogs to snatch with their long bills. Once the prey is caught the heron tips its head and swallows the prey whole. With a wingspan of 44 inches, black-crowned night herons are smaller than great blue herons. The black-crowned night heron has a short wing with gray wings and white underparts, and as the name implies it is mostly nocturnal, roosting in trees in the days. Populations have been gradually dropping over the last 40 years due to the effects of pesticides and loss of habitat. Yellow-crowned night herons also get as far north as Massachusetts, and the adults are slate gray with black head and white cheeks. The yellow-crowned night heron is not seen as often at the black-crowned, and most sightings are in the eastern part of the state and occur in late summer.

One unwelcome visitor seen on the pond is the mute swan, an exotic brought to the U.S. from Europe that now breeds in the wild. Mute swans are quite large, and almost pure white with a graceful S-curved neck. Despite their graceful appearance, they are very aggressive birds and extremely territorial, driving out native birds like the wood duck from preferred nesting areas. They also have large appetites, ripping up vegetation from the bottom of ponds.

MORE INFORMATION

Open year-round, dawn to dusk; no fee; no rest rooms; dogs allowed on leash.

TRIP 41
BORDERLAND STATE PARK

LOCATION: North Easton
RATING: Moderate
DISTANCE: 3.5 miles
ESTIMATED TIME: 1.75 hours
OTHER ACTIVITIES: Birding, fishing, paddling
WINTER ACTIVITIES: Trails are flat and well-maintained, excellent for cross-country skiing

Six ponds and hilly, rocky terrain make this park worth a visit.

Hiking alongside water always makes an outing special, and Borderland State Park has no fewer than six ponds to explore. Add to that the combination of flat hayfields or the option to test your legs on hilly, rocky terrain, and Borderland has something for everyone.

DIRECTIONS

From I-95 take Exit 8 and follow South Main Street 3.5 miles to Sharon Center. Turn right on Billings Street at the traffic signal, then immediately right on Pond Street. Head south on Pond Street for 0.9 mile to a small rotary and continue on Massapoag Avenue. Drive 3.7 miles on Massapoag Avenue and the park entrance will be on the left.

TRAIL DESCRIPTION

It is possible to make either a 3-mile loop via the Leach Pond Loop or a 3.5-mile walk by continuing to make a circle around Upper Leach Pond. From the parking lot off Massapoag Avenue, follow the gravel path through the fields (the mansion will be off to your right). At the T-intersection in the trail, there is an excellent map posted. Go left here to start your walk on the north side of the ponds. (Follow the sign that says Leach Pond.) The trail leads down to the water's edge where a stone building called the Lodge is located. The pond-side trails are wide, flat, and well-maintained, excellent for cross-country skiing. This is also a good spot for viewing waterfowl.

Follow the trail to the left along Leach Pond, passing by the entrance to the West Side Trail (entering left). At various intervals are benches facing the water, offering scenic views of the islands near the pond's center. Near the junction of the Northwest Trail, you will see fields to the right where deer are said to frequent. Farther up the trail on the left is a little stone cave that was probably a farmer's root cellar.

Separating Leach Pond from Upper Leach Pond is Long Dam, built by the Ames family to create Leach Pond. If you wish to limit your walk to 3 miles, turn right here, cross the stream on the wooden footbridge and follow this path until its end, and then go right to reach the parking lot.

For the 3.5-mile loop, continue following the pond-side trail to the northeast. There is an interesting unnamed side trail you might want to explore that runs off to the left through a field. It leads to a dike that separates two secluded ponds—a good place to spot wading birds such as the great blue heron. The main trail takes you around Upper Leach Pond and eventually to the old Tisdale cellar hole, near Mountain Street, where there is a beautiful view of Upper Leach Pond. The trail intersects with Mountain Street, and you must follow

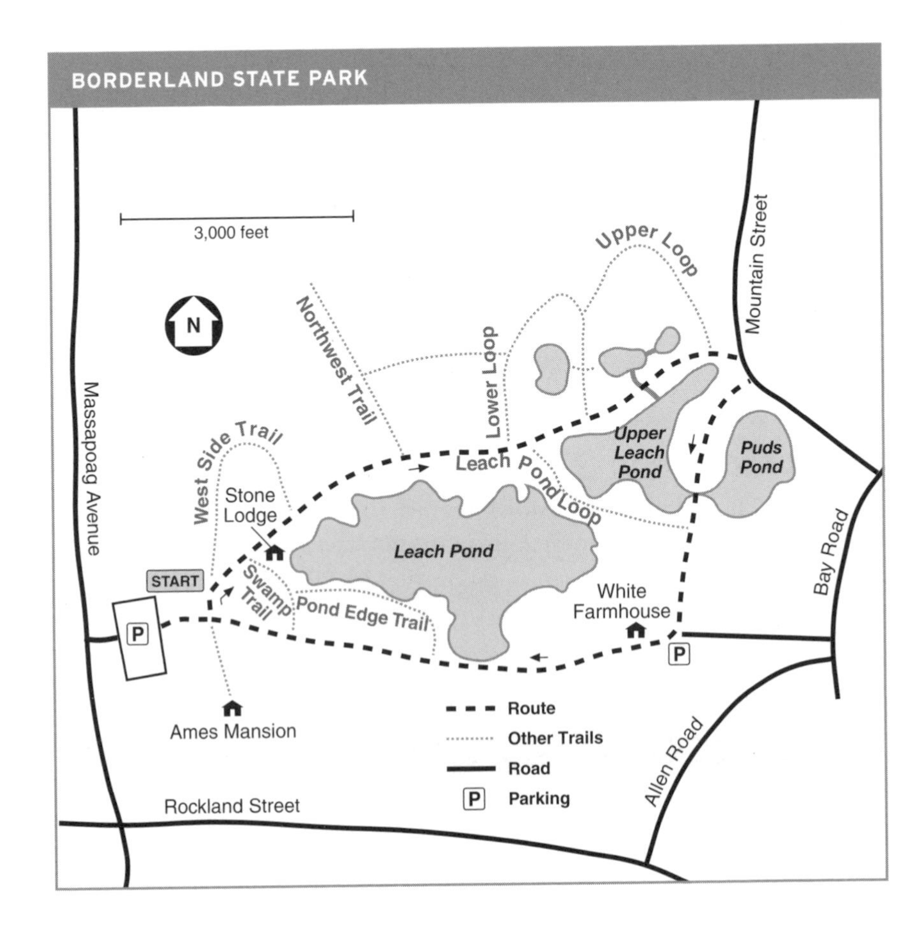

this a few feet to the right before the path leads back into the woods at a gate on the right. This pathway soon takes you to a bridge that spans the outflow stream from Puds Pond.

Follow this trail all the way to the white farmhouse and bear right. The fields and wooden fence here are especially scenic, and I've taken some great photos facing back toward the farmhouse. The wide, level trail next passes by a large cove of Leach Pond (this is where I launched my canoe, parking in the small lot nearby). There are a few rare Atlantic white cedars growing adjacent to the cove, and Pond Edge Trail will be on your right. You can either take Pond Edge Trail, Swamp Trail, or the main trail back toward the parking lot and the Ames mansion.

Borderland can be a popular place, but with 1,570 acres it's easy to find the quiet and solitude that make hiking special.

NATURE NOTES

Borderland was opened as a state park in 1971. Prior to that, it served as the country estate of the Ames family, who named it Borderland because it is on the border of Sharon and Easton. The family constructed the stone mansion in 1910. It is open to visitors for regularly scheduled guided tours in the spring, summer, and fall.

Canada geese in flight. Photo by Jerry and Marcy Monkman.

Prior to the Ames family ownership, the ponds and streams powered a number of different mills in the eighteenth century and early nineteenth century. There was a sawmill, nail factory, cotton mill, and ironworks located here at various times. The nearby land was cleared for farming, and stone walls can still be seen crisscrossing the woodlands.

Small rocky hills cover the northern acres, while flatter land lies to the south. Some of the ponds are covered with waterlilies and blue-flowered pickerelweed in the summer. All are shallow with significant amounts of vegetation growing. As the vegetation dies and fills the bottom of the ponds, swamp shrubs begin to encroach along the shoreline, and the ponds will slowly turn to marsh.

Red-tailed hawks have adapted fairly well to human presence; they can often be seen along our highways, perched in trees and keeping a sharp eye out for any movement in the grassy strips along the roadways. They are one of the few birds that winter here, and their hardiness was acknowledged by Thoreau when he wrote of "the hawk with warrior-like firmness abiding the blasts of winter."

Opossums have also been seen in the area.

MORE INFORMATION

The park also offers organized hikes and birding. For more information, call 508-238-6566 or visit www.mass.gov/dcr.

TRIP 42
ELLISVILLE HARBOR STATE PARK

LOCATION: Plymouth
RATING: Easy
DISTANCE: 3 miles
ESTIMATED TIME: 1.75 hours
OTHER ACTIVITIES: Birding
WINTER ACTIVITIES: Trails are flat and well-maintained, excellent for cross-country skiing

Walk by an abandoned Christmas tree farm on your way to the rocky coastline.

Ellisville Harbor State Park is one of the lesser-known parks in Massachusetts, but if you love beachcombing and watching seals it will soon become

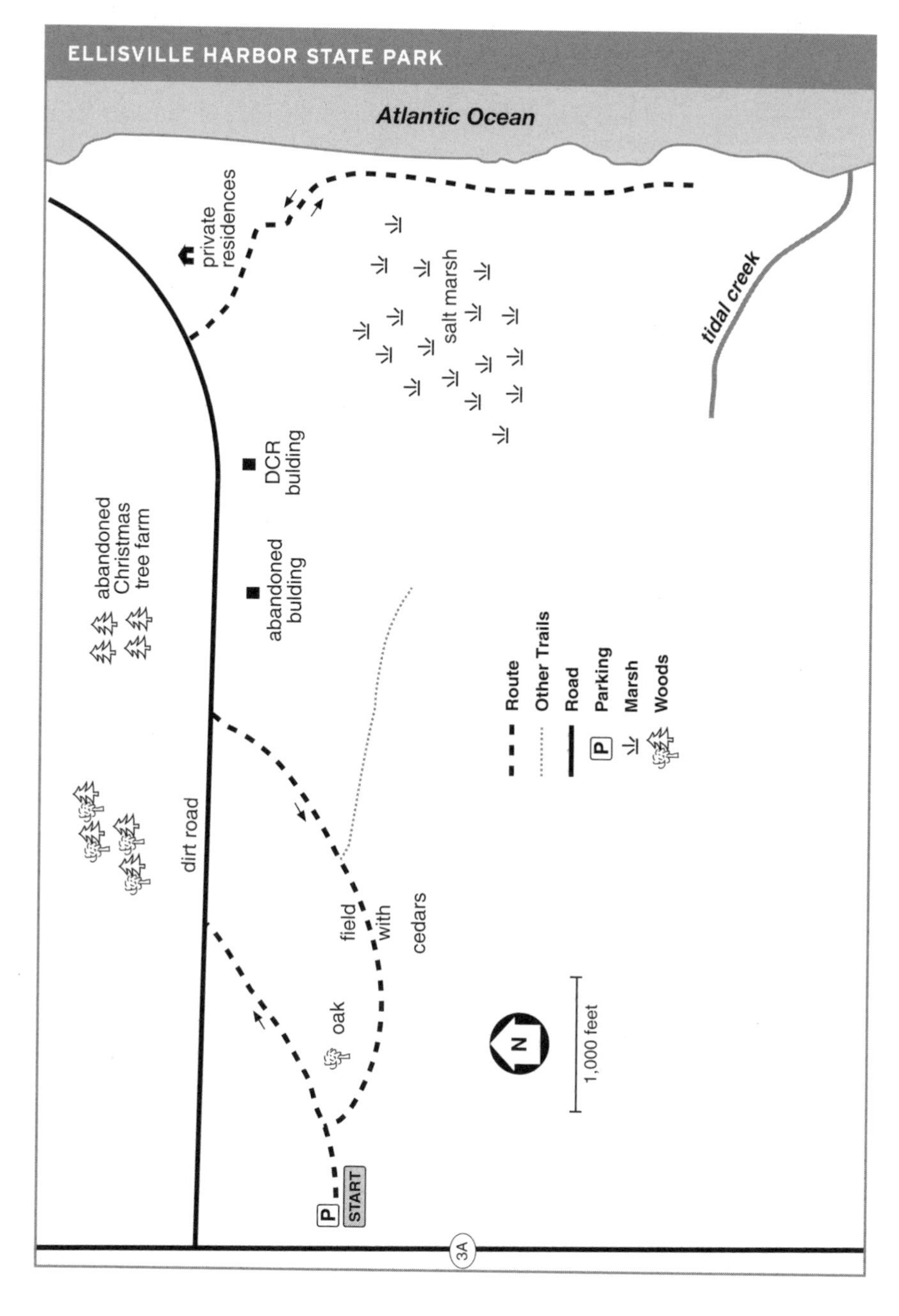

one of your favorites. Located at the southern end of the town of Plymouth, the park spans 101 acres of meadow, woodlands, salt marsh, and shore. This combination of terrain attracts birds of all varieties so be sure to bring your binoculars.

DIRECTIONS

From Route 3 take Exit 2 and follow signs to Route 3A north. Take Route 3A north about 2.2 miles and turn into parking area on the right at the State Park sign.

TRAIL DESCRIPTION

Begin your walk by following the only trail, which leads through a meadow scattered with cedars. About 50 feet from the parking lot the trail splits and you should go left, following blue triangular markers. On your right is a large oak tree with enormous spreading branches that look like groping arms. About 300 feet farther down, the trail intersects with a dirt road. Turn right and walk along the road, which heads directly toward the ocean. On the left will be a patch of woods with scrub pine and oak, and on the right is the meadow where staghorn sumac grows among the cedars. Both the cedars and sumac are opportunistic trees, among the first species to colonize abandoned fields. The field is a good spot to look for kestrels, which hunt in open areas for insects and small rodents. Sometimes they can be seen perched at the top of a cedar tree. Other wildlife that visit the field include white-tailed deer, red fox, and cottontail rabbits.

About a quarter mile down the trail you will see an abandoned Christmas tree farm on the left, where the blue-green Colorado blue spruce mix with the uniformly green balsam fir. You might want to take a few moments and walk the perimeter of this field looking for wildlife, since few people detour from this road. The common crow is one bird you are likely to see here. The other common creature you may see in the field or in the abandoned Christmas tree farm is the groundhog or woodchuck. It makes burrows in the ground and when in danger will make a beeline for its hole.

Continue down the road and within five minutes you will pass an abandoned house and a Department of Conservation and Recreation building on the right. Soon you will come to a sign announcing that the rest of the road leads to private homes (one is directly ahead). At this point a footpath leads away from the road on the right. Follow this. Within a couple minutes the trail descends to the beach and you are rewarded with a deserted shoreline and the blue waters of Cape Cod Bay. To the left the coast has a considerable amount of rocks and to the right the shoreline is more sandy.

With binoculars scan all the exposed rocks jutting from the water for seals. The best viewing for seals is at low tide when more rocks are exposed. You may also see a loon, two cormorants, and buffleheads bobbing beyond the breakers.

Continuing about 400 feet down on your right you will be able to see the salt marsh, where wading birds such as great blue heron can be seen stalking the shallows. In October the autumnal tints of the marsh offer soft hues of gold, rust, yellows, and shades of brown. Be sure to soak up the sounds and smells of the ocean as well as its sights.

Walk the beach for about three-quarters of a mile to arrive at the mouth of the creek that drains and fills the marsh. During low tide the creek carries food such as small fish out to the ocean, and both birds and seals are often stationed just off the creek mouth. To the south the cliffs along the beach are also interesting to view. Scan the water for cormorants diving beneath the surface as they hunt for fish. To return to the parking lot, retrace your steps. You can alter your path by exiting the dirt road on a trail just beyond the abandoned house. This will take you through the field of cedar trees and on the opposite side of the lone oak tree mentioned earlier.

NATURE NOTES

It wasn't too long ago that seals were unwelcome in the Bay State. During the late nineteenth and much of the twentieth century there was a bounty on seals, and fishermen would kill them, fearing that they were eating too many fish. But humans were depleting the fish stocks by overfishing, while seals were feeding primarily on sandlance, a small fish with virtually no commercial

Sand on ocean as far as the eye can see at Ellisville Harbor.

value. The legal killing of seals was finally halted in 1972 with the passage of the Marine Mammal Protection Act.

The seals often seen at Ellisville Harbor are harbor seals, which migrate each winter, heading down from Canada and Maine to Massachusetts. They arrive in October and leave in the early spring. During low tide they sun themselves on the rocks where they are safe from humans on the beach. Known as dog-faced seals because of their pug noses and dog-like looks, they can grow to 5 or 6 feet and weigh as much as 250 pounds. Perhaps one of the best places to see seals in Massachusetts is at Monomoy Island off Chatham. (Both Massachusetts Audubon, 508-349-2615, and the Cape Cod Museum of Natural History, 508-896-3867, offer seal-watching trips.)

In the winter the common loon is sometimes seen here. The loon's underwater feats are legendary, but their flight is equally impressive—they are surprisingly fast for such a large, heavy bird. (The distinctive summertime black-and-white coloring of the loon is replaced in winter by brownish gray feathers.)

MORE INFORMATION

Open year-round, dawn to dusk; no fee; no rest rooms; dogs allowed on leash. For more information, contact Ellisville Harbor State Park, Route 3A, Plymouth, MA, 02362; 508-866-2580; www.mass.gov/dcr.

TRIP 43
FREETOWN/FALL RIVER STATE FOREST

LOCATION: Assonet
RATING: Profile Rock Area, Easy; Rattlesnake Brook Area, Moderate
DISTANCE: Profile Rock Area, 0.5 mile; Rattlesnake Brook Area, 3.5 miles
ESTIMATED TIME: Profile Rock Area, 20 minutes; Rattlesnake Brook Area, 2 hours
OTHER ACTIVITIES: Biking, fishing, horseback riding
WINTER ACTIVITIES: Trails are flat and well maintained, excellent for cross-country skiing

Good vistas, trout fishing in Rattlesnake Brook, and cross-country skiing in the winter and just a few possibilities here.

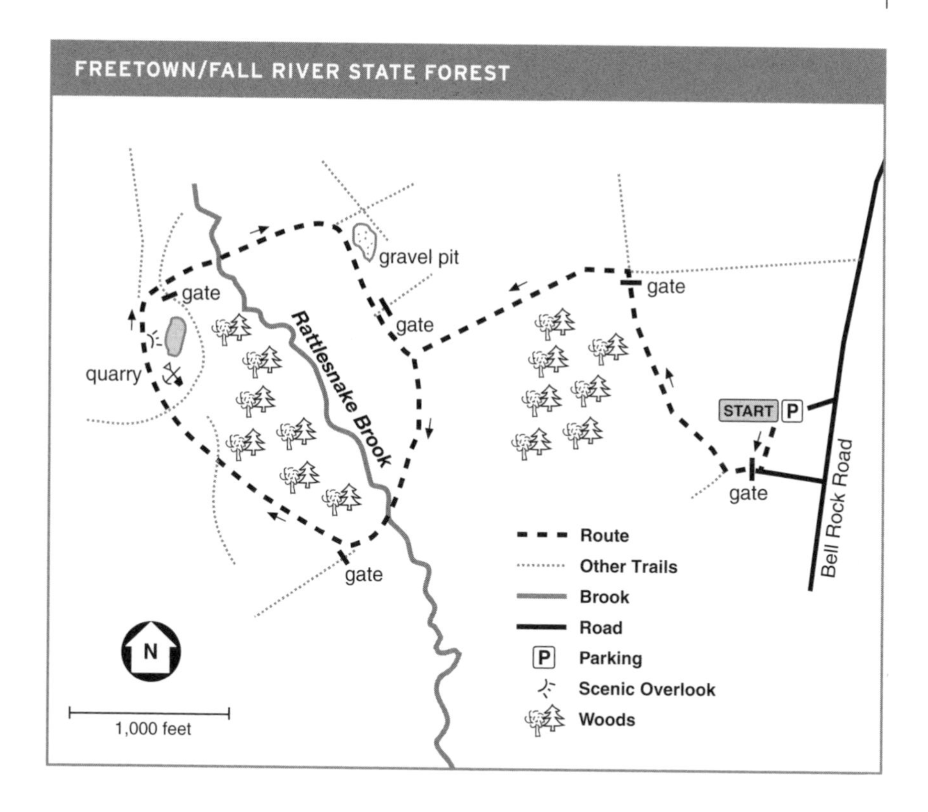

At 5,441 acres, Freetown/Fall River State Forest is one of the larger parks in Massachusetts and offers a wide variety of activities beyond hiking. Snowmobiling, horseback riding, mountain biking, and hunting are all allowed here. This walk focuses on the quieter trails best suited for nature study.

DIRECTIONS

Profile Rock Area. From Route 24 take Exit 10 and go toward Freetown. Travel 0.9 mile on Main Street, then left on Elm Street (following signs for state forest). At 0.2 mile, the road forks; bear right onto Slab Bridge Road and follow 0.6 mile to Profile Rock entrance road on the left. Follow entrance road to parking area.

Rattlesnake Brook Area. From Route 24 take Exit 9 and go south on South Main Street in the opposite direction as Assonet/Route 79 north. (For those coming from the north, the proper turn off the exit will be to the right; if you are coming from the south, turn left.) Follow South Main Street 0.5 mile to Copicut Road on the left. Take a left on Copicut and follow 1.2 miles to its end, then turn right on Bell Rock Road/High Street and follow 0.6 mile to the large parking lot on the right.

If you go to Profile Rock first and then want to go to the Rattlesnake Brook area, you can either get back on Route 24 and follow the directions, or return to the intersection of Slab Bridge Road and Elm Street and look for Route 79. Follow Route 79 south until it turns into South Main Street, then follow the directions for Rattlesnake Brook Area.

TRAIL DESCRIPTION

Profile Rock Area. Profile Rock is located at the northernmost end of the park, and it is a must see. It's only a quarter-mile walk from the parking lot. To reach Profile Rock, take the trail from the parking lot that is lined with stones and begins by two large beech trees. Follow the trail through woodlands of oak, beech, and pine for about 500 yards and you will see Profile Rock ahead to your left. The rock is a 50-foot geological formation that offers 360-degree views of the surrounding countryside.

Although there is no real path to the top, Profile Rock can be scaled with care. Because the surrounding terrain is relatively flat, the views from the summit are excellent. To the west you see a church steeple rising from what seems like an endless expanse of forest.

To return to your car from the summit, simply retrace your steps. There are many trails on the other side of Slab Bridge Road, but the most interesting terrain is just to the south, at the Rattlesnake Brook area of Freetown/Fall River State Forest. The entrance to Rattlesnake Brook area is off Bell Rock Road (see directions).

Rattlesnake Brook Area (southwest area of State Forest). Of the many miles of trails crisscrossing Freetown/Fall River State Forest, this southwest corner may be the best for long walks because of Rattlesnake Brook and an old quarry pond. There is also an overlook above the quarry that provides good views to the east.

Begin the walk by heading to the far left end of the parking area (as you face the woods), where a signboard and trail sign are located. Follow the path by the trail sign for about 40 feet until it intersects with a dirt road at a metal gate. On the forest side of the gate, the dirt road forks, and you should bear right. Continue walking on the dirt road (ignoring smaller side trails) until you reach another gate at a four-way intersection, about a half mile from the start of your walk. Turn left here. The road you are now on will soon fork (about a quarter mile from the four-way intersection) and you should bear left. When you cross the brook, take a moment to follow the path on the right that parallels the water. The little culvert under the road you were on has a stone façade and makes for a nice picture when taken from the streamside path.

As you continue on the dirt road on the south side of the bridge, you have left Freetown and entered Fall River. Ignore the trail on the left with the gate, and stay on the dirt road, which now curves to the right in a northwest direction. The trail will follow a gentle incline, passing an intersection with another dirt road that has large wooden posts on either side. Stay straight on this road, passing an exposed ledge and boulder on the left.

About a half mile after crossing Rattlesnake Brook, you will see an opening on your right with exposed bedrock. If you are walking with young children, hold their hands, as the overlook to your right has a 100-foot drop to a water-filled quarry below. The ledge affords a good view to the east, and it makes a nice resting spot. As you face the view, there will be a trail to your left that descends the overlook and heads down to the quarry. The trail is rough in spots, but is also short, so it should not present too many problems. There is a metal gate directly ahead near the quarry. You should follow the dirt road that goes to the left of the gate. A two-minute walk down this road will carry you over Rattlesnake Brook and then to a fork in the road where you should bear right. Next, you will pass a small gravel pit and gate on your left. About a half mile from the quarry, the trail ends at a T-intersection where you should turn left and follow the road up a slight incline. This is one of the original trails you came in on, and in a quarter mile, you will be back at the four-way intersection with the gate on your right. Turn right here, and you will be back at the parking area after walking 0.5 mile.

Rattlesnake Brook passes beneath a small stone arch bridge.

NATURE NOTES

Rattlesnake Brook is part of the Taunton River Watershed. It flows into the Assonet River, which in turn flows into the Taunton River before mingling its waters with Mount Hope

Bay. The brook is named for the rattlesnakes that once lived here and throughout Massachusetts. Today there are only a handful of timber rattlers left in the state, making them an endangered species protected by law. Rattlers are identified by their triangular head and a rattle at the end of their tails that makes a buzzing sound when vibrated. The body color ranges from yellow-brown to almost black, with dark V-shaped crossbands across the back. They bask during the daytime and hunt at night for rabbits, shrews, mice, chipmunks, and other small animals and birds.

While people almost never encounter rattlesnakes in Massachusetts, there are a number of other snakes that can be seen in our woodlands. Garter snake, milk snake, ribbon snake, and black racer are all found in terrain such as that of the Freetown/Fall River State Forest. The black racer is an especially interesting snake, as it is the only black snake in New England with smooth scales. If it is winter, look carefully for the tracks of animals, such as fox. Massachusetts has both red fox and gray fox. The gray fox is smaller than the red fox and is a skillful tree climber. Hunting in both the woods and fields, gray foxes eat a wide variety of small mammals, supplemented by insects, fruit, snakes, turtles, and frogs. It is said that they establish regular routes, following waterways and valleys on their hunting forays.

Also be sure to look for deer prints. They can be identified by their heart shape, with the pointed part of the track indicating the front of the deer hoof. This allows you to determine which direction the deer was traveling. White-tailed deer are primarily nocturnal, avoiding man by keeping to the thick woods during the daytime, and venturing out to feed at night. They have learned that it is safe to use the trails at night, and it's not uncommon to see tracks going right down the center of the trail for a considerable distance. The population of white-tailed deer is roughly as high as it was when Europeans first settled in America. Their numbers, however, were quite low in the mid-nineteenth century when much of Massachusetts' forest was cleared for agriculture and the deer were hunted year-round for food. Thoreau lamented this in his essay "A Natural History of Massachusetts," writing: "The bear, wolf, lynx, wildcat, deer, beaver and marten have disappeared. . . ."

MORE INFORMATION

Open year-round, dawn to dusk; no fee; rest rooms; dogs allowed. Profile Rock gate usually closes at 6 P.M. from Memorial Day to Labor Day. Hunting is allowed at this state park, so wear blaze orange in season. For more information, call 508-644-5522 or visit www.mass.gov/dcr.

TRIP 44
CARATUNK WILDLIFE REFUGE

LOCATION: Seekonk
RATING: Monument Rock, Easy; Hemlock Grove, Moderate
DISTANCE: Monument Rock, 2 miles; Hemlock Grove, 2.5 miles
ESTIMATED TIME: Monument Rock, 1 hour; Hemlock Grove, 1.5 hours
OTHER ACTIVITIES: Birding

Set on 195 acres with ponds, fields, streams, a small bog area, and boulder-strewn woodlands, Caratunk is a hidden gem just waiting to be discovered.

Caratunk Wildlife Refuge is often overlooked by Massachusetts residents because it is managed by the Audubon Society of Rhode Island. Deer, grouse, muskrat, woodcock, fox, and groundhog are just some of the animals you can see in addition to a diversity of birds. There is a small nature center in the barn adjacent to the parking lot that houses bird exhibits. Behind the nature center is a large field with picnic tables, a butterfly garden, bird feeders, and birdhouses.

DIRECTIONS

From I-95 take Exit 3A onto Route 123. Follow Route 123 eastward for 1.3 miles to a light. Just after the light, Route 123 bears to the left, but go straight onto Thatcher Street. Follow Thatcher Street 1 mile to its end, and then turn right onto Route 152. Follow Route 152 south for 5.5 miles, then turn left onto Brown Street and go 0.8 mile to the Caratunk sign and parking lot on the right.

TRIP DESCRIPTION

Monument Rock. To begin your walk, face the field behind the barn/nature center and walk at an angle across it toward the left side to a break in a stone wall. Follow the trail that heads beyond the stone wall, which is designated by a blue arrow. The path hugs the edge of the field next to woodlands of white pine, red oak, dogwood, birch, and a few large willows. You will pass a trail with a yellow arrow on the right; a little farther on, you will arrive at a trail with a blue arrow. Go just a few feet past the trail with the blue arrow and bear to the right where the trail splits. The trail is lined by grape vines, jewel weed, crab apple, and poison ivy and leads in a northern direction along the edge

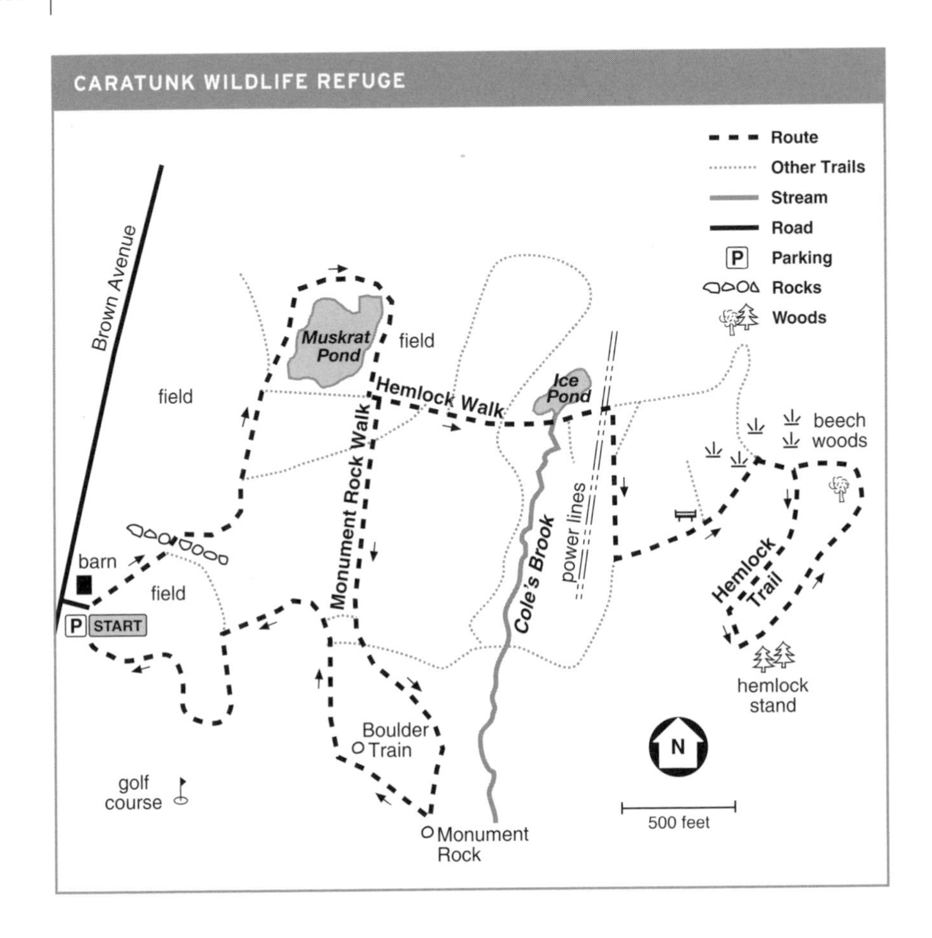

of a shallow pond with a couple small islands. This is Muskrat Pond, home to muskrat, ducks, and turtles.

The trail then continues its loop of the pond, turning first to the east (passing a wooden dock that leads into the water). The trail now turns to the south, passing a stand of poplar trees and a few old oaks before it intersects with another trail at the southeast corner of the pond. Take a moment to look back at the pond and admire the island filled with white birch.

From this point, the walk to Monument Rock is perfect for first-time visitors. Turn left at the trail intersection at the end of Muskrat Pond, go 10 feet and then turn right on the next trail, which is marked by yellow paint dots on trees farther down. Proceed south on this path, which passes through immature woodlands and fields reverting back to woods. Farther down this trail, go straight through a trail intersection, and then in 0.25 mile, pass a trail on the right. (Follow the sign straight toward Monument Rock.) In just one more minute of walking you will reach a T-intersection. Go left, crossing over a ridge of boulders. The trail forks after this ridge to the right. The trail now passes through more mature trees, primarily oaks. Within a quarter mile, you will reach Monument Rock, a 10-foot-high boulder resting against a tree. This narrow slab of rock looks something like a giant tombstone.

Take the trail to the right of the rock and follow it as it parallels a stone wall for almost 0.5 mile, passing a trail on the right. In another minute you'll come to an intersection with another trail. To return to the parking area, bear left here onto the trail marked by red dots. Follow it a short distance to a T-intersection at a boardwalk. Go left here, passing a pleasant area where ferns grow beneath white pines, then over a small stream on two separate bridges. The trail ends at the field behind the nature center and parking lot.

Hemlock Grove. This second hike is a good one for the fall, when you can see the gold colors in a beech grove. It is not a good trail during summer, as it passes through wet areas and dense woods with many mosquitoes. Begin this hike back at the southeast edge of Muskrat Pond, and follow the trail that goes uphill in a southeast direction. You will pass trails on your left and right, then in about a half mile, cross Cole's Brook on a granite bridge. On your left is a small marsh where a pond was once located. (Before the days of electric refrigeration, ice was cut from such ponds and stored in shaded, insulated spots to last into the summer.)

Just after the marsh and former ice pond, turn right at the power lines. The open area beneath the power lines attracts birds and small animals, which in turn attract raccoons and foxes, so be on the lookout if you are here in the early morning. Follow the trail beneath the power lines, then turn left at a narrow path marked by blue paint dots on the trees, ignoring the wider unmarked path that also goes into the woods. The path you are following winds through the woods and has many rocks and exposed roots. Be careful if you're with young children. You'll soon come to a bench and side trail where you should bear right. The ground beneath you is wet in spring, and boards have been laid to assist your footing. In a short distance, you will see a sign for a bog pointing to a side trail on the left. You can detour here to see the bog, but it is rather small.

After viewing the bog, go back to the trail you were on and to where it forks at a sign for the Hemlock Trail. This is the beginning of a loop that takes you to the south and a stand of hemlocks, first passing through a beech grove. The variety of trees at Caratunk is one of the reasons a walk in the autumn is special. You can go either way at this fork and it takes about another 1 mile of walking to complete the loop. After you've admired the hemlock and beech trees, simply retrace your steps back to the parking area.

NATURE NOTES

The field near the parking lot is covered with wildflowers, especially Queen Anne's lace in the summer. Queen Anne's lace is a member of the parsley family, and is also called "wild carrot." It has delicate white clusters of flowers that form a lace-like pattern, growing flat on a two- to three-foot stem. Look for butterflies, bluebirds, and tree swallows flying above the field of flowers. The stone wall is especially handsome, but was originally created for practical reasons rather than aesthetics. When farmers cleared the land of trees in past centuries, they also had to remove the many rocks from the soil. These were dragged from the field in stone boats and then fitted into walls that either marked property boundaries or kept sheep and cattle within the pastures.

Spring migration brings red-winged blackbirds to the area. The male has a distinctive red shoulder patch, while the female resembles a large sparrow but is long-billed and more heavily streaked. They feed, fly, and roost in huge flocks, usually near open fields or marsh. In the summer look for catbirds, cardinals, and herons along the pond's edge.

Swamp maples grow around the pond, whereas cedars begin to appear where the ground rises away toward a field at the pond's eastern end. With binoculars you can scan the field for deer, groundhog, or birds such as kestrel that hunt here. In September, you might see an occasional woodcock flying south just above tree level in the evening. They prefer to breed in areas where there are low wet thickets adjacent to fields, like the area here at Caratunk.

MORE INFORMATION

Open year-round, dawn to dusk (closed Mondays); fee for non-members of the Audubon Society of Rhode Island; rest rooms in the nature center; dogs prohibited. For more information, contact the Caratunk Wildlife Refuge, 301 Brown Avenue, Seekonk, MA; 508-761-8230; www.asri.org/caratunk.htm.

TRIP 45
LOWELL HOLLY RESERVATION

LOCATION: Mashpee/Sandwich
RATING: Moderate
DISTANCE: 2 miles
ESTIMATED TIME: 1 hour
OTHER ACTIVITIES: Biking, birding, fishing, paddling, swimming

Enjoy a walk through primarily wild woods and along scattered beaches.

Lowell Holly was donated to the Trustees of Reservations in 1934 by Abbott Lawrence Lowell, former president of Harvard College. Except for the cart paths constructed by Dr. Lowell, the reservation has been left primarily in its wild state for the past 200 years. The beech trees are large and are quite different from the typical oaks and pines that cover so much of Cape Cod. Their smooth gray trunks stand out like sentinels guarding the peninsula. In winter the lower branches of the beech often retain their dried yellow-brown leaves, contrasting beautifully against the snow. It's a special place where cool breezes coming off the waters of Wakeby Pond and Mashpee Pond pass over the large stand of massive beech trees that shade this peninsula dividing the two ponds. Small pockets of white, sandy beaches, more than 300 native American holly, and several kinds of rhododendrons are just some of the additional reasons to visit the reservation.

DIRECTIONS

Take Route 6 to Exit 2 (Route 130) and go south 1.4 miles. Go left on Cotuit Road 3.4 miles, then right on South Sandwich Road 0.7 mile to the entrance on the right. Proceed down a narrow dirt road, which will bring you to the parking area.

TRAIL DESCRIPTION

To begin your walk, follow the main path, which hugs the right (north) shoreline. Holly trees are scattered about the understory and thrive quite well in the shade of the beech trees. Any walk through the woods is made more pleasant when you can see deep blue water, in this case of Wakeby Pond, through the green foliage.

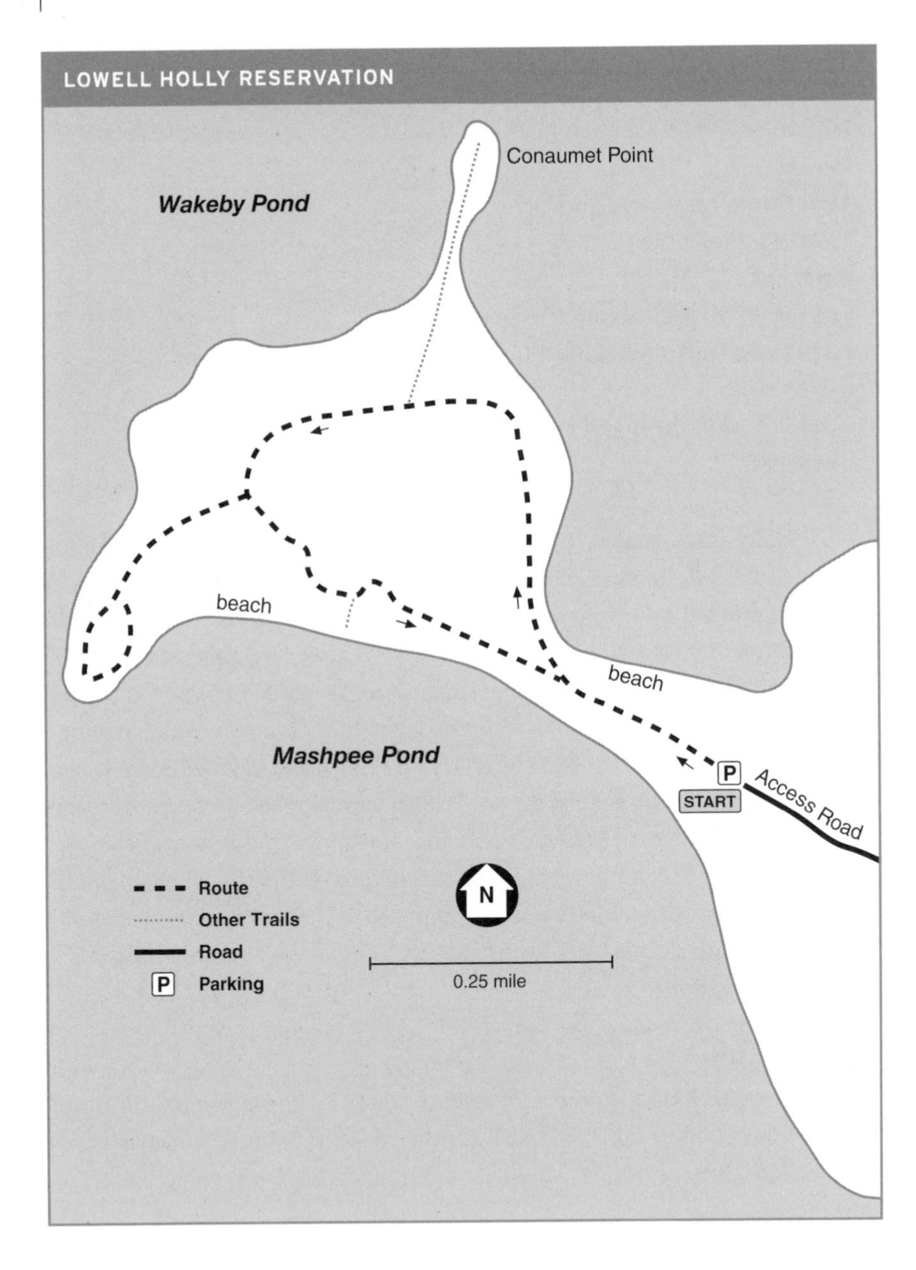

One trail winds its way out to narrow Conaumet Point while another goes to the southern tip of the peninsula. It seems that few of the many visitors bother to walk out to the end of the peninsula, so chances are you will have the woods to yourself. Be warned, however, that the trails are unmarked and get a bit confusing. The trail to the southern end of the peninsula leads to a

60-foot-high knoll near the end of the peninsula. Take a moment to climb down to the water's edge where the two ponds are connected by a narrow passage of water.

Walking back toward the parking area, you can follow the trail that hugs the Mashpee Pond side of the peninsula. There are some very large holly trees on this side, along with more open patches of sandy beaches. In spring the pink-and-white flowers of the rhododendron and mountain laurel are especially handsome.

The pointed, shiny evergreen leaves of the holly tree add color to winter woodlands.

NATURE NOTES

Near the parking area is a small sandy beach and picnic tables that are positioned for views of the water. Mashpee and Wakeby Ponds are well known for their excellent fishing. Trout are stocked in both spring and fall. Warm-water species are also present, including largemouth bass, smallmouth bass, pickerel, and bluegill.

The ponds attract a variety of bird life, including great blue herons, ducks, and Canada geese, and some lucky hikers have spotted osprey. Frequent visitors have told me they occasionally see raccoons and foxes.

MORE INFORMATION

Open year-round; fee from Memorial Day to Columbus Day (a ranger is on duty weekends and holidays during this period); the rest of the year there is no admission fee and only the upper parking lot is open. For more information, call 781-821-2977 or visit www.thetrustees.org.

P 46
T HILL

LOCATION: Eastham
RATING: Easy
DISTANCE: 2 miles
ESTIMATED TIME: 1 hour
OTHER ACTIVITIES: Birding

An ocean-side hike through the Cape Cod National Seashore, with panoramic views.

Treat yourself to a sunrise from the top of Fort Hill, and it will be an experience you won't soon forget. Then top it off with a walk through the hillside fields along Nauset Marsh and return to the hill via the boardwalk that winds through a red maple swamp. You can extend your hike by viewing the historic Penniman House, once owned by a whale-ship captain, and continue back to the parking lot on the trail that runs behind the Penniman House. It's a great way to spend a morning on Cape Cod's National Seashore. The combination of water, boardwalk, and expansive views make this hike a favorite of children. Bring your camera for the spectacular views.

DIRECTIONS

From the rotary where Route 6 and Route 28 meet on the Eastham/Orleans border, drive north on Route 6 for 1.3 miles. Turn right onto Governor Prence Road, then about a quarter mile down bear right onto Fort Hill Road. Follow the signs to the upper parking lot a short distance ahead.

TRAIL DESCRIPTION

Our walk begins from the upper parking lot at the summit of Fort Hill, a small hill with a big view. To the right is Town Cove, which separates Eastham from Orleans; straight ahead is Nauset Marsh, barrier beach; and the Atlantic Ocean lies in the distance.

A trail of shells leads down to the marsh and a huge glacial boulder. Follow the trail to the left in a northward direction for about a half mile until you reach the woods comprised primarily of cedar trees. Bear right and into the woods. In a couple minutes you will arrive at a pavilion with a fine view.

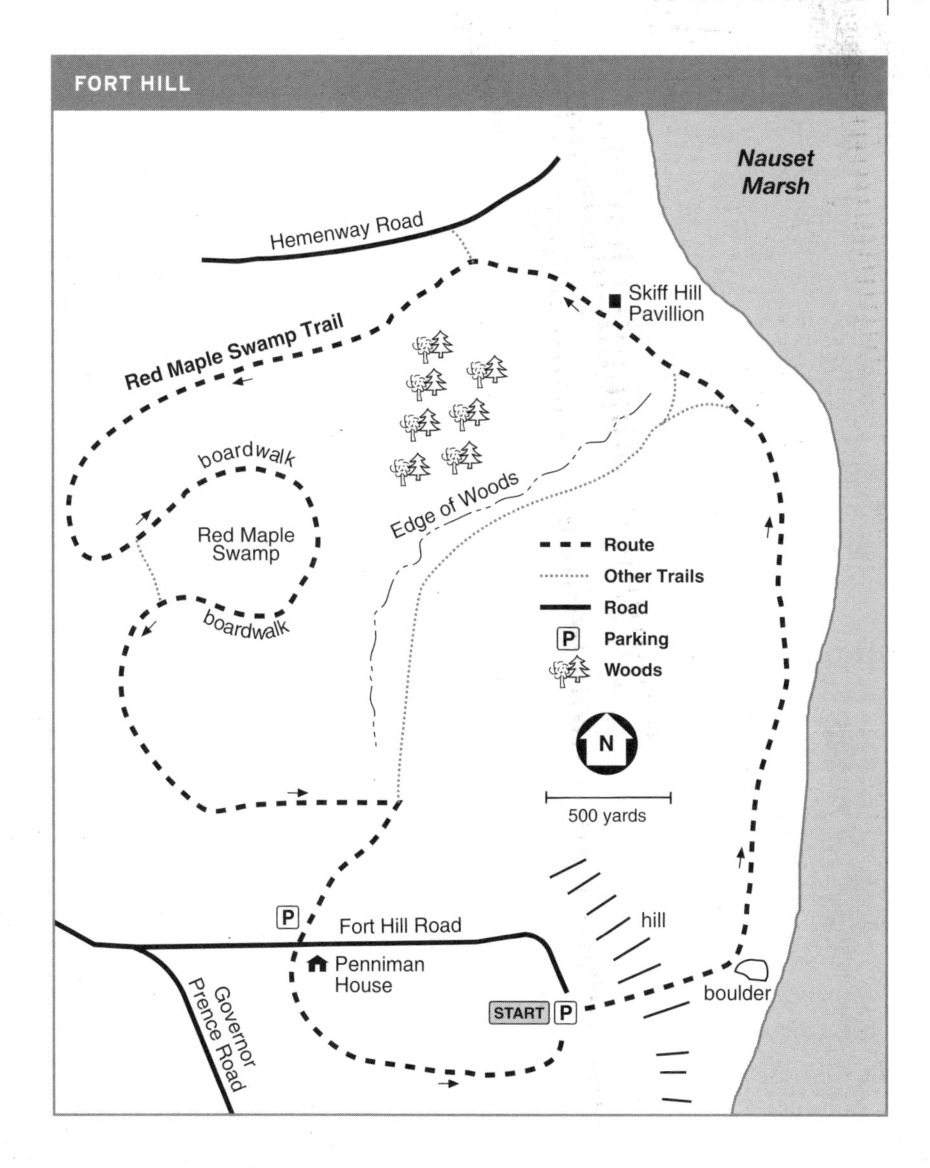

About 300 yards farther along the trail is the beginning of the Red Maple Swamp Trail on the left. A series of interspersed boardwalks help keep the feet dry and children will love the winding wooden paths. The standing water here is fresh water (not salt water), and the swamp maple, or red maple, can tolerate having wet feet and is an extremely adaptable tree.

Follow the trail about a half mile and then at an intersection bear left to enter the darkest recesses of the swamp. The contrast in this dark and shaded wetland from the sunny fields at the beginning of the walk is one of the features that makes this walk special. Interpretive signs along the trail identify plants such as highbush blueberry, netted chain fern, and fox grapes. There is also winterberry (a low plant with bright red berries eaten by birds) and sweet pepperbush (which gives off a fragrant aroma from its flowers in August).

After walking an additional 0.75 mile you will reach another fork. You should bear left. After another five minutes of walking you are back at the fields of Fort Hill. (Scan the fields for meadowlarks or bluebirds.) Turn right here and follow the trail to the lower parking lot, then cross the street to the Penniman House. You can't miss this historic home because at the front of the yard is an enormous archway formed by the jawbones of a whale. Captain Edward Penniman took to the sea at eleven years of age, eventually circling the world seven times. His home, built in the French Second Empire style with cupola overlooking both the bay and sea, became a local landmark. Behind the house you can pick up the trail that will lead you in an easterly direction through low-lying woods for about a third of a mile back to the main parking lot.

NATURE NOTES

Henry Beston wrote *The Outermost House*, chronicling the natural year, while living in a cottage on the barrier beach. For nature lovers, the book is a must-read.

The first boulder you encounter is a glacial erratic, deposited during the last Ice Age. Look closely at its south side and you will see a spike embedded in the rock, perhaps used as an anchor for small boats or to pull bales of salt hay out of the marsh.

In the pavilion is Indian Rock, a boulder used by Nauset Indians to sharpen fishhooks and tools. The abrasive qualities of this fine-grained metamorphic rock were perfect for grinding and polishing implements. Let children run their fingers over the grooves in the rock, and explain how the Indians sharpened their tools in those same grooves. This glacial boulder was originally farther out in the marsh but was moved here for viewing.

Bayberry, black cherry, honeysuckle, and salt-spray rose grow along the edge of the marsh. Autumnal tints here are subtle but pleasing to the eye, with golden marsh grass ringed by russet vegetation.

The open fields are great for picnicking, kite flying, and birding. You might spot a snow bunting, a small bird that looks a bit like a large sparrow until it reveals a belly that is almost pure white. This ground bird is about 6 inches long, and is seen on tundra, dunes, and open fields. Other birds you might see are harrier hawks hovering above the salt marsh, searching for prey, and herons or greater yellowlegs feeding in the mudflats.

MORE INFORMATION

Open year-round, dawn to dusk; no fee; no rest rooms; dogs prohibited. Red Maple Swamp Trail is handicap accessible. Contact Cape Cod National Seashore Headquarters, 508-349-3785; www.nps.gov/caco/places/forthill.html.

TRIP 47
WELLFLEET BAY WILDLIFE SANCTUARY

LOCATION: South Wellfleet
RATING: Easy
DISTANCE: 3 miles
ESTIMATED TIME: 1.5 hours
OTHER ACTIVITIES: Birding
PUBLIC TRANSPORTATION: Take the Commuter Rail to Brockton, then the Plymouth/Brockton bus

Excellent birding and diverse plant life abound as you walk along Silver Springs Brook.

Wellfleet Bay Wildlife Sanctuary is one of Cape Cod's most popular outdoor destinations because of its extensive trail system along the edge of Wellfleet Bay and its salt marsh. To the north of the Nature Center is the Bay View Trail, a 1.4-mile loop trail, and to the south is the Goose Pond Trail and Try Island Trail/Boardwalk that together cover about 3 miles. There is also a short trail along the edge of Silver Spring Brook that runs for 0.6 mile. All are worth exploring, but Goose Pond Trail and Try Island will be the focus of this walk. Both have great vistas and diverse plant life. The birding is also excellent—more than 250 species of birds have been seen at the sanctuary.

DIRECTIONS

Follow Route 6 for 0.3 mile north from the Eastham-Wellfleet town line to signs at the entrance road on the left. Follow the entrance road, crossing West Road, to the Sanctuary parking lot 0.4 mile away.

TRAIL DESCRIPTION

To begin your walk and exploration of the Goose Pond Trail follow the signs from the Nature Center directing you to the trail that heads in a southwesterly

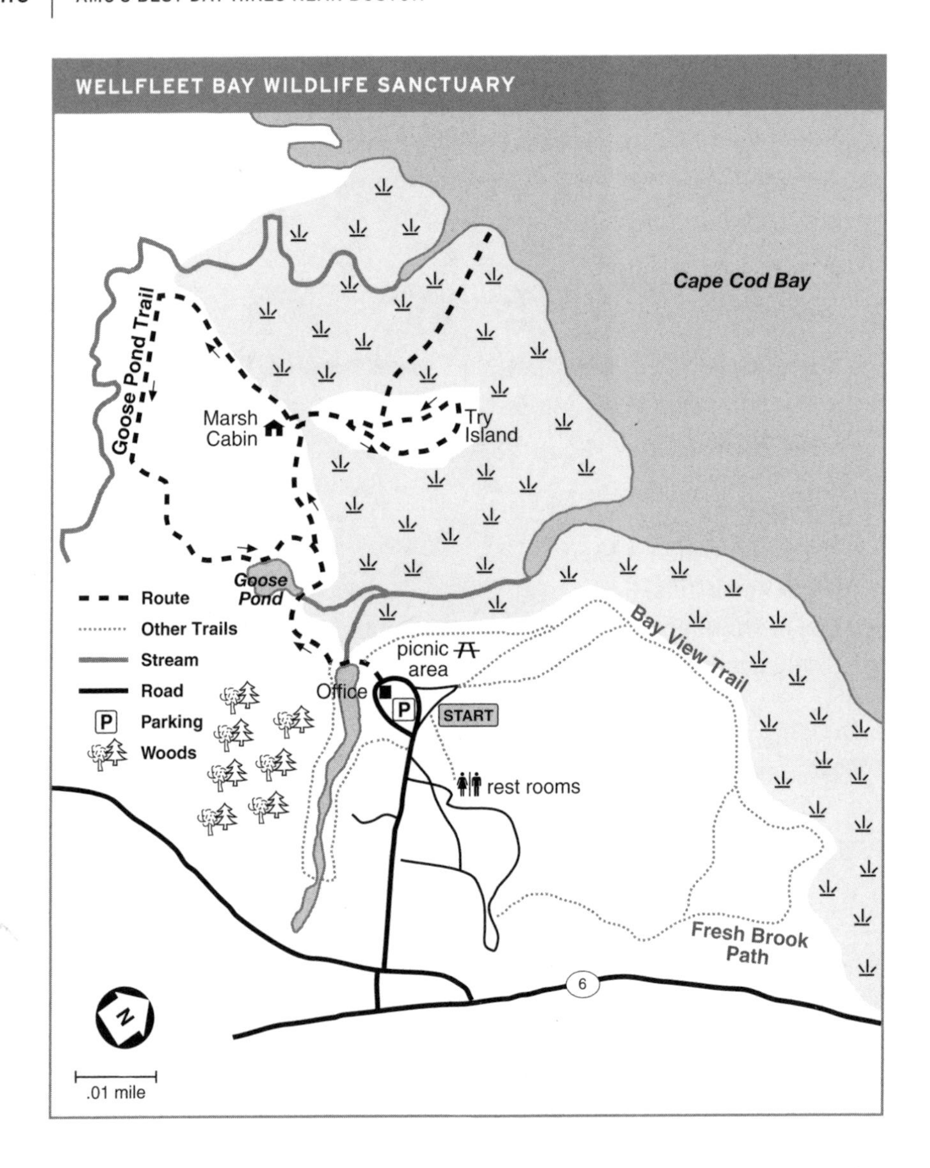

direction. A side trail, called the Fresh Brook Pathway, soon heads to the right, but you continue straight. Catch a glimpse of Try Island as you cross Silver Spring Brook, which has been made into a pond by the small dam you traverse. The shoreline of the pond on your left is surrounded by marsh fern, white poplar trees, swamp milkweed, and purple loosestrife, a non-indigenous plant that crowds out native vegetation. The loosestrife is easy to spot because of its bright purple flowers that bloom in the summer.

If you want to see more of the water, turn left after crossing the dike for a half-mile loop trail around the pond that will bring you back to the parking lot where you can resume your walk.

When you cross the dam over Silver Spring Brook on the Goose Pond Trail you will emerge into an area of pines, including white pine, pitch pine, red pine, and Scotch pine. All were planted here to stabilize the sandy soil. It's interesting to note that when the Pilgrims landed at Cape Cod, the peninsula was covered with trees, but by the time Thoreau made his four explorations of the Cape he lamented that the land was literally blowing away because almost every single tree had been cut.

Follow the path through the pine woods for two or three minutes and then bear right over a small bridge. Goose Pond will be on your left. Many species of birds visit here, including the great blue heron and kingfisher. (As you face the pond there is a small bird blind set up for observation on the left side of the pond to the east.) Continue westward on the main path past the pond and a white spruce on the right. Continue straight, passing a trail that comes in on the left. Red cedars will be scattered through the woods and a small observation deck will be on the right overlooking the marsh. About a quarter mile from Goose Pond, take a right on the trail opposite the "marsh cabin" that leads through the marsh and over to Try Island. Kestrels, harrier hawks, and red-tailed hawks can all be seen in this area.

Just a minute or two through the marsh you will come to a fork in the trail. Bear right, following the sign to Try Island. Soon you will reach the island's wooded eastern end. Follow the trail to the very end of the island where a bench has been erected on a bluff offering a great view of the bay and the salt marsh. From the bench at the end of the island, turn around and follow the path on the right that runs parallel to the ocean, passing by another bench with a view. Within two or three minutes you will reach the intersection with the boardwalk. Turn right onto the boardwalk to head toward the beach. It's about a quarter-mile walk to the shore, passing by the fine bladed high-tide grass that colonial farmers used for cattle feed, and past beach grass with narrow backs rolled at the sides to reduce area of surface evaporation from coastal winds. The beach grass has an extensive and wide-spreading root system than helps hold the sand on the dunes and beach.

After exploring the beach retrace your steps over the boardwalk and then bear right to exit Try Island. Once you cross the marsh, you will be back at the T-intersection by the marsh cabin. Turn right to complete your loop of the property. The path is wide and sandy, with fields and woods to your left and the salt marsh to your right. Look for Virginia rose and salt spray rose with curved thorns and pale pink blossoms in the early summer. Sea lavender, also called marsh rosemary, grows at the upper edge of the marsh, staying close to the ground to conserve moisture. It has tiny white flowers that stay on the plant into the fall.

About a quarter mile down this path is an arrow pointing you to the left at a fork. Bear left, heading into the fields. After walking through the fields and woods for a quarter mile you will be back at Goose Pond. Turn right to return to the parking lot (it takes about another ten minutes to cover the half-mile distance). Before you go into the Nature Center to examine the many exhibits be sure to pause by the beautiful butterfly and hummingbird garden.

NATURE NOTES

The box turtle and the black racer are two reptiles that might cross your path in this upland meadow. The box turtle has a high-domed shell with yellow, orange, and black markings. Be sure not to disturb box turtles, as human development has led to loss of turtle habitat and their numbers are down. The black racer is a rather large, extremely quick snake. It can grow over 5 feet long, and can be seen basking in the sun or hunting for small rodents. The black racer is not poisonous (nor are any of the ten species of snakes that live on the Cape) and it too should be left undisturbed.

Goose Pond has red-wing blackbirds from March to October, and the male can be identified by its red shoulder patch. The females are dark brown and they nest in the wetlands, in grass-and-weed nests usually set in low bushes. They feed on insects and marsh plants. Warblers also visit the thickets around the pond during migratory periods. Other pond dwellers include turtles such as the snapping turtle, with its dark green-black shell with ridges, and the painted turtle, with smooth black shell and a head streaked with yellow markings.

In the marsh you also might see the greater yellowlegs, a 14-inch-long wading bird with long yellow legs and grayish back and white underparts. Tree swallows, which have a glistening blue-black coloring above and white below, can be seen swooping through the air, catching insects above the marsh in mid-flight. They prefer nesting boxes in open areas, often competing with bluebirds for choice boxes.

Beach plums, which have pink-white flowers in May before the leaves are fully out, grow in the sheltered spots of the field. They yield deep purple fruit in September, which is eaten by red fox, raccoon, and birds. Other plants seen here include black locust, pokeweed, goldenrod, spindle tree, and golden aster. If you look closely you might be able to see the tall, green, fern-like leaves of asparagus, the wild descendants of farming that was done here more than 60 years ago. One of the dominant trees here, the oak, will carry its rusty leaves well into November when many other trees have lost their foliage.

Crooked stems of bur-reed, with their ball-like flowers. Photo by John Hayes.

MORE INFORMATION

Nature Center. Memorial Day to Columbus Day: Daily, 8:30 A.M. to 5 P.M. Columbus Day to Memorial Day: Tuesday through Sunday, 8:30 A.M. to 5 P.M.; rest rooms.

Trails. Open every day, 8 A.M. to dusk (8 P.M. in summer); small fee for non-members of the Massachusetts Audubon Society; rest rooms; dogs prohibited. For more information, contact Wellfleet Bay Wildlife Sanctuary, 291 State Highway, Route 6, South Wellfleet, MA, 02663; 508-349-2615; wellfleet@massaudubon.org; www.massaudubon.org.

TRIP 48
GREAT ISLAND

LOCATION: Wellfleet
RATING: Moderate
DISTANCE: 4 miles
ESTIMATED TIME: 2.5 hours
OTHER ACTIVITIES: Birding

The combination of pine woodlands and coastal dunes makes Great Island a special place to walk.

The estuarine tidal flats formed by the Herring River drainage are rich habitat for marine life such as fiddler crabs, quahogs, and oysters. There are no roads on the reservation; the only sound you will hear is the lapping of the waves and the call of the birds. Because the island is large and often overlooked by visitors, you can look out over the water and enjoy Great Island in relative solitude. Be sure to bring drinking water and a hat, as the walk is relatively long and much of it is in the sunshine.

Great Island is a knob of glacial debris that is currently connected to the mainland by a narrow hill of sand. (Winds and tides have continually reshaped this area.) In the late 1600s and early 1700s, a tavern served mariners on Great Island, and the walk goes to this historic site.

DIRECTIONS

From Route 6 take the Wellfleet Town Center exit and follow the sign toward the town center. At 0.2 mile turn left onto East Commercial Street and follow that for 0.8 mile to the town pier. Turn right onto Kendrick Road and follow it about a mile to its end. Turn left onto Chequesset Neck Road and go 1.7 miles to the Great Island parking lot on the left.

TRAIL DESCRIPTION

From the parking lot, follow the trail next to the map and sign welcoming you to the Cape Cod National Seashore. The trail passes through a stand of pitch pine (identified by the three rigid needles) that are all about the same age due to the replanting activity here at the end of the nineteenth century. Early settlers cut most of the old timber that once covered much of Cape Cod, and without its diverse covering of trees the Cape was literally blowing away,

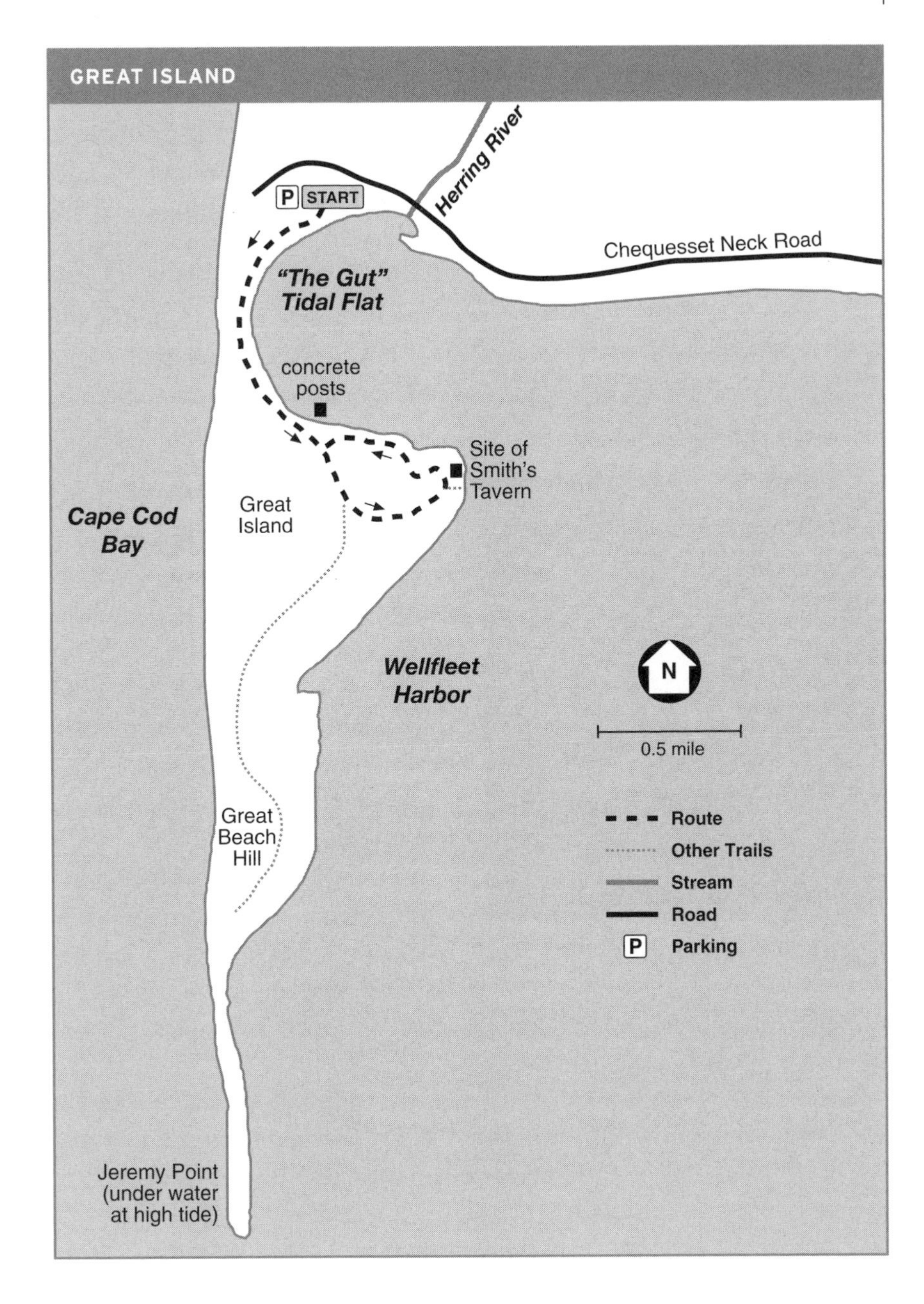

before planting efforts began to stabilize the soil.

Within three or four minutes you will arrive at the water's edge on the Wellfleet Harbor side of the island. Turn right here and follow the shore in a southerly direction. A sign tells you the mileage of the various walks on the island. The salt hay growing along the shore was used by early settlers as cattle feed.

A view over the salt marsh.

On a winter walk here, you might get lucky and see a harbor seal swimming in the bay or sunning on the shore.

As you walk the shore look for oyster shells. During high tide the shoreline walk can be a bit muddy, so wear boots during cold-weather months. About fifteen minutes into the walk there is a path on the right that leads to wooden stairs spanning the dunes to the beach on the Cape Cod Bay side of Great Island.

After you check out Cape Cod Bay, return to the Wellfleet Harbor side of Great Island and continue walking southward. Follow the curving contour of the shore around the tidal flat known as The Gut. You might see sideways-moving fiddler crabs, which burrow into the sand. The males have a large singular claw that they use in battle during mating season.

Continue along the coast for about a half mile and you will pass concrete posts and then a Great Island destinations mileage sign. Take a right on the path that comes from the interior of the island. On hot days the pitch pines in the woods provide welcome shade.

Follow this interior path for about a quarter mile until you reach a fork in the trail. Go left on the narrow path to the east-southeast. You will find that you make better time on this woodland path because you are walking on firm ground rather than in sand. After about a half mile of walking you will arrive at a sign for the tavern. (There is also a short trail to the right that quickly brings you to a small bluff overlooking the water, which makes for a good resting spot.) The view before you is impressive. The sparkling blue water of Wellfleet Bay stretches north and east toward the Cape Cod mainland.

The Smith Tavern site is marked by a sign and boulder. It once served as a meeting place for weary mariners. A recent excavation of the site revealed more than 24,000 artifacts including wine glass stems, clay pipes, and even a lady's fan. Whalers frequently visited the tavern, both those on ship and shore whalers. Using small boats equipped with harpoon and lance, shore whalers stayed close to shore, often driving the whales up on the sand where they could easily be killed and butchered.

Retrace your steps back from the bluff to the Smith Tavern sign. Bear right to complete your loop back to The Gut and toward the parking lot. After five minutes of walking there you'll see a faint trail to the right, but you should continue through the woods heading northwest. In about five more minutes you will be back at the shore by the concrete posts. From here, turn left and retrace your earlier steps along the shore and around The Gut to return to the parking lot.

If you enjoyed this 4-mile walk you may want to return and try a more ambitious walk farther out on Great Island—a rise of land known as Great Beach Hill. This would be a 6-mile round-trip walk. Jeremy Point, at the southernmost end of Great Island, is not recommended as a walk because it is under water at high tide.

NATURE NOTES

Wellfleet oysters are known for their excellent quality. Oysters were important in the diet of the Native Americans that lived here, and later to the settlers who commercially harvested them for food and used their shells to make lime. Over-harvesting, and perhaps other unknown factors, caused the disappearance of the Wellfleet oyster. In an attempt to reestablish oysters in the bay, oyster stock from the southern U.S. has been introduced.

Even before the arrival of the white man, the Native Americans were on the lookout for shore-stranded whales to use as a food source. When the Pilgrims landed on the Cape prior to settling in Plymouth, they came upon Indians butchering a whale on a beach near Great Island. Thoreau witnessed a similar scene on one of his four walks through the Cape, when he saw 30 blackfish (a small whale) stranded on the beach: "They were a smooth shining black, like India-rubber, and had remarkably simple and humplike forms for animated creatures, with blunt round snout or head, whale-like, and simple, stiff looking flippers."

The whales were so plentiful here prior to the 1900s that lookouts were posted on the high ground at Great Beach Hill. The lookouts alerted the whalers who pursued the great mammals in small boats. Whale houses (in which gear was stored) and try-works (used to boil out the whale oil) were built around the perimeter of the island. The height of whaling activity in New England was reached in the 1840s, when there were more than 700 American whaling vessels at sea. But with the discovery of the mineral oil in Pennsylvania, the demand for whale oil dropped. Today, visitors to Cape Cod see whales on whale-watch excursions and concerned people are trying to protect the whales, which are still killed by some foreign countries for commercial purposes.

MORE INFORMATION

Open year-round, 6 A.M. to midnight; no fee; portable rest rooms provided seasonally; dogs prohibited. For information, contact Cape Cod National Seashore Headquarters, 508-349-3785; www.nps.gov/caco/places/greatisland.html.

TRIP 49
SANDY NECK CIRCUIT

LOCATION: Barnstable
RATING: Moderate
DISTANCE: 1.6 miles, 4.7 miles, 9 miles, or 13 miles
ESTIMATED TIME: The 4.7-mile option takes 4 hours, 40 minutes
OTHER ACTIVITIES: Birding

Sandy Neck is a 6-mile-long barrier beach bordering Cape Cod Bay.

A choice of trails offers options ranging from a 1.6-mile-long nature walk to a hike of more than 13 mile along the protected marsh and 100-foot-tall dunes to the open waters of Cape Cod Bay.

DIRECTIONS

To reach Sandy Neck from US 6 (Exit 5), head north on MA 149, turn left onto MA 6A, then right onto Sandy Neck Road. Follow Sandy Neck Road to the parking lot at its end. A fee is charged for parking in season.

TRAIL DESCRIPTION

Begin this circuit on the Marsh Trail; the trailhead is located in the parking area opposite the check-in booth. The trail initially passes through an area of red pine and scrub oak, then opens up by the great marsh. Large square blue boxes line the marsh—these are traps to control the green fly. The dunes to the left obstruct the view of the ocean. Stay on the sandy trail to avoid ticks

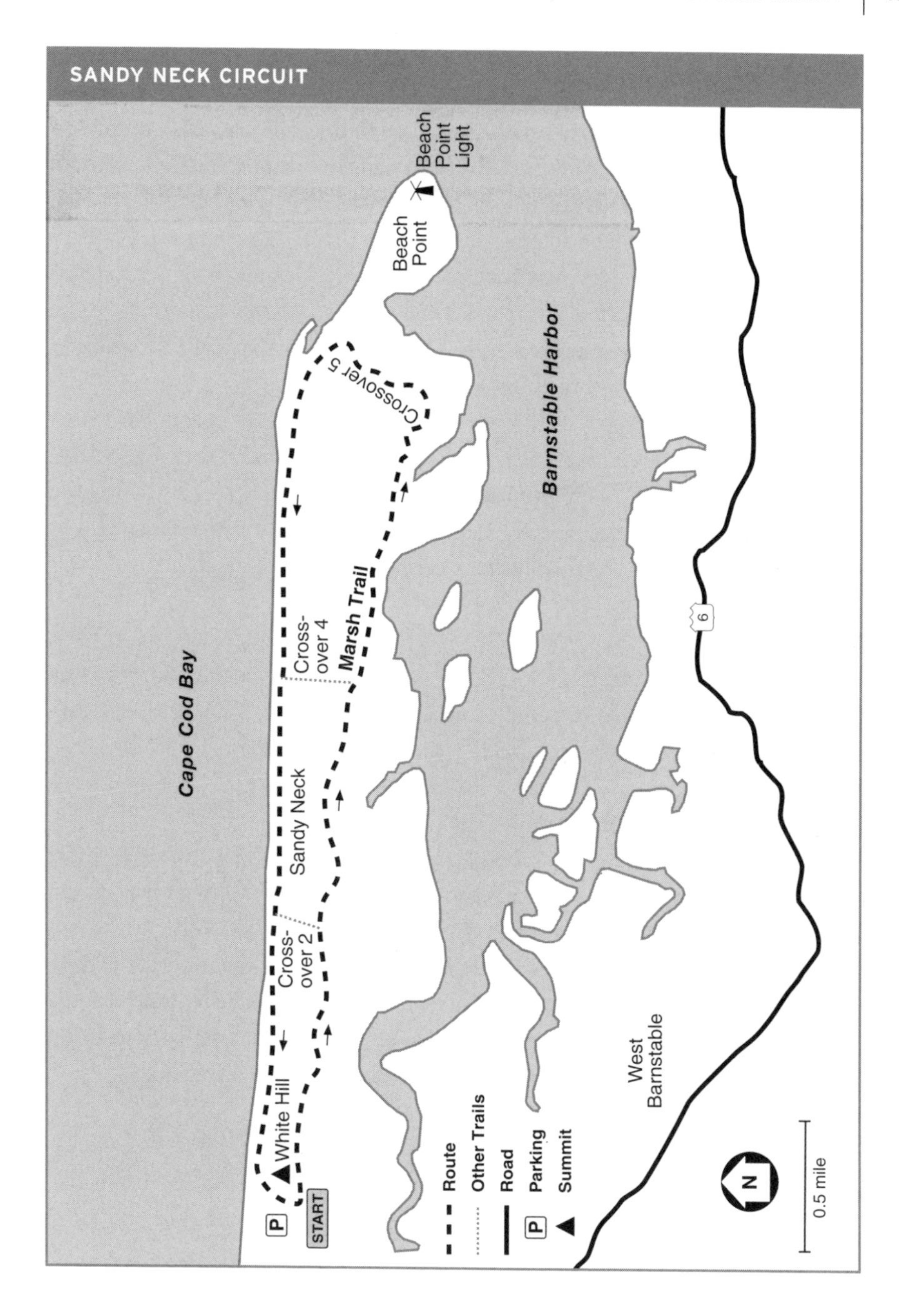

and poison ivy, and to avoid destroying the beach grass and other fragile dune plants. At 0.5 mile a junction is reached. A left turn here leads 1.1 miles back to the parking lot via the beach. Alternately, continue straight ahead to signpost 2 at 1.5 miles. Poverty grass displays its yellow blooms in early June, and pale purple patches of sea lavender grow prolifically along the trail.

As the trail approaches crossover 2, Scorton Creek comes into view, meandering the bay. Turn onto crossover 2 to return to the trailhead and complete a 4.7-mile hike. For a 9-mile hike continue straight to signpost 4 (there is no 3). Along the way is a dune cottage with no less than 20 swallow houses! Watch for horseshoe crab molts and deer and coyote prints. The historic cottages on Beach Point and the decommissioned Sandy Neck Light House come into view as the trail approaches signpost 4. Turn left at crossover 4 to return to the parking area and to complete a 9-mile hike, or continue straight for another 1.5 mile to crossover 5 and turn left for a 12-plus-mile hike.

A horse trail intersects trail 5. Cross straight over it to reach the shore. Private land lies between the path here and the tip of Sandy Neck. To extend the hike, continue east along the beach to the lighthouse before retracing the route and returning to the parking lot along the shore. Be aware that a trip to the lighthouse extends the mileage by a couple of miles.

NATURE NOTES

Sandy Neck provides habitat for several endangered species, including piping plovers, diamond-backed terrapins, and spadefoot toads. The dunes are covered with wildflowers, wild cranberries, and hardwood trees.

MORE INFORMATION

Four-wheel-drive vehicles are allowed in certain areas, and hunting is permitted during the appropriate season. Check tide charts, as low-lying areas on the marsh side may be flooded at exceptionally high tides, especially in the area adjacent to the start of the Marsh Trail. Hikers are not allowed to enter private property or areas marked Erosion Control and must stay off the dunes, crossing over only on designated trails. Because of the exposure, be sure to bring adequate water and sunblock; allow time for slow going in soft sand.

TRIP 50
MYLES STANDISH STATE FOREST: EASTHEAD TRAIL AND BENTLEY LOOP

LOCATION: Plymouth/Carver
RATING: Moderate to strenuous (due to distance)
DISTANCE: 3 or 7.5 miles (depending on choice of trail)
ESTIMATED TIME: 2 or 4 hours (depending on choice of trail)
OTHER ACTIVITIES: Biking, camping, paddling, swimming
WINTER ACTIVITIES: Trails are flat and well-maintained, excellent for cross-country skiing

At more than 14,000 acres, Myles Standish State Forest is one of the largest reservations in the state park and forest system and offers many recreational opportunities.

The forest offers universally accessible rest rooms, five camping areas (Fearing Ponds 1 and 2, Charge Pond, Barretts' Pond, and Curlew Pond), and sixteen ponds. A portion of Charge Pond is set aside for equestrian camping. There are 15 miles of cycling paths, 35 miles of equestrian trails, and 13 miles of hiking paths (blazed with blue triangles) that venture deep into this unique area. The recreational opportunities here seem endless. In addition to hiking, the forest offers camping, bicycling, canoeing, and swimming. The terrain is excellent for mountain biking, and the sport is very popular here.

DIRECTIONS

To reach the forest from the north, take MA 3 south to Exit 3. Turn right (west) onto Long Pond Road and travel about 3 miles to the entrance on the left. Park headquarters is located on Cranberry Road. To reach the headquarters from the west (I-495), take Exit 2 (South Carver) to MA 58. Turn north onto MA 58, continue straight on Tremont Street where MA 58 bears left, and proceed for a little less than a mile to Cranberry Road on the right.

TRAIL DESCRIPTION

The original Easthead Trail is a 3-mile loop circling Easthead Reservoir. In 1991 the 4.5-mile Bentley Loop was added at the northern end of the original loop. Both the original trail and the Bentley Loop are clearly blazed with blue trail markers or blue paint slashes and are well-maintained.

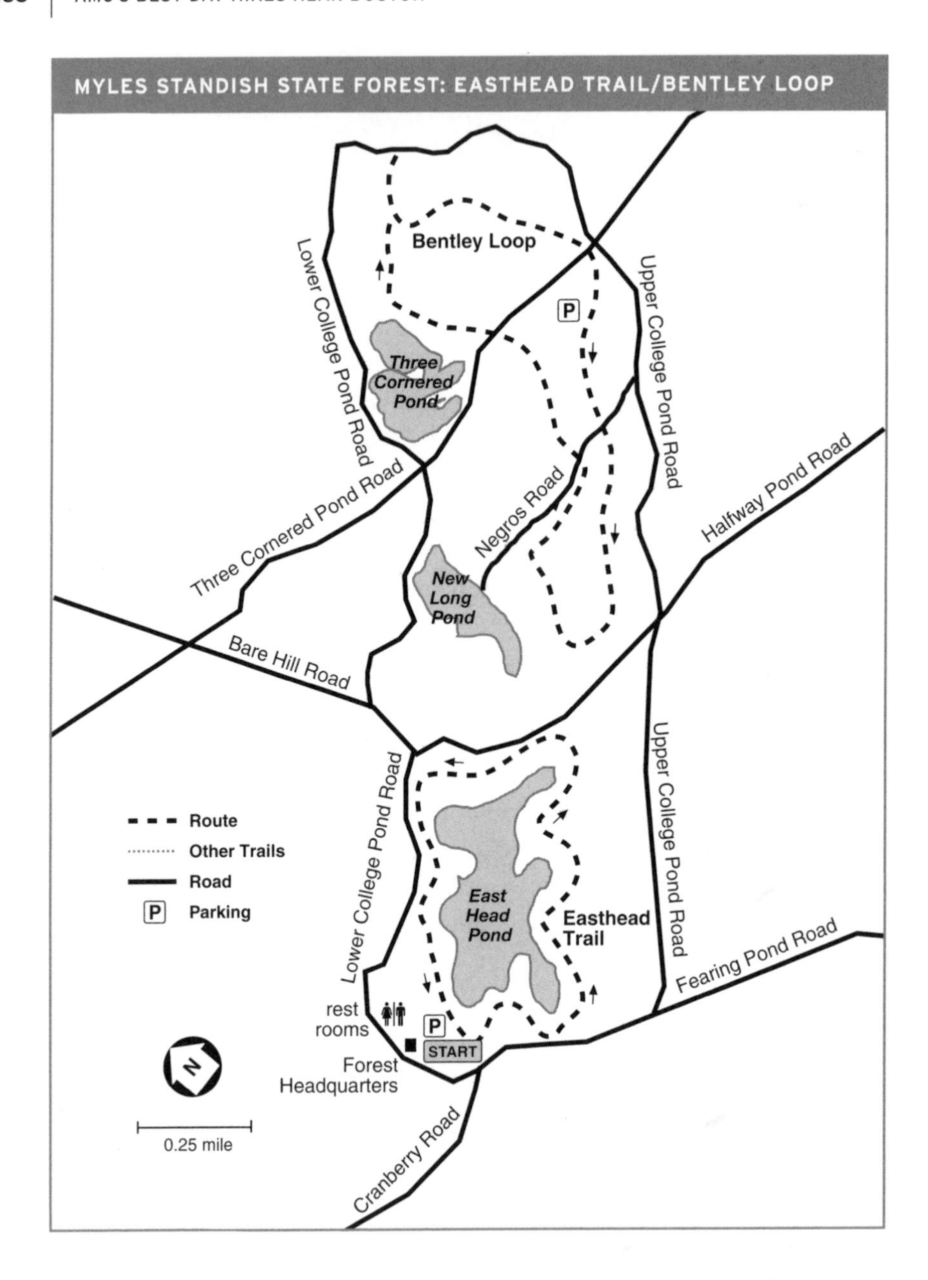

The Easthead Trail begins on the north side of Cranberry Road, about 150 yards east of park headquarters. A sign indicates the entrance to the Easthead Nature Trail. Entering the woods, the trail proceeds north, roughly following the eastern side of the reservoir. In about 1.4 miles, the trail turns left onto a well-used bridle path that follows a gas pipeline. In a short distance the trail reaches two junctions. At the first, the original Easthead Trail loop turns left to begin its return to the starting point via the western side of the reservoir.

To continue on the Bentley Loop, walk a few yards right onto a paved road. Follow the paved road a short distance, and then turn onto the first dirt road on the left (with a metal gate numbered 75). The trail continues a short distance along this dirt road and then turns right onto a woods road. At the end of this road, just before a meadow, is a trail junction where the Bentley Loop heads both left and right.

Turn left at the junction and follow the well-blazed trail. (Use caution, as there are many unmarked paths that cross the trail in this section. If no trail marker is seen after a short distance, retrace the route to the last intersection.) The trail skirts the edge of New Long Pond, bears right then left, and passes Three Cornered Pond on the left. Beyond the pond the trail traverses the first of several meadows. It proceeds almost straight across this meadow (there is a 5-foot post in the middle), then turns left just before a second meadow and heads north toward College Pond.

The trail turns left at another meadow and continues some distance along its left edge. The path turns left into the woods at another marker and quickly reaches its northernmost point at a junction. The path heading north leads to the College Pond parking area, while the Bentley Loop turns right and proceeds south.

After about 50 yards the trail turns left and descends the hill, turns sharp right, and comes to a meadow (the first since turning south). Traverse the meadow and exit left at the far end. Soon College Pond Road is visible on the left. The trail skirts the edge of a parking lot, then turns right into the woods.

Cross another meadow and the trail enters into the woods for a short time before proceeding straight across yet another meadow at the bottom of a hill. From here the trail takes a very winding course to arrive back at the loop's starting point.

To return to the Easthead Trail, walk down the woods road, turn left at the dirt road, and proceed to the gate at the paved road. Turn right onto the paved road, follow it to the bridle path, turn left onto the bridle path, and then make a quick right to continue on the second portion of the Easthead Trail. Follow it for about 1.5 miles around the reservoir back to the starting point. At one point along this section, the trail follows the road for about 100 yards and then reenters the woods.

NATURE NOTES

Myles Standish State Forest contains some of the largest areas of pitch pine–scrub oak plant community in New England. The forest is also well known for its kettle ponds, created as huge chunks of glacial ice became partially embedded in the ground and then melted when the ice ages ended. The holes left behind filled with water and became round ponds. There are many fragile natural areas in the forest, such as the shores of the kettle ponds, and these are marked with signs—please stay on the trail in these areas. In summer, interpretive programs include cranberry bog explorations, pond trips, and fire tower visits.

MORE INFORMATION

For more information, visit www.mass.gov/dcr.

Appendix A

THE BAY CIRCUIT TRAIL

IMAGINE BEING ABLE TO WALK IN A COUNTRY SETTING all the way from Plum Island on Boston's North Shore to Duxbury on the South Shore. Of course Boston blocks the direct coastal route, but one day you will be able to hike the Bay Circuit Trail, a long-envisioned "emerald necklace" arcing through Boston's outer suburbs between Route 128 and I-495. Ward Reservation, Moose Hill Reservation, and Walden Pond, all in this book, are considered three "jewels" in the necklace. Many other reservations in this book will have portions of their trails designated as part of the Bay Circuit, and it will be possible to walk from one reservation to another in an arc of green.

It is a permanent recreation trail and greenway corridor extending through 21 towns in Eastern Massachusetts and linking the parks and open spaces surrounding metropolitan Boston. As of press time, according to the Bay Circuit Trail and Greenway: "Efforts to close the final few gaps in the trail are under way. Recent successes include a trail easement across a cranberry bog in Pembroke, state agreement to a route across former Tewksbury Hospital land, and completion of state design plans for the Bruce Freeman Bikeway along a former railroad connecting Lowell and Acton. Although the trail is primarily through woods and fields, some sections follow scenic country roads, passing by many points of historical interest. Spurs branching off from the main trail will lead to more wild tracts of land or historic places. For more information, contact the Bay Circuit Trail and Greenway at www.baycircuit.org.

The concept of walking in peace and solitude through so large a portion of highly developed eastern Massachusetts is an exciting one. In many respects it will allow the nature lover to go back in time to when the Native Americans followed footpaths from one tribal land to another or from inland hunting grounds to the coast. The idea also has the potential to galvanize the public into action that will protect more of our open spaces before it's too late.

The idea itself is not a new one. Charles W. Eliot II first envisioned a network of easily accessible trails through adjoining conservation land in 1929. But it wasn't until the 1990s that the effort really got going, and more and more of the Bay Circuit emblems are starting to appear at reservations. This state has a number of long north-south-running trails: the Appalachian Trail in the Berkshires, the Robert Frost Trail in the Connecticut River valley, the Mid-State Trail in central Massachusetts. Now it's up to us to carve out our own path of green here in eastern Massachusetts.

Appendix B

CROSS-COUNTRY SKIING

THERE IS NOTHING GLAMOROUS OR HIGH-TECH ABOUT IT. Then again, there is no noise, no engines, no waiting in line. Only a pair of skis and the rhythm of your own pace, under your own power. Cross-country skiing has been described as the horse and buggy of the sporting world. That may be true; gliding on skinny skis is the essence of simplicity, and that's why I love the sport.

With the graying of the baby boomers, cross-country skiing has seen something of a decline in participation. Because it involves a strong aerobic workout, many have let their skis gather cobwebs. Yet the sale of NordicTracks and other fitness equipment is booming. This contradiction strikes me as even more strange when you consider that cross-country skiing brings you the pleasures of hiking, while a stationary ski-track offers you the choice of staring at a wall or a TV.

One of the nice things about cross-country skiing (besides being inexpensive) is that you don't have to travel far to find some great trails. In eastern Massachusetts there are a number of lesser-known reservations and sanctuaries that have flat terrain conducive to cross-country skiing.

For groomed trails, one has to look a little harder, but the selection increases as you head west. Here are few places to check out:

EASTERN MASSACHUSETTS

- Great Brook Farm Ski Touring Center in Carlisle has 10 miles of trails for beginner, intermediate, and expert skiers. Night skiing, rentals, and lessons are available (978-369-7486).
- Weston Ski Track on Park Road in Weston is located on the DCR Leo J. Martin Golf Course. There are 9 miles of trails for all levels of skiers. It offers night skiing, snow making, rentals, and lessons (781-891-6575).

- Although Lincoln Guide Service does not own or groom trails, it is located near 57 miles of trails on town conservation land in Lincoln. There are a variety of trails suitable for beginners through experts, with lessons available (781-891-6575).

CENTRAL MASSACHUSETTS

- Wachusett Mountain Ski Area in Princeton has groomed trails and limited rentals (800-SKI-1234 or 978-978-2300).
- Northfield Mountain Ski Touring Center is just east of the Berkshires in Northfield, with more than 40 kilometers of groomed trails. Excellent grooming and large selection of rentals (413-659-3713).
- Brookfield Orchards in North Brookfield has 12 kilometers of trails through the orchards and surrounding hills. It also features a country store (508-867-6858).
- Red Apple Farm in Phillipston opens its fields on weekends to skiers. They have 10 miles of trails and offer lessons (978-249-6763).
- The Rocking M Ranch in Charlton (near Sturbridge) has skiing on their 60 acres on weekends and school vacations. They have rentals, a heated clubhouse, and groom by snowmobile. Because of their southerly location it's best to call ahead for snow conditions (508-248-7075).
- The Massachusetts Department of Conservation and Recreation grooms trails at selected locations in the Bay State. Here are a few selected areas popular with cross-country aficionados: Rutland State Park in Rutland; Wendell State Forest in Wendell; and Otter River State Forest in Baldwinville (near Templeton and Winchendon).
- Blackstone River and Canal Heritage State Park have some gentle trails that were once canal towpaths in Uxbridge and Upton. A good starting point is at the River Bend Farm parking area on Oak Street in Uxbridge. Because of its southerly location it's best to call ahead for conditions (508-278-6486).
- There are acres of open meadow at North Common Meadow in Petersham, off Route 32 in the center of town. There is no grooming, but for those who like to blaze their own trail it's a wonderful area, just east of the Quabbin.

THE BERKSHIRES

The Berkshires are especially conducive to cross-country skiing because the region receives more snow than the rest of the state and the scenery is often spectacular.

- Hickory Hill Ski Touring Center in Worthington features 650 acres of wooded terrain crisscrossed by 25 kilometers of double-tracked trails.

They use state-of-the-art grooming equipment. Ski lessons, rentals, and a large barn with a fireplace are also provided (413-238-5813).

- Brodie Mountain in New Ashford is known for its downhill skiing but also has a full ski-touring center with rentals and instructions (413-443-4752).
- Bucksteep Manor Cross-Country Ski Center in Washington has 16 trails totaling 20 kilometers. Lessons, rentals, a country inn, and dining. Located at an elevation of 1,800 feet, they often get snow when it rains elsewhere (413-623-5535).
- Canterbury Farm in Becket, at an elevation of 1,600 feet, has groomed skiing through 200 acres of rolling hills. Rentals, lessons, and a bed-and-breakfast (413-623-8765).
- Butternut Basin in Great Barrington offers 7 kilometers of cross-country skiing on groomed trails adjacent to the alpine area (413-528-0610).
- Notchview Reservation in Windsor is a true wilderness area with about 16 miles of trails passing through spruce and hemlocks. Look for wild turkeys, coyotes, and deer as you round the bend. Trails are not groomed (owned by the Trustees of Reservations).
- Two Audubon properties in the Berkshires allow cross-country skiing on their extensive trails: Canoe Meadows Wildlife Sanctuary in Pittsfield and Pleasant Valley Wildlife Sanctuary in Lenox.

Cross-country skiing is a sure cure for cabin fever—get outside and give it a try. For up-to-date reports on ski conditions at many Massachusetts cross-country ski areas, visit www.xcskimass.com/conditions.

Appendix C

FISHING

MANY OF THE WALKS IN THIS BOOK are located near bodies of water that provide some great opportunities for fishing. Before casting your line into that brook, pond, or lake, make sure you have any licenses that are required. Additionally, here are some tips on catch-and-release and fishing with kids.

CATCH-AND-RELEASE

There's an old saying that a fish is too valuable to catch only once. That's never been truer than today. Freshwater fish bear the dual pressures of decreasing habitat and increasing numbers of anglers.

When I was a kid I kept every fish I caught, though only one in ten was actually eaten. The reason I kept them was to show my mom and dad. Today I release most fish I catch. I've learned a photograph is the best way to capture the memory.

Many anglers now practice catch-and-release, and increasing numbers of trout streams have designated catch-and-release sections. Yet even with the best intentions, some of the fish that are released die anyway. Here are some tips to ensure the health of the fish you release:

Use Artificial Lures. Fish rarely survive being hooked with bait, because they tend to swallow the hook along with the bait. Artificial lures and flies, which fish bite but don't swallow, typically hook a fish in the mouth and are therefore much easier and less damaging to extract. Consider purchasing barbless hooks, or debarb your hook by pinching the barb back with a pair of pliers. (Some anglers believe you can catch more fish with a barbless hook because it is easier to set the hook.)

Play the Fish Fast. It is best to play the fish quickly, rather than exhausting it. If the fish is worn out, it has used valuable energy, and the stress will reduce its chances of survival.

Net Knowledgeably. If you use a net, use one with cotton mesh. Nets with a hard plastic mesh can scrape the fish and remove its protective mucous film. The proper way to net a fish is to have the net half in the water and then lead the fish into it headfirst.

Extract The Hook Deftly. You might be able to remove the hook without ever taking the fish out of the water, although more often than not the fish must be handled and removed from the water. The critical factor to remember is that the fish should spend only five or ten seconds out of the oxygen-bearing water. (Your hands should be wet before handling it to protect the fish's mucous film.) A set of needle-nose pliers can be helpful when removing hooks from bass, and a hemostat will help release a fly from a trout's mouth. If the hook is set too deeply to easily remove, it's best to cut the line: the juices in the fish's mouth will dissolve a metal hook in a few days.

Revive And Release Gently. Never throw a fish back in the water or release it into a strong current. It's best to slide the fish back into the water with its head facing the current. If the fish appears very tired hold it in the water for a moment, moving it slowly back and forth to help water flow through its gills. You can do this by cradling it under the stomach with one hand and holding it above the tail with the other. The fish should be recovered to the point where it can easily swim away under its own power.

There is nothing wrong with taking an occasional fish for the dinner table. But first consider if the fish is a native or one that has been stocked. A wild or native fish should be released because it has a better chance than a stocked trout to reproduce. Stocked trout can be distinguished from natives because their coloring is dull and pale, and often their fins are clipped or deformed. Always release fish during their spawning period so that they have a chance to lay or fertilize eggs.

Angling is a wonderful way to introduce children to the magic of the natural world. By showing them the practice of catch-and-release, we show them a practical and simple method of conservation at work.

FISHING WITH KIDS

Every year without fail a story about the joys of taking a child fishing is published, and I always wonder if the kids described are real. Sure there are some tender moments, and fishing is something every dad or mom should introduce their children to, but my advice is to do it with low expectations.

Kids have short attention spans, and fishing is a slow sport. The child does not understand patience, so plan your trip accordingly. Here are my do's and don'ts, learned the hard way, for children under six years of age.

Do:

- Find a pond that has bluegills or sunfish, and use worms. Children don't know the difference between a trout, a bass, or a sunfish and don't care—they simply want the thrill of catching a fish.
- Plan on being on the water for 30 minutes tops; chances are, after 15 minutes the child will be thinking about home.
- Find a sandy beach to fish from. The child can play in the sand, throw stones (to scare the fish away), and wander around.

Don't:

- Take more than one child; it's simply too much for the parent to be untangling lines, preventing fights, and explaining why one child caught a fish and the other didn't.
- Take more than one child in a boat.

Perhaps the most important thing you can do while taking a child fishing is to roll with the punches and have fun, even if the trip lasts only ten minutes. The child is learning not from the act of fishing, but from your reaction to this new experience.

My last outing with my four-year-old went something like this. We cruised around the pond in my canoe, and Brian wanted to cast the line (we did, into a tree), paddle the canoe (we did, in circles), and play with the worms (he did, and dropped a few over to feed the fish). Dad caught a pickerel. Minutes went by and Brian caught nothing. Brian asked, "How much longer?" and "When can we see Mom?" Dad said a prayer for another fish. Dad's line had another pickerel on, so he immediately switched poles with Brian and helped him reel it in. Dad took pictures of Brian and fish before releasing (the fish, not Brian). Dad put on a lure and immediately caught a bass, followed by another, quickly realizing this was going to be an incredible day of fishing. Brian then picked up the paddle and announced it was time to head home. Dad cried silently, knowing that if ever he was going to catch the big one, today was the day.

When we got home, however, Brian ran into the house, and shouted, beaming, to his mother, "Mom, it was awesome. I caught a pickle!"

Appendix D

WILDLIFE WATCHING

THE RESERVATIONS, SANCTUARIES, AND CONSERVATION LANDS reviewed in this book are all rich in wildlife. Seeing that wildlife, however, depends on both luck and one's knowledge of the creatures themselves. We can't do much about luck, but there are a number of steps you can take to increase your odds of spotting the birds, animals, and reptiles that live in eastern Massachusetts.

Thoreau was an expert "wildlife watcher," patient and full of curiosity. He would think nothing of sitting for an hour to watch a bird or animal gather food. "True men of science," he wrote, "will know nature better by his finer organizations; he will smell, taste, see, hear, feel, better than other men. His will be a deeper and finer experience." I have certainly found that nature reveals more of her subtleties when I focus all my senses into the natural surroundings. Try following Thoreau's example and let yourself become absorbed by the forests, fields, and water—even if you don't see wildlife, the walks themselves are more rewarding and refreshing.

Two of the key components of wildlife watching are knowing where and when to look. The best time to see most wildlife is at dawn or dusk. Many creatures are nocturnal, and there is also some overlap at dawn and dusk with the daytime birds and animals. Spring and fall are the two best seasons, especially for migratory birds. Animals that hibernate will be active during the spring after a long winter, and in the fall they will eat as much as possible in preparation for the cold months to come. Winter has the least activity but it does offer some advantages, such as easier long-range viewing (no foliage) and the potential to see some animals crossing the ice (such as coyotes); also, animals are often easier to spot against a background of white snow.

When people ask me where to look, I say "everywhere": in the fields, on the forest floor, on the water or ice, along shorelines, in trees, and in the sky. But if

I had to pick the most productive single spot for seeing wildlife, I'd say it's the edge of fields. Hawks and owls often perch here, and many animals make their dens and burrows where the woods meet the meadows. Creatures feel safer around the edges—deer often stay close to these fringe areas before entering a field at nightfall. Red foxes and coyotes hunt the edges, and they can sometimes be seen trotting through tall grass on their rounds.

Another productive area is along riverbanks and shorelines. Minks, weasels, muskrats, and raccoons, just to mention a few, are commonly observed foraging next to water. And of course shorebirds, wading birds, and ducks are found here. Scanning a shoreline with a pair of binoculars can be extremely rewarding—during a visit to a lake early one morning I once saw an owl, a heron, and an osprey all within five minutes. Many of the wild areas in this book offer excellent canoeing, and this too affords opportunities for nature study at close range.

Obviously, when walking through the woods you must do so quietly if you hope to get near wildlife, but being quiet is not enough. Most creatures would prefer to hide than run, and they will sit tight and let you walk right by. You should give the surrounding areas more than a casual glance. For example, when trying to spot deer I look for parts of the animal between the trees rather than for the entire body. I look for the horizontal lines of the deer's back contrasting with the vertical trees. Knowing the size of the animal also helps; when scanning for deer most people would do so at eye level, yet deer are only about 3 feet high at the shoulder.

Many animals blend in with their surroundings so well it's almost impossible to see them. The American bittern, for example, sometimes hides by freezing with its head in an upright position to match tall reeds and vegetation around it. A snapping turtle in shallow water looks just like a rock, and ruffed grouse can be indistinguishable from the fallen leaves on the forest floor. Even great blue herons will stop feeding and wait, silent and unmoving, until perceived danger passes.

Another key factor to consider is wind direction, which can carry your scent to wildlife. If I'm traveling down a trail and the wind is coming from my left, I tend to look more in that direction since my scent is not being carried there. And if I have a choice when beginning my hike, I always travel into the wind. The same holds true when approaching a known feeding area. Serious wildlife photographers even go as far as wearing rubber boots to stop the scent from their feet from escaping into the air!

It is important, by the way, that humans do not approach too closely, or birds like the heron will take wing, thus expending valuable energy to avoid us. Many creatures will allow us to observe them, so long as we do not walk directly at them or linger too long.

Some animals are almost never seen because they are nocturnal and secretive. But you don't have to see them to know that they are present. They leave clues. You will find the tracks of otter, heron, raccoon, and deer along the soft margin of a river or lake. Hiking after a snowfall can be especially rewarding as fresh tracks can easily be seen. Some astute trackers can also identify creatures by the droppings they leave behind. The burrows and dens of animals reveal where such animals as the fox and groundhog live. Owls disgorge pellets, which can identify their presence and what they have been feeding on. Look for them underneath large pine trees. Deer leave a number of signs: the trails they use between feeding and resting grounds and the scrapes and scars on saplings caused by a buck rubbing its antlers. Peeled bark can mean deer, mice, rabbit, or others, depending on the teeth marks and the shape and height of the marking.

The time and patience required to find and identify clues can be significant, but so too are the rewards. It is satisfying to solve the wildlife "puzzle," not only in learning of a species' presence but also to deduce what its activities were. Children especially seem to enjoy this detective work.

Besides using your sense of sight, you should use your hearing to help in wildlife identification. Many of us have heard the hooting of an owl at night or the daytime drumming of the male ruffed grouse. It appears that more and more folks in the outer suburbs will soon be hearing the wild and eerie yapping and howling of coyotes. Some animal sounds are quite surprising. Creatures you wouldn't expect to make a peep can be quite vocal at times. I've heard deer snort, porcupines scream, and woodchucks grunt and click their teeth.

Knowing the behavior of birds and animals can often explain their actions. For example, if a ruffed grouse pulls the "wounded wing act," you can be sure its chicks are near and it is trying to draw you away. The mother grouse makes a commotion, dragging its wing in a way sure to get your attention. After watching the mother's act, take a moment to scan the forest floor and you just might see the chicks (look but don't touch, and be careful where you step).

Another example of behavior that's important to understand is the warnings certain creatures give if you get too close. A goshawk guarding its nest will give a warning of *kak, kak, kak*; don't go any closer, it may attack you. (Never get too close to nesting birds or chase or corner an animal. Often the best way to get a second look at an animal is to remain perfectly still. They may return out of curiosity.)

Nature study is all the more fascinating when you learn the habits of each wild animal: what it eats, where and when it feeds and rests, whether it is active in the winter or hibernates. Birds can be studied in a similar way, and of course migration patterns are crucial to understanding when and for how long certain birds are in our region. Reptiles, being cold-blooded, are active only in the warm-weather months. Their temperatures vary with that of the surrounding atmosphere, so they cannot survive freezing temperatures. The relatively few reptiles that live in Massachusetts must hibernate in holes or burrows below the frost line during winter. The best time to see some of them is in the late spring; for example, that's when the snapping turtle comes out of the water to lay its eggs on land.

For wildlife photography, you need a zoom lens and a tripod. High-quality shots are extremely difficult. It's hard enough just locating an animal or uncommon bird, but finding a clear shot for a picture can be quite frustrating. Patience is the key—that's why professional wildlife photographers often spend days in the woods working from a blind.

Finally, don't discount dumb luck. Much of the wildlife I've seen has been by accident, but I greatly increased my odds by repeat visits to favorite reservations. After tramping hundreds of miles, I think I've now seen just about every species that's in Massachusetts.

But there are still a couple creatures, like the bobcat, that have eluded me and will keep me walking for another few hundred miles, I'm sure.

Appendix E

LEAVE NO TRACE

THE APPALACHIAN MOUNTAIN CLUB is a national educational partner of Leave No Trace, a nonprofit organization dedicated to promoting and inspiring responsible outdoor recreation through education, research, and partnerships. The Leave No Trace Program seeks to develop wildland ethics—ways in which people think and act in the outdoors to minimize their impacts on the areas they visit and to protect our natural resources for future enjoyment. Leave No Trace unites four federal land management agencies—the U.S. Forest Service, National Park Service, Bureau of Land Management, and U.S. Fish and Wildlife Service—with manufacturers, outdoor retailers, user groups, educators, organizations such as the AMC and the National Outdoor Leadership School (NOLS), and individuals.

The Leave No Trace ethic is guided by these seven principles:

- Plan ahead and prepare
- Travel and camp on durable surfaces
- Dispose of waste properly
- Leave what you find
- Minimize campfire impacts
- Respect wildlife
- Be considerate of other visitors

The AMC has joined NOLS—a recognized leader in wilderness education and a founding partner of Leave No Trace—as a national provider of the Leave No Trace Master Educator course. The AMC offers this five-day course, designed especially for outdoor professionals and land managers, as well as the shorter two-day Leave No Trace Trainer course, at locations throughout the Northeast.

For Leave No Trace information and materials, contact: Leave No Trace Center for Outdoor Ethics, P.O. Box 997, Boulder, CO 80306; toll free: 800-332-4100, or locally, 303-442-8222; fax: 303-442-8217; www.lnt.org.

INDEX

T

W

ABOUT THE AUTHOR

MICHAEL TOUGIAS is the author of several books about New England, including the following:

- *Ten Hours Until Dawn: The True Story of Heroism and Tragedy Aboard The Can Do*
- *King Philip's War: The History and Legacy of America's Forgotten Conflict* (co-author with Eric Shultz)
- *Until I Have No Country* (a novel of King Philip's Indian War in New England)
- *New England Wild Places* (chronicles fourteen journeys to remote regions)
- *Autumn Rambles of New England* (back-road foliage trips)
- *Quiet Places of Massachusetts* (off-the-beaten-path destinations)
- *Country Roads of Massachusetts*
- *There's a Porcupine in My Outhouse: Misadventures of a Mountain Man Wanna-be*
- *A Taunton River Journey*
- *The Blizzard of '78*

Mr. Tougias has written the following for AMC Books:

- *River Days: Exploring the Connecticut River from Source to Sea*
- *Nature Walks in Eastern Massachusetts*
- *More Nature Walks in Eastern Massachusetts*
- *Nature Walks in Central and Western Massachusetts*
- *Exploring the Hidden Charles*

Mr. Tougias leads visually impaired people on nature walks and is involved in protecting open space in Massachusetts. He gives slide lectures for all his books, visit www.michaeltougias.com.

The Appalachian Mountain Club

Founded in 1876, the AMC is the nation's oldest outdoor recreation and conservation organization.The AMC promotes the protection, enjoyment, and wise use of the mountains, rivers, and trails of the Northeast outdoors.

People
We are nearly 90,000 members in 12 chapters, 20,000 volunteers, and over 450 full time and seasonal staff. Our chapters reach from Maine to Washington, D.C.

Outdoor Adventure and Fun
We offer more than 8,000 trips each year, from local chapter activities to major excursions worldwide, for every ability level and outdoor interest—from hiking and climbing to paddling, snowshoeing, and skiing.

Great Places to Stay
We host more than 135,000 guest nights each year at our AMC Lodges, Huts, Camps, Shelters, and Campgrounds. Each AMC Destination is a model for environmental education and stewardship.

Opportunities for Learning
We teach people the skills to be safe outdoors and to care for the natural world around us through programs for children, teens, and adults, as well as outdoor leadership training.

Caring for Trails
We maintain more than 1,400 miles of trails throughout the Northeast, including nearly 350 miles of the Appalachian Trail in five states.

Protecting Wild Places
We advocate for land and riverway conservation, monitor air quality, and work to protect alpine and forest ecosystems throughout the Northern Forest and Highlands regions.

Engaging the Public
We seek to educate and inform our own members and an additional 1.5 million people annually through AMC Books, our website, our White Mountain visitor centers, and AMC Destinations.

Join Us!
Members support our mission while enjoying great AMC programs, our award-winning AMC Outdoors magazine, and special discounts. Visit www.outdoors.org or call 617-523-0636 for more information.

THE APPALACHIAN MOUNTAIN CLUB
Recreation • Education • Conservation
www.outdoors.org

AMC BOOK UPDATES

AMC BOOKS STRIVES to keep our guidebooks as up-to-date as possible to help you plan safe and enjoyable adventures. If after publishing a book we learn that trails are relocated or route or contact information has changed, we will post the updated information online. Before you hit the trail, check for updates at www.outdoors.org/publications/books/updates.

While hiking or paddling, if you notice discrepancies with the trail description or map, or if you find any other errors in the book, please let us know by submitting them to amcbookupdates@outdoors.org or in writing to Books Editor, c/o AMC, 5 Joy Street, Boston, MA 02108. We will verify all submissions and post key updates each month.

AMC Books is dedicated to being a recognized leader in outdoor publishing. Thank you for your participation.